Broadcast News Writing, Reporting, and Production

Broadcast News Writing, Reporting, and Production

Ted White
Virginia Commonwealth University

Adrian J. Meppen
WCBS–TV News

Steve Young
CBS News

Macmillan Publishing Company
New York
Collier Macmillan Publishers
London

To

Rita Butler and Edith Danaher

Morris, Adele, Arlene, Roberta, Michelle, and Sarah Meppen

Gertrude and Irving Young

Copyright © 1984, Macmillan Publishing Company, a division of Macmillan, Inc.

Printed in the United States of America

Macmillan Publishing Company
866 Third Avenue, New York, New York 10022

Collier Macmillan Canada, Inc.

Library of Congress Cataloging in Publication Data

White, Ted,
    Broadcast news writing, reporting, and production.

    Includes bibliographical references and index.
    1. Broadcast journalism. I. Meppen, Adrian J.
II. Young, Stephen B.   III. Title.
PN4784.B75W5   1983   070.1'9'0973   82-4707
ISBN 0-02-427010-5

Printing: 4 5 6 7 8   Year: 8 9 0

ISBN   0-02-427010-5

Preface

Because the broadcast world is changing so rapidly, it was a challenge in writing this book to keep up with all the new developments and techniques, particularly the changes in technology. But we are confident that our advice about writing, reporting, and producing will be as valid in five or ten years as it is today.

The basic creative process that goes into a good news script or field report for radio or TV has not significantly changed since the pioneering days of such great broadcast journalists as Edward R. Murrow, Elmer Davis, H. V. Kaltenborn, Raymond Gram Swing, and Lowell Thomas. Their traditions were carried on by such people as Walter Cronkite, Eric Sevareid, David Brinkley, and the late Frank Reynolds and Chet Huntley. Those traditions are alive and well today with the help of such talented journalists as John Chancellor, Pauline Frederick, Charles Kuralt, James Lehrer and Robert MacNeill, Bill Moyers, Roger Mudd, Charles Osgood, Dan Rather, and Howard K. Smith—all good writers and reporters.

The major emphasis in this book will be on developing your writing and reporting skills. The book is designed to help young people who wish to become writers, reporters, and producers for radio and TV news. Although we include considerable detail concerning the technical aspects of TV news, it is not our intention to help train you to be a technician or director. But you will have to learn some basic technical skills if you are to be successful in both the classroom and the professional world.

It will be difficult for you to accomplish much, for example, in your broadcast news courses unless you can operate an audiotape recorder and video camera and understand how to edit both audiotape and videotape. You also should be familiar with good lighting techniques.

In most broadcast courses you will need to develop these skills if you wish to complete your reporting assignments. Few, if any, universities will provide technicians to handle the lights, cameras, and microphones. And, of course, you may be required to use some of this equipment every day in the small markets in which you will find your first job.

Another reason for learning how to operate equipment is that you will come to understand its capabilities and limitations. When you reach a station that is large enough to support a technical staff, you will know what the technicians can and cannot do with their equipment. This will be important when you explain to your cameraperson (and lighting and audio technicians in the major markets) what kinds of shots and effects you are trying to achieve. You will win professional respect from your technical crews if you show an understanding of their problems and an appreciation of their skills.

Many challenges await you. Similarly, organizing this book was a challenge for us. After much deliberation, we decided to deal with radio news first and then with television. The difficulty is that much of what we discuss in the radio section of the book also applies to television. From an instructional point of view, we believe it makes more sense to teach you about the less complex aspects of radio news before moving into television. Once you know how to write news copy for radio, the transition to writing for television is rather simple. Also, learning how to prepare a voice report for radio is excellent preparation for television reporting.

In parts of the book we are critical of some of the methods and techniques employed by radio and TV news organizations. We make these criticisms so that you will be aware of some of the profession's shortcomings and in the hope that when you join that profession you will aim for high standards. Despite our criticisms, we are bullish on the future of broadcast journalism. We think you have chosen an exciting and challenging career. It will not be easy, but it will never be boring.

Ted White
Adrian J. Meppen
Steve Young

Acknowledgments

During the three years that we worked on this book, we relied on the assistance, resources, and support of many people. It is doubtful that this book would have been ready as soon as it was without the assistance of Kathy Morrison, who retyped the complete manuscript and also provided perspective based on her own experience as a television assignment editor, reporter, and anchor. Her moral support at a difficult time will always be remembered. Bob Thomas was very helpful, particularly in the early stages of the manuscript when we needed assistance with our research. He also helped with the typing, as did B. J. Wiltshire.

We spoke with many people—news executives, reporters, anchors, and educators—while working on the book. The following individuals spent more time than they probably could afford answering our questions: Don Hewitt, Richard Mutschler, Charles Osgood, Sanford Socolow, and Howard Stringer of CBS News; Chris Borgen, Joe Blanco, and Jan Lurie of WCBS–TV; Jack Whitaker of ABC Sports and Jeff Gralnick and John Stossel of ABC News; Paul Greenberg of NBC News; Bill Ballard and Steve Greenwald of WBTV, Charlotte; Gordon Barnes, Rob Barnes, Judy Borza, Ted Kavanau, Ed Turner, and Sam Zelman of CNN; Ron Miller of WWBT–TV, Richmond; Howard Kelley of WTLV–TV, Jacksonville; Spence Kinard of KSL–TV, Salt Lake City; Ed Cavagnaro of KCBS, San Francisco; Michael Bille of WQAD–TV, Moline; John Spain of WBRZ–TV, Baton Rouge; Ray Depa of KETV–TV, Omaha; Ken Srpan of WRDV–TV, Raleigh; Bob Greene of *Newsday*; Jack Taylor of *The Denver Post*; John Ullmann of Investigative Reporters and Editors, Inc.; and Professor Clark Mollenhoff of Washington & Lee University.

Special thanks also to CBS News correspondents Charles Kuralt and Charles Osgood and ABC News commentator Paul Harvey for permitting us to print samples of their writing, and to Professor Vernon Stone of Southern Illinois University for providing us with some of his research material. Professor Philip Keirstead of Florida A&M shared his insights with us, as did Chuck Novitz, President of Sigma Delta Chi. Electronic experts Dave Cunningham and Greg Endsley of Integrated Technology and Peter Kolstad of Basys contributed much to our understanding of the new computer technology. Our appreciation to Robert Kaplan of CNN and Lionel Phillips of CBS News who shot many of the photos used in the book.

Throughout the years there have been many colleagues to whom we owe thanks for their help and advice and support; CBS News President, Ed Joyce; Executive Vice President, CBS Broadcast Group, Van Gordon Sauter; and CBS News correspondents Reid Collins, Walter Cronkite, Morton Dean, Douglas Edwards, Richard C. Hottelet, Alexander Kendrick, Dan Rather, and Dallas Townsend.

Appreciation also to Mike Stein of ABC News and Jack Pluntze, former news director for WNEW Radio. For moral support we thank Mark Dulmage, Don Gallagher, and Randy Harber of CNN; Jim Branon of WCBS–TV News; Mike Lynn of CBS News; Jack C. Levine, formerly of WOR News; and former CBS newsmen, Lee Otis and Zeke Segal.

We value highly the assistance and counsel from our associates in the academic world, particularly George T. Crutchfield and William H. Turpin at VCU; Howard B. Jacobson of the University of Bridgeport; Hillier Krieghbaum, professor emeritus of New York University; the late John Patterson of the Columbia Graduate School of Journalism; and Professor Irving Rosenthal, formerly of City College of New York. Two of our former students, Rob North of WFLA–TV, Tampa, and Gerry Penacolli of KYW–TV, Philadelphia, supplied valuable information about "getting started" in TV news.

And finally, sincere thanks to our executive editor, Lloyd Chilton, and his staff at The Macmillan Company for guiding this book to its completion.

About the Authors

Ted White is currently an associate professor in the School of Mass Communications at Virginia Commonwealth University in Richmond. He has worked as a writer, editor, reporter, and producer for a variety of news organizations, including CBS News, WCBS Radio and TV, ABC News, WOR Radio and TV, WINS Radio in New York City, the Voice of America, and the Cable News Network. White is also coauthor, with Bob Siller and the late Hal Terkel of CBS, of *Television and Radio News*, published by Macmillan in 1960.

Adrian J. Meppen began his career in broadcast journalism as a writer for WCBS–TV, the network's flagship station in New York City. He has produced the nightly Eleven O'Clock Report for WCBS–TV and coproduced the Six O'Clock Report. He has written for *The Wall Street Journal* and *Newsday* as well as for WQXR, the radio station of *The New York Times.*

Steve Young has been a CBS News correspondent since 1968. Before that he worked for WNEW Radio in New York City and WICC Radio in Bridgeport, Connecticut and was for six years an adjunct faculty member at Columbia University's Graduate School of Journalism.

Foreword

Once, long ago and far away, I looked over a report written by Eric Sevareid and said to him, "Eric, this is the best piece of reporting I have seen about this war. How did you ever learn to report and write so well under such pressure?"

He answered with a smile, "Practice, hard work and a lot of tough miles."

Many things have happened to both of us since that night in Saigon. None of them has convinced me that he was kidding.

On the contrary, the further I go the more I know he was, as usual, serious and right.

Sevareid is, of course, a legend and one of the standards against whom everyone else in the craft should be and is judged. Few, if any, reporters past or present can measure up. But the goal is worth striving for and his words are worth remembering as you go through this book, written by three people who have worked their way up in the Sevareid school.

This is a how-to-do-it book by people who have done it.

They have written for people interested in the real work of broadcast journalism rather than the perceived glamor.

That work can be and often is challenging, exciting and rewarding. It is seldom glamorous. To do it well requires a solid grounding in fundamentals, practice and experience. Reporting is best learned by going out and reporting stories. Writing is best learned by writing. Nothing original or profound about that. But it may help to have it in mind as you go through this book, which can provide that "solid grounding in fundamentals" for those who read and heed it.

Dan Rather

Contents

7   More Style Rules   65

8   Originality and Color   80

16 Beats and Assignments for Television   163

17 Electronic News Gathering   183

18 Constructing the TV News Story   189

22 The Lineup 246

23 Investigative Reporting 265

24   **Looking Ahead and Summing Up   291**

1

Introduction to Broadcast Journalism

The Prerequisites—A Good Foundation

What's the best way to get started in journalism? That question has been debated for decades by professionals and educators. The argument was more heated when the traditional, green-eyeshade editors occupied most newspaper city rooms. "Bunk," is what most of them would have said about journalism education. "The only way to learn how to write and report is to work on a paper," would have been another typical comment. The suggestion that one could learn reporting and writing skills in the classroom was alien to them.

Much of that hard-nosed attitude disappeared along with the eyeshades. Many newspaper and broadcast editors, reporters, and producers have moved into college and university classrooms as adjunct and full-time professors. There are still many working journalists who question the value of journalism programs, arguing that the best preparation for a career in journalism is a strong liberal arts education. That is why the majority of successful college and university programs in journalism limit the time devoted to the major to about 30 semester hours and require 90 or more semester hours in the sciences and liberal arts.

1

The popularity of journalism programs in recent years is apparently, in part, a reflection of the growing concern among many young people that the traditional liberal arts program is "not enough" to compete in today's highly competitive marketplace. Many students view journalism programs that include a heavy emphasis on liberal arts as the "best of both worlds." And there seems to be some evidence to support this. Most newspaper and broadcast managers are looking for young "street-ready" men and women who show an ability to cover a news conference or city council meeting and have some familiarity with a police blotter and the court system. Most news directors will take the time to polish the young college graduate who has intelligence, strong motivation, and some basic journalistic skills. But few news directors have the time or patience to explain the principles of news, how to write a good lead sentence, or how to conduct an interview in a professional manner. These are a few of the skills that broadcast news executives will expect you to bring to your first job.

So prepare yourself well. In that first job, you will be expected to demonstrate persistence, tenacity, an insatiable curiosity, and an abundant supply of energy. These same attributes also will make you a good student. And the interest and work you demonstrate in the classroom and laboratory will be matched by your teachers.

It would be best if you bring some basic writing ability and, perhaps, some journalistic theory to your first broadcast journalism course. Most major programs insist on English writing courses and, often, an introductory course in the journalism department as prerequisites for upper-level courses in the major. Any form of writing—any discipline that forces you to work with words—is important for your development as a journalist. Good writing is the most essential skill that you must develop if you are to succeed in broadcast journalism.

Virginia Commonwealth University (V.C.U.) broadcast news student uses a Convergence editing console to edit her story.

This book is designed mostly to help those students who show some ability to deal with words and grammar and, preferably, have a knowledge of journalistic principles. But some of you will be dealing with journalistic concepts for the first time. For that reason, this book includes considerable basic journalistic theory along with detailed explanations and instruction in broadcast news writing, reporting, and production.

Getting Started

In the 1950s and, to a lesser degree, during the 1960s, the broadcast journalist was often a converted newspaper reporter or editor. Attracted by the glamor of the position or the higher salaries, hundreds of newspaper people deserted the print world for jobs in broadcasting. They brought with them the tradition of an inquisitive, skeptical reporter. They knew how to dig deep to get the facts that made each story credible and vivid.

But today most young broadcast journalists are a product of their own medium—the generation that grew up on TV. Although they are familiar with the technical production details, they often lack the newspaper reporter's skill with words and ability to dig out a story. The young TV reporter often finds it difficult to cut to the heart and meaning of a story so as to make it understandable in a limited time span.

Today's journalism students can develop those necessary reporting skills by combining classroom instruction with job experience. This will help them acquire those "street smarts" most TV and radio news directors are looking for.

Students often get their first experience in broadcasting by working for a college radio station. This experience is invaluable. Many colleges and universities have active intern and work-study programs that encourage and often require students to spend part of their time working for radio and TV stations. Some universities have working arrangements with radio and TV stations in their area that permit students to produce and broadcast news programs for the public as part of the curriculum.

If you take part in such programs and get your degree in journalism, you will have an edge over others seeking jobs. Most station managers are reluctant to pay much for intern services, but even time you contribute without pay could be a worthwhile investment. Many students begin this way on a part-time basis before getting a paycheck from a radio or TV station.

Some broadcast news executives believe that colleges and universities are turning out too many journalists. They say there are not enough jobs to go around. Of course, not everyone who gets a degree in journalism is going to find a job at a newspaper, radio, or TV station. But the same is true of other professions as well. Journalism school graduates who have talent, are prepared to work hard, and are willing to relocate will find jobs. Relocating often is a major factor. You will probably discover that most of the jobs will not be in your hometown.

V.C.U. broadcast news student views some videotape before editing his story.

Most writers, producers, and reporters working in major markets began their careers in smaller cities. Working for a newspaper in a small town always has been a good way to learn the newspaper business, and it is no different in broadcasting. The best beginning jobs are on small-town TV and radio stations.

One of our recent graduates obtained a position as a street reporter for a TV station in Toledo, Ohio. Within six months he had moved to Cincinnati and later to Tampa, Florida. He had trained well for his career while in college, working both at the campus radio station and for commercial stations near the university. He spent many hours putting together an audition tape. It was a good audition tape that illustrated his reporting talents and his ability to edit videotape. More than anything else, it was that audition tape that landed him the job in Toledo. But the real accomplishment was his ability to produce the tape and show off his TV reporting skills. And that is one of the things this book will help teach you to do.

Understanding Many Roles

Young people often are confused about the roles they see themselves playing in radio and TV news. Some indicate no interest in television. Many prefer a career in radio, perhaps because their first contact with the medium was in high school or at the college radio station. Others think of themselves as working behind the scenes, not as a personality.

Some students mistakenly believe they lack voice and diction quality and their physical appearance is not sufficiently glamorous for television.

Voice quality, diction, and appearance can be improved. Increasingly, good journalists are beginning to succeed in broadcasting on merit rather than on appearance. Too many people are in front of TV cameras because they are attractive, but there are signs that some news directors are seeking intelligence and good news judgment first and a pretty face second. They are demanding that their reporters and anchors be experienced journalists.

It also is important to remember that you can change the direction of your career in broadcast news. Many veteran broadcast journalists have functioned in different news positions during their careers, and sometimes they have held different positions at the same time. Just because you start out in one job does not necessarily mean you will keep it forever. It is quite common, for example, to start out in radio and later move to television.

Regardless of what you decide to do in broadcast news, you really should know how to function in almost every role. No one expects you to be a TV anchorperson, an expert camera operator, a graphic artist, and a street reporter. But you should know as much as possible about each of those jobs and every other position in broadcast news. Unless you understand graphics, it will be difficult for you to know what you can and cannot do as a producer of a TV news program. Unless you know the capabilities and limitations of cameras and the crews that are using them, you will be hard put to run the news assignment desk.

V.C.U. broadcast news student checks out camera before going on assignment.

One thing is certain in broadcast journalism, as in most professions: you must learn the fundamentals. Few people in broadcasting will edit news before they learn how to write it properly. One usually does not acquire the title of producer without putting in time as an associate producer and writer.

It takes more to succeed in broadcast journalism than a nice smile and a gift for clever phrases to toss at the weatherperson. Both of those could be assets once you have proven that you can function as a journalist.

Your first job likely will be with a radio or TV station in a small market where you will be expected to handle a number of roles. If your first job is with a radio station, you will have to know how to write and read a news script on the air, how to ad-lib a report from a telephone or mobile unit, how to conduct an intelligent interview, how to run an audio console, how to edit tape, and how to handle complaints from the public on the phone.

These are only a few of the things you might be expected to do. You probably would read commercials and might be asked to do remotes from shopping malls and fairs. With luck, you would get an opportunity to devote most of your time to news in that first job, but there would be no guarantee. Some teachers and journalists believe that graduating students should take only those jobs that will permit them to spend all their time working on news. Ideally, that may be true. But taking on some of the other, nonjournalistic chores may be a good idea. Perhaps if broadcast journalists learned more about the other operations in broadcasting, more of them would attain executive positions. Too many time salesmen have become general managers and not enough news people occupy those positions. Perhaps the commitment to extensive, in-depth news, so lacking at many of the nation's radio and TV stations, would be stronger if more news people moved into the executive suites. In any case, the decision may not be yours. If the competition for a job in broadcast news forces you to locate in a small market, you usually will be required to do more than cover the news.

CBS News Correspondent Charles Osgood recalls that when he was a senior at Fordham University he knew he wanted to work in some aspect of radio. But he is quick to add that if he had made a list of probable things he wanted to do in radio, "I'm sure that news would not have been on it."

When he was graduated from Fordham, Osgood got a job in Washington working at WGMS, a classical music station. "I was interested in music," he said. "I was never involved in news."

Osgood became program manager and later general manager of that all-music station, which was owned by RKO-General. The company also owned a TV station in Hartford where Osgood was sent as general manager. Osgood remembers, "I was only 29 and over my head. After the longest year of my life . . . I was told they were going to get someone else to take over."

An old college friend, who was about to go to work for ABC, helped Osgood get a job there that started him off on a new career in journalism.

CBS newsroom in New York. (Photo by Lionel Phillips)

The point, says Osgood, is that you "can't always plot in advance what you are going to do in this business . . . as you can in some others. I discovered opportunities that I didn't know existed for me, and I found out that I had abilities I wasn't aware of."

When asked for advice on how to get started in broadcast journalism, Osgood suggested "staying loose, keeping your mind alive and involved in what's going on in the world." He added, "Be flexible, be willing to try new things, and take advantage of the opportunities when they come up."

Regardless of how you start out, remember that nothing is forever. As soon as you feel secure in your ability, you probably will be spending a lot of time reading *Broadcasting* magazine's classified section and sending out audition tapes.

Working Conditions

If working nine to five and having weekends off are important to you, then perhaps you should consider a profession other than journalism. Regular working hours are rare in the news business. Lunch and dinner are usually consumed on the way to or from a news story or delivered to your desk in a paper bag. Often you will be too busy to think about eating. Most journalists eat too much junk food, smoke too much, consume too much coffee, and often drink too much. Add to this the pressure of deadlines and the frustrations of missing out on a story—or blowing one—and you get some idea of the constant tension that is involved. You can expect late night calls from the assignment editor telling you to take the place of a sick reporter on your weekend off. And then there are the running battles with the news director and other executives who frequently are second-guessing your performance in the field, at the desk, or in producing the newscast. If you are the news director, the general manager will be looking over your shoulder.

If peace of mind, tranquility, and a good night's rest are vital to your existence, do not covet a working press card. On the other hand, if you thrive on excitement and have a curiosity that is impossible to satisfy, this world may be right for you. You will need more than a dash of aggressiveness and a thick skin. You also will develop a sense about how far you can push people and how to detect when a "no" really means *no*. It would be naive to believe that you could survive in journalism without drive.

You will be lucky to earn more than a minimum wage in your first broadcast job. One of the reasons for the low starting salary is that it is a buyer's market, a glamorous and exciting business in which many

CBS News correspondent Dan Rather, anchor and managing editor of the CBS Evening News. (CBS News photo)

young people want a piece of the action. News directors and station owners realize this and often take advantage of the situation. If they run a small station, they know you will not remain with them long. You will be "using" them too—using them to develop your skills and to prepare the audiotape and videotape auditions that will allow you to move to a larger market. Of course, not everyone wants to live in New York City or Chicago, and there are many advantages to taking root in one of the smaller cities. Working in a community of 100,000 can be gratifying, especially when civic leaders and a large percentage of the people in the community recognize you on the street and call you by your first name. That recognition and respect are often missing in the larger cities unless you are a top anchor. Many reporters and all those working behind the cameras in large cities are merely faces in the crowd.

Many of you will be thinking of making it to the very top. Everyone wants to know how much he or she can earn when anchoring the news for a network or one of the top stations in New York or Chicago. Many of these anchors earn a quarter of a million dollars or more, and a few have contracts two or three times that amount. But these obviously are exceptions. Some on-the-street reporters and producers in New York may earn $50,000 or more a year. But the pay for most unionized editorial positions in a major city is about half that amount. And in the majority of the nation's radio and TV stations that have no unions the salaries are significantly lower. So when you read that Dan Rather or Barbara Walters has signed a multi-million-dollar contract, think of them as you would the handful of star quarterbacks or tennis pros who are making it big. But do not forget the hundreds who do not go to the Super Bowl or to Wimbledon.

Professor Vernon Stone, in a report for the Radio and Television News Directors Association, noted that on average the pay for entry level positions in television was only slightly higher than in radio, but that the TV news veteran could expect to earn twice the salary of his radio counterpart.[1]

Changing Attitudes

Some broadcast managers in medium-sized markets are changing their attitude about salaries. Broadcast consultant Albert Primo, creator of the Eyewitness News format, says most managers once believed that a person ought to consider himself lucky to have a job. But he says even in the smallest markets, news, weather, and sports personalities are now demanding higher salaries. Primo notes that management is meeting those demands and treating its people with "respect and care."[2]

Broadcasting magazine also reported that the larger salaries have filtered down to the smaller markets and "surprisingly large salaries are now likely to turn up almost anywhere."[3] The magazine noted that in

Albuquerque, New Mexico (the 77th market) one anchor switched stations when his salary was doubled to $80,000 dollars.

Consultant Primo believes that anchors are still most important for TV news operations, but he says in many markets the weather person has become increasingly more valuable. He says that on many TV sets the weather personality is becoming more important than the sports anchor.[4] We will examine both of these positions later in the book.

A Typical News Staff

According to the Radio and Television News Directors Association (RTNDA), a typical TV news operation has more than a dozen full-time employees and two part-timers. The RTNDA survey showed that stations in the top ten markets have news staffs of 40 or more people, and markets ranked 11 through 50 employ 20 or more. RTNDA says this represents an increase of about 2 percent over a seven-year period. The survey found no increase in the size of radio news staffs during the same period.

RTNDA says the typical radio station employs one full-time and one

ABC News correspondent Barbara Walters interviewing the late Egyptian President Anwar Sadat. (ABC News photo)

The "pit" at Cable News Network (CNN) headquarters in Atlanta. Assistant director at switcher sits next to director. (Photo courtesy of CNN)

part-time newsperson.[5] But many radio stations in major markets employ three or four full-time news people, and some other stations, especially those owned by the networks, employ dozens of newswriters, editors, reporters, anchors, and producers. WCBS Radio in New York, for example, has a news staff of 50 and that does not include technical personnel. The networks each employ hundreds of writers, producers, and reporters. Many new editorial positions became available when the Cable News Network went on the air in 1980. More jobs became available when CNN began a second news service, CNN Headline News, in 1981 and Westinghouse-ABC launched its own 24-hour Satellite News Channel (SNC) a few months later.* Hundreds of additional positions also became available when CBS, NBC, and ABC extended their morning news programs and began broadcasting new, overnight newscasts. The expansion of local news to two hours or more in some markets also has increased the number of available positions. Many more jobs are expected to open up for young journalists as cable operations expand nationwide. The change in the Federal Communications Commission (FCC) regulations that will allow additional radio and TV stations to operate also could mean more work for young journalists.

*SNC sold out to CNN in 1983.

Satellite News Channels newsroom in Stamford, Connecticut, before its sale to CNN in 1983. (Group W Satellite Communications photo)

The Unions

Reporters at small stations and even some larger ones usually are not required to be union members. But in most major markets and at the networks (except CNN and SNC) you will be compelled to work under a master contract negotiated by the American Federation of Television and Radio Artists. A condition of employment is that you be a member of the union known by its members as AFTRA.

This requires an initiation fee, and on a semiannual basis you will be asked to pay dues on a sliding scale according to your earnings within AFTRA's jurisdiction.

AFTRA negotiates certain minimum payments for reporters, sports reporters, weather people and so forth. Any journalist with the experience and reputation to command an above-scale salary is free to negotiate on his own.

The union has little to do with editorial aspects of a reporter's work. AFTRA will not intervene on behalf of a reporter who believes he is not getting choice assignments. AFTRA will not intervene if a reporter thinks his scripts are being too heavily reworked. These aspects are subjective, contentious, and not regarded by the union or management as areas in which the union can become involved. Work assignments are considered to be the sole prerogative of management. AFTRA will get involved, however, if a reporter is required to work excessive hours.

At some of the nation's biggest local TV news operations, reporters sometimes work 12 hours a day and longer because they are required to do stories and appear on-camera in the studio for both the evening and late night news. In most instances, reporters are not compensated for overtime and there is no such requirement under the AFTRA contracts. Some correspondents have been required to work several weeks without a day off. Admittedly, these are severe examples, but the problem of excessive hours can be a recurring and irritating one.

Part of the problem stems from everyone's inability to plan when and where the news will happen. Management argues that it cannot afford to have a long enough bench of reporters, editors, producers, and camera operators to cover every possible contingency.

Over the years some resentment has been expressed by broadcast journalists that they have to belong to any union. Some see them as providing basic protection. One of the most frequently voiced comments is that some unions represent too many diverse interests. AFTRA, for example, represents not only local and network news people, but also actors, singers, dancers, and others. The majority of AFTRA's members are not journalists.

In addition to AFTRA, there are a number of other unions representing workers in broadcast news operations: the Writers Guild of America (WGA); the International Brotherhood of Electrical Workers (IBEW); the National Association of Broadcast Employees and Technicians (NABET); and the International Alliance of Theatrical, Stage Employees, and Motion Picture Machine Operators (IATSE).

These unions represent thousands of workers throughout the country, but the vast majority of radio and TV news personnel are not represented by these or any other unions. If you find yourself in a union shop, you will discover that in most instances your days of handling more than one job are over. In New York, writers, editors, and producers often cannot touch equipment at radio and TV stations.

One of the advantages of serving your apprenticeship in a smaller market is that you get a chance to learn how to do almost everything. Unfortunately, the lack of union representation in those markets is also one of the reasons your paychecks will be smaller.

Minority Opportunities

The broadcast industry offers tremendous opportunities for women and minorities. Under pressure from the federal government, more women, blacks, and Hispanics have entered broadcast newsrooms. But there still are complaints that not enough women and minorities occupy decision-making positions at the networks and local stations. And blacks have fallen behind women in obtaining lower-echelon news jobs.

Reporter-anchor Renée Poussaint of WJLA–TV, Washington D.C. (WJLA–TV photo)

Professor Vernon Stone said there has been a sharp increase in the number of women news directors in the past decade. The RTNDA research chairman said that more than 50 TV stations now have women running their news operations. In the early 1970s, there were only two female TV news directors, according to Stone. He added that by 1982, about 97 percent of TV stations in the country had women on their news staffs, compared to 57 percent in 1972. In radio, newswomen held jobs at only about 20 percent of the newsrooms ten years ago. Stone said by 1982 that figure had jumped to 59 percent.[6]

But former FCC Commissioner Tyrone Brown said there is still a lot of frustration among minorities and women trying to advance in broadcasting. Speaking at a Washington conference on minorities in broadcast management sponsored by the National Association of Broadcasters (NAB), Brown noted that, 20 years after federal equal employment legislation, blacks and minorities had "made little progress" in reaching management positions. Brown called on broadcast companies "to search out and find potential [minority] shining stars and get them on a fast track within the companies."[7]

The importance of this for women and minorities is that the potential is still great as long as the federal government continues to look over industry's shoulder. In all fairness, some broadcast news managers, realizing their moral obligation, have voluntarily employed more women and minorities in recent years. In many cases, they also realized it was good business. Black anchors, for example, are likely to attract and hold larger audiences in communities with large numbers of blacks.

It would be an exceptional city now that does not employ at least one female and black anchor or reporter. In many cities, more Hispanics are showing up on the screen. But perhaps the greatest opportunities still await Spanish-speaking broadcast journalists. Journalism programs at most colleges and universities have failed to attract large numbers of Hispanics.

Ethics

No introduction to broadcast journalism would be complete without some discussion of ethics. In becoming a broadcast journalist, you are really accepting a public trust. The classical argument is that this trust is all the more important because "broadcast space" on the air is limited. It is as if newspaper, magazine, or book publishers could function only if the government granted each applicant a license to operate a printing press. Some say that changing technology is diminishing the need for a broadcast journalist to take special pains to be objective and fair. This argument holds that because cable television, superstations, and the videodisc promise greatly expanded video opportunities and the emergence of "narrowcasting" to special interest audiences, strictures on broadcast journalists should be no more, or less, rigorous than those applied to print journalists.

At any rate, it is essential that you understand some issues of ethics that will be reviewed here. Some are and will remain unique to broadcast journalism. Others are common to all forms of journalism.

There will be times when you will bash heads with a broadcast salesman. Radio or TV journalists are constantly asked by sales departments to cover a store opening as a news item because it will help generate broadcast advertising revenue, or they are ordered to cover the opening of Bill Whiz Bang's Auto Supermarket.

In theory there should be a division between news departments and sales departments. But the separation often is blurred and there may be times when your sales people will ask you to do a favor for a client. In a word, resist. Accommodate them if it means your job or if you can convince yourself that there is a legitimate news story in what they are peddling. Otherwise, try to get them to understand that if you do such self-serving puffery promotions and miss the real news, your audience will become suspicious and turn elsewhere for credible news, and the station will lose audience, advertising, and money. The managements of some stations have established policy against such practice of business department interference, and such policy is a measure of a station's professionalism.

Gratuities

Never accept anything of value from someone who has an interest in being seen or heard on the air. That is the most fundamental kind of compromise. Your policy should be to have your station pay your own way. Do not even open the door to the possibility that someone will say you were influenced in how or if you reported a story, or how prominently it was played, because you received something valuable. There are reasonable exceptions. For example, if you are reporting a luncheon speech, it would not be improper for you to accept a free lunch. Some news organizations insist that their theater critics purchase their own tickets to avoid any possible conflict. But most news directors are reluctant to purchase theater tickets or buy books for their reviewers. No real ethical problem is involved here. Publishers and theater producers are not likely to expect any special favors from reviewers because they have sent them free tickets or books. But if a bottle of Scotch suddenly arrives at your door from a publicist, return it immediately.

Some ethical decisions require considerably more thought. Think about what you would do in the following circumstances. These are not hypothetical situations; they all occurred.

1. You are working at a small radio station with a news staff of five. A downtown shopping center is being built. The sales manager of the radio station would like to win new advertising business. He tells the news director, who also is the morning news broadcaster, that the news department must do some stories about the businesses that are moving into the shopping complex. The news director goes along with this and directs you to produce one or two stories a week. Do you go along?

2. A gunman is holding hostages inside a local bank. You telephone the bank and the gunman answers the phone. You are recording the conversation. The gunman demands that you broadcast his message of discontent concerning state politics or he will harm the hostages. Do you consult the police? Your management? Do you broadcast the message?

3. Iran is holding American hostages and wants billions of dollars of Iranian assets in exchange for the release of the hostages. You have been assigned to the story and have learned that the amount of frozen Iranian assets exceeds American claims on those assets by approximately six billion dollars. The White House Counsel (the president's lawyer) tells you, "I would discourage you from reporting that story." He does not deny the accuracy of the information but suggests that such a story might impair the ability of the United States to conduct its foreign policy. Do you report the story or withhold it?

4. You have discovered through a long period of investigation that the

leader of a Ku Klux Klan group in a northeastern city is Jewish. Do you report it?

5. You are working on a story about the rivalry between Addidas and Puma, the West German companies that produce shoes and other clothing for athletes. The setting is a summer Olympic games. You learn that as part of the rivalry one of the companies has offered $25,000 cash to an assistant U.S. track coach to have his star sprinter switch shoes so that the company can reap publicity benefits. You confront the coach. He implores you not to proceed, saying the story would wreck his career.

As mentioned earlier, these are all real incidents. The reporter in the first situation resisted the command that there be one or two stories about the new tenants at the shopping plaza. The reporter ultimately resigned, complaining that there was no management commitment to news.

The gunman holding hostages did not get his wish. The message was not broadcast. Some of his comments concerning the circumstances inside the bank were paraphrased. Ultimately, the police were able to apprehend him. The reporter did not consult the police.

The Iranian assets story was broadcast despite the not-so-subtle White House suggestion that it be withheld. The information proved to be accurate, and there was no indication that the story had impaired the work of U.S. diplomats.

The reporter and his newspaper proceeded with the Klan story. Soon after it appeared, the subject of the story committed suicide. No recrimination ensued from the victim's family or others.

The bribe to the U.S. coach was reported at length. The coach was shown pleading with the reporter but his plea was not heard because he refused to give an interview. The story impaired but did not cripple the coach's career.

Each reporter must, of course, follow his or her own conscience when such questions of ethics arise. Not every reporter will make the same decision, and the decisions are not always clear-cut. It is important to make the decision that you believe is honest. Your integrity is your most valuable asset. If you lose that, your work as a journalist will not be worth much.

Staging

Another thorny issue is "staging." That is whether or not to ask people to change in any way what they would have done had you not been present. In one sense, this is an abstract issue because reality is inevitably altered, however subtly, by the intrusion of a microphone or television camera.

But we are talking about bolder manipulation. It is summed up in the expression newspaper photographers use, "making a picture," not "taking a picture." They are referring to the practice of putting objects in people's hands, or telling them what to wear, or how to look in what are represented as spontaneous news pictures. This is deceitful and dangerous.

If you are covering a strike and arrive while pickets are sitting around having their lunch, do not encourage them to pick up their placards and begin marching again because you have a deadline to meet. It would be better to record your interviews or shoot your videotape while they eat rather than to stage a demonstration. If shots of picketing are necessary for your story, return later or wait for the pickets to finish their lunch.

It is important for viewers to have confidence that what they see on the screen reflects events as they actually occurred. You should therefore refrain from telling people what to do, how to do it, or when. That is called "staging an event" or just "staging." While virtually all news directors are opposed to this sort of deception, some regard it as ethically permissible to have someone re-enact something they have already done. For example, is there really anything dishonest about asking a basketball coach to extend a practice session for you if you arrived late? If your camera malfunctioned while some children were tossing bread to some ducks, would you be deceiving your audience if you asked the children to do it again? Probably not. But there is an obvious difference between re-enacting such shots and deliberately deceiving your audience, for example, by suggesting to a rioter that he toss another rock through a window because you missed it the first time.

Set-up Shots

You will encounter other situations that are not so well-defined, and you or your news director will have to decide whether it is staging. A good rule to follow about re-enacting or staging is—when in doubt, don't.

It is suggested that you "set up" shots whenever possible. That means asking in advance what can be expected so you and your camera operator can get the necessary shots to tell the story. For example, if you were going to videotape a feature about glassblowing, you would want to ask the artist to show you how she would be moving about her studio during the process. The camera operator also would ask the artist to open the door of the kiln before the actual shooting to determine if the light could possibly damage the camera's picture-taking tubes.

News Judgment

One of the most difficult things in journalism to define is news judgment—the ability to decide what news is worth reporting. Various definitions have been offered over the years. Some people describe it in terms of an intangible: "Some people are just born with it." Others do not subscribe to that point of view.

Impact, Interest, and Information

If a story is worth covering, it will usually include at least one of three elements—*impact, interest,* or *information*. What do these three words mean?

Impact is concerned with what effect the story has on the lives of your viewers or listeners. It does not matter whether or not your audience numbers in the hundreds, thousands, or millions. What matters is whether or not this particular story concerns something that could have an effect on their lives. Some examples are a cut or increase in taxes, a gasoline shortage, a war in the Middle East, an increase in crime, a drug rehabilitation center being built in a residential neighborhood, a rezoning that will affect the character of a certain section of your city, or the granting or denial of money to your city from the state or federal governments.

A news story has impact if it concerns some event that will affect the lives of a great number of people who live in your viewing or listening area.

Interest often can be defined by asking yourself, "Is this a story that people can't help talking about?" Usually, stories with a great deal of interest will also be those that help people escape for a brief moment from the pressures or routine of their everyday lives. If a movie star is stricken with cancer, that story will not have any great impact on the lives of most people. But death is a basic fear. People frequently discuss death, especially when someone famous dies. If a man tries to cross the Atlantic in a rowboat, people may talk about the daring feat although it has no effect on their lives.

All feature stories are interesting, but some also have *impact*. The naming of the first woman rabbi to lead her own congregation was an interesting feature story that also had impact. It highlighted the controversy over the role of women in religion at a time when the fight over the equal rights amendment was making headlines.

Some stories give viewers and listeners useful *information*. Many TV and radio stations now have consumer and medical reporters. They tell you how to shop wisely in the supermarket; how to bargain with a dealer over the price of a new car; how to avoid being cheated by home improvement firms; and give medical advice about jogging and early detection of physical problems. Such stories provide information that people can use in their everyday lives. Often such stories also combine impact or interest. When former First Lady Betty Ford developed breast cancer, she discussed her mastectomy with a candor that encouraged other women to take tests for breast cancer.

In addition to these three elements of news judgment, a fourth—*visual*—applies only to television news. Television news allows the viewer to see and to hear the news event or, at least, a carefully and objectively edited version of it.

Because of the *visual* element, a fire that would not merit two paragraphs in the daily paper or even a brief mention on the radio is worth 20 seconds of precious air time on television. Considerable criticism has been leveled against an overemphasis on pictures when an event scarcely justifies coverage. This will be discussed in more detail later in the book. But television is always looking for the story that makes a good picture. Even in the largest of markets, most one-hour TV newscasts will present only about ten reports from the field, and the selection usually is keyed to what is best visually.

Second-Guessing

News judgment is subject to lots of second-guessing. If you were to check what story the other station or stations in town led with or decided to cover throughout their news broadcast, you would discover that the product turned out each night by the Action News team and the Eyewitness News crew would be both different and the same. The material will, for the most part, be basically the same but served up in a different manner.

Newsroom at WBBM–TV, Chicago. (WBBM–TV photo)

News directors and producers at competing stations usually react to the same wire bulletins and newspaper headlines, cover the same events, and develop much the same features. The difference is in the manner in which it is presented. One station might lead with the report of the mayor's news conference during which he announces the firing of a department head because it took the city a week to dig out of a snowstorm. Another station might lead with a story about a child being killed in a local fire. If you polled the Action News staff, half probably would say, "We goofed. Eyewitness News had the better lead." The other half probably would comment, "We sure beat the competition tonight."

Of course, the same comments were being voiced in the Eyewitness News studios. Both stations would have had legitimate reasons for leading their newscasts with either story. There really is no loser or winner. You can be certain that both stations would include the two stories during their 30 or 60 minutes of news. If one of the stories was missing, then someone would be guilty of bad news judgment.

Probably the greatest debate in the broadcast newsroom centers around the choice of lead story for the newscast. Should it be local, national, or international? There is an old theory that a flood killing hundreds in India is less interesting than a policeman being killed on Main Street. That is why most stations lead with a local story.

News judgment also extends to good taste. A newswriter or producer who routinely leads off a newscast with stories about crime and sex in the belief that it will hold a larger audience is doing a disservice to the community.

Foresight

Often good news judgment is knowing when to move fast on a breaking story, not waiting to see what the competition does. For example, an assignment editor at Channel A dispatches a reporter and camera crew more than 50 miles to the scene of an oil spill on the Hudson River. Meanwhile, the assignment editor at Channel B takes no action. The editor with foresight realizes that the oil will soon flow toward his city and be a major story. The editor at the other station rationalizes that the oil spill is outside his 50-mile viewing area, so he does not send a reporter or crew. His news judgment is questionable. The oil does make its way to the city and is an important story.

Another more obvious lapse of news judgment concerned a story about an auto accident involving Senator Edward Kennedy of Massachusetts. In preparing a review of the week's news for one of the radio networks, a producer failed to include a story about Senator Kennedy driving off the bridge on Chappaquidick. When questioned by the editor about this omission, the producer explained that it was "merely an auto accident" and was not important enough for a review of the week's news. The death of a young woman in the accident was not immediately known, but the editor correctly insisted that the story be included in the weekly review. His instincts told him this might be more than just an auto accident. The Chappaquidick story made more than one week-in-review in the next decade.

Developing News Judgment

You must develop sound news judgment to survive in broadcast journalism, and you will have to work on developing it in your first job, whether it is as a desk assistant in a major radio or TV station or as a young reporter in a small town. A desk assistant in a big city newsroom will be expected to recognize important news as it moves on the wires and to bring it to the attention of the editor immediately. An alert desk assistant who demonstrates an ability to recognize important news is an asset to a busy editor. And an appreciative editor often can shorten the apprenticeship for a young journalist.

That same ability to recognize news will be just as essential for the young journalist at a small radio station, where he will most likely be expected to write newscasts and function as a reporter the first day on the job.

You must remember that what may be news in one community will not necessarily be so in another. The guest speaker at a Rotary meeting in a small town could produce a page of copy and perhaps a recorded interview. But such guest appearances usually go unnoticed in a city of any size.

The birth of twins could be one of the major news developments of the day in a community of 5,000, but the delivery of anything less than quadruplets would probably go unreported in Los Angeles.

Local news developments can be expected to get more attention in a smaller market than in a larger one. A radio station with limited power can be expected to concentrate much of its news coverage on its immediate area. The result often is an abundance of local news and too little national and international news. But if you find yourself working as a newsperson in such a market, you must remember that your audience will, for the most part, want to hear more about those twins and the Rotary's guest speaker than about a congressional debate over foreign aid.

One of the best ways to develop news judgment is to compare your instincts with those of senior journalists. Watch what happens to the wire copy that is delivered to the editor. Which stories are assigned to writers and reporters? Which stories are ignored and why? Most editors and reporters will take the time to explain their decisions to a young journalist who shows interest in learning.

Another basic rule in the development of news judgment—and for survival—is to learn from mistakes. Most news directors and editors will tolerate some errors by beginners, but do not test their patience by repeating the offense. If you make a mistake, examine why and be determined not to do it again. That is part of the learning process and part of developing good news judgment. If you understand that you failed to see the impact of a story or did not ask a key question during an interview, that in itself has value. Next time, you should know better.

In a small news operation, your news director will give you assignments, but you will be expected to show enterprise by developing some stories of your own. It also is important to remember that your news director probably is anxious to move on to a larger market. So if you show enough initiative, you may move into his job within a few months. If that happens, you will be looking for someone to help you and, for the first time, you will be making assignments for someone else. That will be the most important test of your news judgment, and how you perform may decide your future.

From there, you probably will move up to bigger stations with larger staffs. You will become one of a team of reporters. Where you go and how you grow depend in large measure on your training, motivation, and ability.

3

Sources of News

Having laid the foundation in Chapters 1 and 2 with an introduction to broadcast journalism and a discussion of news judgment, this book, as mentioned in the Preface, will first deal with radio broadcast and then TV news. Chapters 3, 4, and 5 discuss news gathering and news sources; Chapters 6 through 9 treat in detail and in sequence the important steps in broadcast news writing, points of style, rewriting, lead sentences, and lead-off stories. The final portions on radio broadcast, Chapters 10 through 12, discuss organization of news copy, editing and timing newscasts, and some technical aspects of audiotape inserts.

A newsroom should be thought of as a central clearinghouse of story ideas from a variety of sources. Most important are the wire services, which report all the day's happenings in your city, state, nation, and the world. Various institutions and individuals will also be fighting for your attention, trying to get part of the time allotted for your broadcast. Tips will also come in from viewers and listeners. And you will be alerted to various crime and fire stories from the police radio. Let's examine in detail what broadcast news organizations receive from various sources.

Wire Services

The two major wire service organizations in this country are the Associated Press (AP) and United Press International (UPI). They offer several different types of wires. First is the radio wire, written for use on the air

WCBS–TV wire room. (Photo by Lionel Phillips)

without any editing or rewriting. Almost all broadcast news operations subscribe to the radio wire because it provides a distilled coverage of the major stories of the day. AP also provides a TV wire which in many ways is similar to the radio wire. It provides headlines and brief summaries of the news.

It is unfortunate that the majority of broadcasters never see the newspaper or "A" wires. Only stations in larger markets buy both the broadcast services and the "A" wires that provide extensive details. It is not only a cost factor. The majority of stations do not have sufficient news staffs to rewrite the newspaper wire into broadcast style even if they could afford both wires.

So to accommodate the thousands of smaller stations, the wire services tap out hourly broadcast summaries. These are known as the "rip and read" wires.

We cannot condone the "rip and read" approach to news. One of the main purposes of this book is to help you develop your own broadcast writing style. But we recognize that broadcast wires are here to stay and that you probably will find yourself "ripping and reading" until you land a job in a larger market.

The "A" wires provide the major international and national stories. The regional wires concentrate on news in a large area covering several states. The state wire provides news within an entire state. In some large cities, a local wire supplies news in that metropolitan area. These local wires provide two main listings of possible news stories. The first is a morning index of scheduled events, known as a daybook, which covers stories that take place during the morning and afternoon. It lists a number of stories that the wire will cover and other stories that it will not staff. Do not throw away the stories that the wires list but will not cover. You and the wire services will not always agree on which stories are worth air time. In the early afternoon, the wires will provide a night-book, listing events scheduled for that evening. This will provide ideas for nighttime stories to update your late broadcast.

The wire services also offer high-speed machines that deliver more than 1,000 words a minute, 20 times faster than the conventional wires. The high-speed wires also are designed to feed computers which are beginning to appear in greater numbers in radio and TV newsrooms. A report on the use of computers—the electronic newsrooms—will be included later in the book.

A variety of other wires concentrate on business, sports, and weather information. Some of the larger broadcast news operations also take Reuters, the British news agency's wire.

Photo Services

The wire services also provide most of the still photographs used on television. The photos are fed to newsrooms on Laserfax (AP) and Unifax II (UPI) machines via telephone lines. AP and UPI also provide customers with slides of people and events in the news to flash on a small insert beside the TV anchorperson.

Newspapers

Newspapers are another major source of stories for radio and TV news operations. Newspapers receive the same wire services news from AP and UPI as do radio and TV stations. What radio and TV news can get from the papers in the way of story ideas are mostly features and investigative reports that their newsrooms might not otherwise know about. There is nothing wrong with taking a story idea from the papers, but some news directors try to avoid making a habit of it. News organizations, however, regularly raid each other's ideas.

Broadcasters also check the newspapers to see which stories are making the front page. This should help you to make sure you are not missing or underplaying any stories in your newscast.

If the newspaper has a genuine exclusive, then you must credit it as the source of the story. That is only fair. But do not be too generous with those plugs for your competition. Use your own initiative. Many times it requires only a telephone call to verify that the newspaper "exclusive" is true—or false. Once you have determined that, you can use the story without attributing it to the newspaper.

Other Radio and TV Stations

Newspapers are not the only competition that radio and TV monitor. They listen to the radio stations in town and monitor competitive TV broadcasts in much the same way as they check newspapers. Some stations avoid feature stories that have already run on competing stations.

Press Releases

The daily mail will provide more story ideas than any station can broadcast. The volume of press releases is overwhelming. Broadcast coverage is more coveted than attention from newspapers because of the larger audience.

Most press releases end up in the wastebasket. Some, however, provide interesting story ideas or advance information on legitimate news events.

Without the press release, the assignment desk may never know that Disneyworld is in town auditioning for chorus girls. Of course, it is free publicity, but it also offers visual appeal for TV viewers. Press releases announcing an antique or automobile show will bring TV cameras out for more features. And if someone decides to go cross-country on a bike, TV and radio will no doubt cover the event, perhaps mentioning the bike manufacturer in the process.

A newsperson must decide, "Is this just a free ad for the business or product or is it also a valid news story? Does it provide impact, information, or interest?" Television also is concerned with the story's visual potential.

Obviously, press releases fill a need and not all are pushing a product or a point of view. A release from a hospital dealing with a new heart surgery technique could stimulate the assignment editor's interest and provide an interesting radio and TV story. A press release from the police department about an award ceremony for civilian heroes has obvious audio and video possibilities.

The only danger with press releases is that they sometimes become a crutch. Don't rely on too many of them to fill up the six o'clock news.

Network and Syndication Feeds

If the station you are working for is owned by or affiliated with a network, you will be offered a daily supplementary service of news stories and features, known as syndication or news feeds. They provide radio and TV stations with additional coverage of major national and international events for use on local newscasts. For many stations, this is the only way to get some audiotape or videotape of an event before it is presented on a network broadcast. It is collected by the networks

WWBT–TV intern monitoring news feed from New York.

from their affiliates and then distributed to them. On a day when your
area may be short of material, these can be a lifesaver.

But what about the independent television news stations that are not
affiliated with a network? It was to serve these TV stations that the Independent Television News Association (ITNA) began supplying hard
news, features, sports, weather, and other reports to its member stations
via satellite. By the end of 1982, only 13 independent TV stations were
supplying and receiving daily feeds from ITNA. That is only a small
number of the approximately 200 nonaffiliated TV stations in the country.

One of those independent stations, WPIX in New York, formed a network news service of its own, Independent Network News. In 1982, INN
was feeding a half hour of network news to 75 TV stations via satellite
during prime time (9:30 P.M.). Most stations record the feed and play it
back at 10 P.M. along with 30 minutes of local news.

AP and UPI also provide audio material for any station that wants to
buy it. Reports and actualities (voices of newsmakers) are designed so
they can be used in locally produced newscasts. The broadcast wires run
descriptions of the audio material before feeding it out to the stations so
they will know what to expect. The stations receive the audio material
on telephone lines. Many news operations have automated equipment
that records the feeds as soon as they start. Most stations record the entire feed as a precaution but often use cartridges to record specific material they know they will want to use. A tone between each cut gives the
stations time to insert new cartridges into their machines.

The audio operation is a two-way street. Both AP and UPI buy reports and actualities from radio stations and stringers to supplement the material from their reporters and editors. Both wires maintain separate news staffs to handle the audio services.

Another source of news for local stations are the network broadcasts. Most TV affiliates routinely record the network newscasts throughout the day, extracting material for use on their own local newscasts.

Local Angles to National and World News

The sources previously mentioned provide many top stories outside a local broadcast area. These are stories of national or international interest. Ideally, radio and TV try to find local angles to these stories. For example, when the Solidarity labor movement was causing problems for Poland's communist leaders, many broadcasters went into local Polish communities. They interviewed neighborhood leaders and people on the streets for their opinions about what was happening in their homeland.

When an Air Florida jet crashed soon after takeoff from Washington National Airport, killing 78 people, radio and TV news staffs were particularly interested in discovering how many of the dead and survivors were from their cities. As tragic as the story was for listeners and viewers everywhere, the crash was especially painful and significant for residents of Washington, D.C., Virginia, and Florida because the majority of those killed were from those areas. The accident also had a special significance for some small communities such as Lorain, Ohio, and Peabody, Massachusetts. For them, the story became a local one—not national—when two passengers from those towns were reported on the list of dead.

Phone Tips

In any good newsroom, the telephone always is ringing. It is not considered a nuisance. Phone tips are often how most stations learn about breaking news. They can give you the jump on both the competition and the wires. In many areas, radio and TV stations offer cash prizes for the best news tip of the week or month.

Police and Fire Radios

You cannot always rely on phone tips to get you to a breaking story ahead of the competition. All alert assignment desks monitor police and fire scanners. You might not beat the competition to the scene, but you won't miss the story. The wire services eventually will run the story, but often too late for you to gather good audio and visual material.

V.C.U. broadcast news student monitors police and fire scanner while she works on a news script.

The Eyes and Ears of the News Staff

Members of the news staff can also make a contribution. Their eyes and ears can see much that will provide good stories for radio and television. They also meet other people in their business and social lives. Once it becomes known they work in broadcasting, news people can expect to hear about "good stories" from acquaintances.

Do not be afraid to make suggestions for stories to your assignment editor. Even if you are not assigned to cover it for some reason, it will very often get on the air.

Futures File

How do broadcast newsrooms keep track of all these ideas for news stories? Obviously, stories that are breaking that day will be decided upon as they come in. But what about the feature story that can wait a day or two? What about a press release for an event that will take place next week? What about the murder trial set to start next month?

The answer is a futures file. It can be as simple as 31 manila folders, one for each day of the month. Into each folder go story ideas that will take place on that day. Assignment editors check the futures file for a particular date at least one day before. This is so they can weed out stories they do not want and plan for coverage of the others.

Once a futures file is established, it should be placed where everyone can look at it. It is no good locking the file in the boss's office if reporters, editors, and desk assistants are to put advance material in it. The entire staff should be encouraged to feed the futures file.

If the news director finds little or nothing in the file, he may have trouble finding enough assignments for reporters. This is particularly true on weekends when news is usually slow. It is said that most wars begin on weekends. But little else seems to happen with the exception of natural disasters. So anything left in the futures file for the weekend is especially appreciated.

Information Gathering Techniques

Reporters employ three techniques—interviews, observation, and documentation—in gathering information. And news sources engage in certain practices—the news conference, off-the-record talk, background briefings, leaks, and trial balloons—in generating information. Let's consider each of these, starting with information gathering techniques for reporters.

Interviewing Techniques

The interview is a basic tool for developing a news story. In preparing for an interview, you must first ask yourself, "What sort of information do I want to collect?" The information you seek will be different, for example, if you are at a fire, a dinner for a doctor who is being honored, talking to a new member of the city council, or interviewing a poet who has just won a national prize.

At the fire, you will want to find out what happened. You will question the fire chief, people who escaped from the building, those who live or work across the street from the fire, and anyone else who can shed some light on how and why the fire started.

But at the dinner for the doctor who has served his community for 50 years, you will be looking more for emotional response than for facts. How does the doctor feel about his 50 years of service and about the honor his fellow citizens and patients are bestowing on him?

At the city councilman's office, you will be trying to discover his views on one or more issues. You will want him to talk about his beliefs and goals.

Your interview with the poet who won a national prize will attempt to find out how he writes and lives. You will want him to discuss his life-style and the creative process.

These are only a few of the interview situations you will encounter. Usually, you will interview people who have some special knowledge; celebrities, politicians, business, and community leaders; and your fellow citizens to whom something good or bad has happened.

At first you probably will find it unsettling to interview the famous and the powerful. It may help to remember that often you represent something those people want—access to wider recognition through your news organization. You need not be timid. Be courteous, not arrogant, but ask solid questions.

Richard Salant, then president of CBS News, once sent a memorandum to all CBS news correspondents at a time when Howard Hughes was very much in the news. He urged correspondents to think about what they would ask Howard Hughes should they somehow corner the famous recluse. The point is well taken. Frequently, far more effort is spent arranging an interview than preparing for one.

Leading Questions

How you frame a question depends on the purpose of an interview and how it will be used. Generally, you should avoid asking leading questions, because you then appear to be fishing for a particular answer rather than searching objectively for what is on the interviewee's mind.

Some examples of leading questions that are to be avoided are as follows:

1. Will you carry a gun now that you have been robbed?
2. Are you going to stop working now that you've won the lottery?
3. Are you going to move away now that the mud slide has destroyed your home?

Those questions could be worded in a nonleading manner. Thus,

1. Will you do anything to try to avoid being robbed again?
2. How will you spend the money you won in the lottery?
3. What will you do now that the mud slide has destroyed your home?

But sometimes leading or rhetorical questions can be useful, especially if the subject is shy, hostile, or feels intimidated. The interviewee may respond more openly if he feels you understand or sympathize with him. In such an instance, what usually would be regarded as a leading question may be a way of drawing the interviewee out and making him feel comfortable. For example, in interviewing an elderly woman who has been mugged, you might find it helpful to ask, "It must have been a frightening experience for you?"

A Time for Silence

It is important to sense when not to ask a question. Frequently a question will step on the interviewee's response and destroy an established mood. If you simply remain silent and wait, the person you are interviewing will often restate something in clearer form or go on to make a point about an important question you had not thought to ask.

When conducting interviews, beware of overlapping or stepping on the interviewee's answers. This can be confusing, especially in radio interviews with more than one person. It can be particularly troublesome when conducting telephone interviews or tape recording them for later broadcast. Much of the equipment used in recording such interviews contains devices that smooth out sharp changes in volume. If you speak before the answer is completed, or an interviewee responds before the question is finished, part of the answer or question may go unrecorded.

Telephone Interviews

One of the most useful pieces of equipment in the radio newsroom is the telephone. Properly used, it can be a tremendous asset in making radio newscasts more interesting and exciting. The telephone also makes it possible for small stations to compete with those that have larger budgets and staffs. As long as you have a phone, you have as much chance as the competition to reach an eyewitness to an explosion in Tennessee or a sheriff in Wyoming who has captured a notorious criminal.

Conducting a good telephone interview requires special skills and finesse. For example, that sheriff may be great with a shotgun but a dull personality on the telephone. He also may be a "yes" and "no" man, which means you must find some way to get him talking or ruin the interview. Your job probably will be even more complicated because a dozen other reporters may be in his office waiting for their chance to speak with him. What follows are a few techniques that will help you get good actualities.

You should warm up or relax the person on the other end of the line. You are likely to get more colorful tape out of the reticent sheriff if you tell him that thousands of people probably will be listening to his story on radio.

If his responses are limited to "yes sir" and "no sir," you might find

WRVA desk editor-reporter John Ennis.

it helpful to pretend that the telephone connection is not too good and to ask him to repeat what he said. Chances are he will respond in detail. The essential thing is to so phrase questions that they cannot be answered by a "yes" or "no." If you ask the sheriff if he had much trouble nailing his man, you probably will get a "yes" or "no" reply. But if you ask him, "Exactly how did you corner the outlaw?" you may get a good piece of tape.

It is important to keep him talking until you are certain that you have enough good material for broadcast or are convinced that it is a hopeless cause—that the sheriff definitely is a man of action, not words.

Remember also that a recording of good technical quality is just as important as content. Before you get your interviewee started, make sure your telephone line is as good as possible and be certain that your recording level is right.

Editors often must "kill" tape recordings that had good information but were not broadcast quality. If you have difficulty understanding a person on the phone, or later when you listen to it on the playback, you should not use it on the air. If you must put your ear up against the speaker to make sense out of a recording, you should forget about it. By the time it travels to the car or home speaker it will be unintelligible.

Here is a final and important note on the use of the phone for recordings: it is not a legal requirement that a beep or tone device be attached to a phone. Some stations still use this intrusive signal on all the telephone recordings they air, because they do not understand the law or they fear possible legal suits. The simple way to resolve this is to advise the person with whom you are speaking that you are recording the conversation. Some stations record that warning as well as the interview, but most stations do not bother with this formality. If the interviewee requests that his voice not be used, that request must be honored. Any reporter who ignores that request deserves to be sued. And remember there is never an excuse for not identifying yourself properly and advising the individual on the phone that you plan to record his voice. If you do not so advise him and play that material on the air, you could be guilty of invasion of privacy.

Ending the Interview

Young journalists seldom know when to end an interview. Often that is because they are concerned about missing something or that the boss will think of a question they did not ask. As your experience and confidence increase, the more secure you will be in knowing when you have enough material. In time, you will develop a sense that will tell you, "that's it, I have what I need."

Meanwhile, you can help develop that sense by preparing properly for the interview. Make a list of important questions. Listen carefully to the answers. Make a mental note (or if you feel more secure, keep written notes) each time you record good quotes. When you believe you have all the material you possibly can use, and think you have covered the most salient points in your interview, end it. You must avoid returning to the station with an endless amount of tape. It is defeating to have a good interview that cannot be broadcast because you did not have enough time to edit it.

Observation

Observation is the second reporting technique employed by journalists to gather information. It can support and strengthen the information developed during an interview. And at times—when interviews are not available—observation is all that a reporter will have to work with.

Broadcast reporters do most of their observing while covering a breaking story in the field. Record your sense impressions of sights—colors and forms—sounds, and smells at the scene of a fire, storm, or other disaster so you can describe an event vividly for your listeners. If you are covering a hurricane, try to describe how the wind sounded as it howled through the trees. If you cover the demolition of a library building tell your listeners how the ground rumbled and shook when the dynamite went off.

Observation is a critical skill in what many reporters regard as one of the most stressful situations, broadcasting an event live as it happens.

Such situations might include the aftermath of a plane crash, a police shoot-out with bank robbers, and the campaign headquarters of a candidate on election night.

You must ad-lib such on-the-spot reports because there is no time to write a script. Your eyes become the eyes of your listeners who cannot see what you are seeing.

You can prepare in advance for some live news events, such as the inauguration of a new mayor, a Fourth of July parade, or a funeral. Make a list of facts to be included in your live broadcast, but avoid writing a finished script. Keep those notes you prepared in advance within easy reach so you can refer to them when you must fill during lulls until the next part of the event takes place.

Documentation

Reporters generally agree that the most reliable method of collecting information is through documents. Although interviews are helpful, and observation strengthens a reporter's story, public records and other documents are probably the most forceful tools that a reporter can use. Documents can be used to verify or reject information the reporter has been told or has observed.

For example, a reporter may be told by a source that a certain lawyer is fixing drunken driving charges for his clients. A confrontation interview with the lawyer probably will produce a denial. But if the court records show that no driving-while-intoxicated case handled by that attorney ever came to trial, the reporter is in a strong position to develop the story further.

More about documents and public records will be discussed in Chapter 23, "Investigative Reporting."

Let us turn now to techniques that news sources utilize. Often, newsmakers employ these practices to seek some advantage in the public eye, but reporters who prepare in advance and ask solid questions can develop good stories.

The News Conference

The news conference has become common practice in all but the smallest markets or towns because it is a fast, inexpensive way for a newsmaker to get a point of view across to the public.

That's important for the person holding the news conference. What often is important for you is getting access to a newsmaker who otherwise might not be available to individual reporters. But remember that a news conference is a staged event. Reporters should ask solid and intelligent questions and should not be lulled into complacency. Too often, the news conference becomes a free podium for the person who calls it.

Often you will be sent to a news conference without much warning as you shuttle between stories. Frequently, all you will know is that the mayor, governor, city council member, or industry spokesman wants to meet with the press. The subject may be a well-kept secret. At other times information about the news conference will be leaked in advance. And there will be occasions when the person holding the news conference will reveal why it is being called.

If the subject is known, prepare yourself. Read whatever background information you can find. Dig through back issues of newspapers. If your station maintains a morgue, use it. Ideally, you will have sufficient information when you arrive at the news conference to ask relevant and intelligent questions.

The caller of a well-organized news conference will likely provide a news release covering the subject of the meeting and sometimes a full text of remarks to be made. Read them carefully. Look for what, if anything, is truly news. Seek your angle, how to advance the story you are covering.

Remember that the person who calls the news conference intends to use you and probably knows the subject better than you do. Assume that some reporters will ask soft questions that yield only self-serving answers. Assume this not out of arrogance but because a news conference is no more productive than the quality of the questions asked. Uninformed, naive questioning by even a few reporters can lower the level of a news conference.

Because many reporters participate in a news conference, the opportunity for a newsmaker to manipulate the situation is far greater than during a one-on-one interview. Be alert and listen carefully to the questions and answers. Take careful notes. Look for inconsistencies. Use any background information you have that contradicts the speaker. Follow-up questions are important but it's difficult to get the opportunity to ask them in a roomful of reporters, some of whom ask irrelevant questions just to be seen or heard. You will have a better chance of asking that follow-up question if you sit as close to the speaker as possible. Get to the news conference early so you will get a good position.

During the news conference, try to take the most complete notes possible. List the questions by number and write a summary of the answers. Verbatim text of key quotes is best, if you are fast enough to do it. Note the time the news conference begins and check your watch each time you hear a significant remark. This will help you locate the material quickly when the news conference is over. Another way to flag good quotes is to note reference counter numbers that appear on most audio recorders.

Off-the-record Talk

When a source gives you information with the understanding that you cannot quote or paraphrase it, that is known as "off-the-record" talk. Such information may lead you to other on-the-record sources who may verify what you were told off the record. You should never use off-the-record information directly because if you violate a confidence, you will never get a story from that source again.

Sources sometimes try to block the broadcast of a story by purposely telling you something off the record so you cannot report it. It may be better to refuse off-the-record information if you think you can develop the story on your own. That is a decision you must make on a case-by-case basis. Off-the-record information, however, eventually can be helpful, and you learn in time how to make it work to your advantage. It can help you to ask others the right questions—as long as you do not reveal your off-the-record source.

Background Briefings

When a source gives you information that may be used only without direct attribution, it is known as a background briefing. These often lead to stories in which sources are generalized by such phrases as "according to a reliable source," "an informed source told us," or "an industry spokesman said." Background briefings, usually initiated by government or industry, have legitimate value in preparing the media for comprehensive reporting in the future. Reporters, however, should keep alert to their misuse or abuse for personal or political advantage.

Leaks and Trial Balloons

Still other tactics employed in passing information to reporters are leaks and trial balloons. A leak usually involves sensitive information which the source often shares with only one reporter. A reporter should weigh that chance for an "exclusive" against the reliability of the source on the basis of past experience. The reporter should also consider whether the source has a personal axe to grind, and should make every effort to verify the accuracy of the information leaked. The individual who leaks information sometimes seeks to influence others, such as city council members' or legislators' votes on an issue. Sometimes the source of a leak is motivated by conscience to expose wrongdoing by another in the public interest but lacks the courage to do so openly.

A trial balloon is an attempt to test public reaction to an idea before a public official formally announces a proposal or policy. Again, with no direct attribution, an official or someone else in his administration "floats" the trial balloon by mentioning a certain course of action as a possibility or potential solution to a problem. If the trial balloon meets with a public outcry and editorials in opposition, the idea most likely will never be formally proposed and the official escapes blame or criticism. If, on the other hand, public reaction is favorable and editorials endorse the idea, the official publicly announces the plan.

5

Beats and Assignments for Radio

On almost any given day of the year news organizations will be able to get a story from the police, fire departments, the courts, or some agency of the government. News directors have found that assigning a reporter to cover one of these on a regular basis—called a beat in journalism jargon—pays ample dividends. The reporter on the beat gets to know the subject, develops good sources of information, and receives early tips.

Other beats besides those mentioned include education, science and health, consumer information, and business. Let's concentrate on the types of beats to which you may be assigned as a young reporter.

City Council

As we have stressed several times, most of you will find jobs in smaller markets when you get out of college. This is good because at those small stations you will get an opportunity to do so many things that will be required of you during your career. Among the important beats you will learn to cover is city council meetings and, depending upon the location, possibly meetings of the county and state legislative bodies.

In the smaller markets, the city council usually is a frequent source of news. The same sometimes is true in larger markets, especially when the mayor and the majority of the council are of different political parties.

Learning about the workings of a city council is likely to be one of the first challenges that you as a young reporter will have to face. Prepare yourself as best you can now in college. Some journalism programs offer courses on local government. If yours does not, the political science department probably will.

You may be required by your professors to cover the city council, which will give you valuable experience. Former students often comment that they wish that they had known more about the workings of the city council when they got their first job. It is important, for example, to know how a piece of legislation goes through the council, the political makeup of the council, and the problems that exist in the various districts that the council members represent.

Ken Srpan, News Director of WPTF, Raleigh, North Carolina, recalls that a newspaper reporter helped him when he began covering the city council in Richmond, Virginia. "It's great," Srpan said, "if you can find someone who has covered the council for a year or two, who can tell you about the idiosyncrasies of each council member . . . what they're like and what they're after." Srpan said if you are replacing a reporter who has been covering the city council, you should "get him to tell you all he knows about the council before he leaves town." Unfortunately, the person you are replacing will often be gone by the time you arrive. But, Srpan said, most of the other reporters will be glad to help you out even if you are competing with them.

Srpan said you really have to spend a lot of time at meetings before you understand what makes the council tick. "And you have to attend the committee meetings as well," he added, "because you often find out more about how they really feel on an issue at those meetings than you do at the formal sessions of the whole council."

Srpan also said it is important to know in advance what the council and its committees are going to be discussing. "That way," he said, "you will have an idea what is likely to make news rather than going in blind."

This sort of preparation means that you can plan on recording those parts of meetings that are likely to produce some fireworks. Most reporters like to watch, listen, and take notes so that they can interview certain members of the council following the debate rather than trying to record the entire meeting. But if you anticipate some heated debate, make sure your tape recorder is working so that you do not miss the natural sound.

These pointers will help you to solve the main problem for radio reporters at local government sessions—getting good, meaty sound cuts that will attract the listener's attention. Often, the issue being discussed can be made more interesting if the reporter interviews people who will be affected by the lawmakers' decisions. Many times you will be able to "butt" together sound bites from people with opposing views, creating the effect of a debate. This is called intercutting. A lively exchange could rescue what otherwise might be a dull story.

The Police

The police beat is more common at local stations than at the networks. The reason is that a lost child in a community may make a good local story, sometimes even a lead story. So will a major bank robbery or a violent crime. But it is rare that a police story merits national attention. It would require a prominent victim, an unusually large dollar loss, or some weird angle before the story would be covered for a national audience.

Digging up police news is easier to do for radio than for television. Many small radio stations make what they call "the telephone rounds." The reporter phones police and fire departments, checking to see if there have been any car accidents, fires, burglaries, crimes, or anything else of local interest. Often a police officer will be available for audio interviews or can put you in contact with one of the officers on the case.

In the largest cities, there may be a police wire similar to an AP or UPI news wire that will let you know about police activity. In some large cities or counties, the police department also has a public relations staff. One of its many duties is to help reporters get information on crime stories.

Learn to translate what the police tell you. Police tend to talk in a jargon. There are certain recurring phrases in the vocabulary of a police officer that you should banish from your copy. Examples are "alleged perpetrator" and "read his rights," as in "the alleged perpetrator was read his rights."

Under our system of law, an accused person is innocent until proved guilty. An arrestee may be called "the accused" or "a suspect," but it is better to say the person was "arrested by police in connection with . . ." Later, if the suspect has been arraigned, you can identify that person by name as being "charged with the crime" (for that is what "arraigned" means).

You should be careful when police identify someone as the person who committed a crime. For example, 20 officers at the scene of a bank robbery all claim that they saw a suspect hold a gun to the head of a bank manager and pull the trigger. Twenty witnesses sounds impressive, but their word is not conclusive until they testify in court and the jury convicts.

Even when there are millions of witnesses to a crime, responsible journalists do not shortcut the judicial process. President Kennedy's alleged assassin, Lee Harvey Oswald, was killed by Jack Ruby on live national television. Millions saw it happen. Millions more saw the tape replays. But responsible news reporters did not call Ruby "Oswald's killer'' until after Ruby was convicted. One could always imagine a scenario in which Ruby fires a blank pistol while the real killer fires bullets and escapes because attention is focused on Ruby.

A Crime in Progress

One of the most dramatic forms of crime reporting occurs when the event is still taking place. A bank robbery involving hostages is an example. The police radio usually provides the earliest tip on this kind of story as well as details on how the police are handling it. But remember that what you hear on police frequencies is for your guidance, not for direct rebroadcast. You may use it to decide where to place yourself and others in your news team, or you may paraphrase the information. But it is a violation of the rules of the Federal Communications Commission (FCC) to report verbatim what is said in what amounts to a private radio transmission. The same is true of conversations on Federal Aviation Administration (FAA) frequencies.

Sooner or later, when covering a crime in progress, you may face the dilemma of whether to attempt to get information from the criminals if it could possibly interfere with the work of various authorities. An airline hijacker or rioting prison inmates may try to use you. You must use common sense. Consult your supervisors. Remember, the criminals usually will have access to radios and will be able to hear what you are reporting. Check the guidelines of your station, if they exist, or check first with the news director or producer. Police departments ask for voluntary restraint in such situations. They argue that the reporters may complicate the policemen's efforts to end a crime quickly with a minimum of harm.

The Courts

Most crimes lead to the courtroom, which is another regular source of local stories. Covering a trial in court really will test your abilities as a newsperson. It takes lots of concentration, energy, and patience.

So much goes on in a trial that you have to keep asking yourself:

1. "What is important and what is not?"
2. "What is the heart of the prosecution's case?"
3. "What is the main argument for the defense?"
4. "Is the judge (or jury) leaning toward one side or the other?"

Always be ready for those moments that write their own headlines—a shouting match; a shaken, crying witness; or a scornful lawyer. Watch faces in the courtroom. The defense and prosecution do, and so should you. Often, the reactions of the jury, the judge, the lawyers, the defendant, and the spectators will make good copy.

Working for radio, your task is to note selective quotes for your narration. Do not try to write down all that is said in the courtroom. Your writing hand will become numb and so will your mind. Summarize the less important points in your notepad while keeping alert for full quotes on the key points of the testimony. The opening statements by the prosecution and the defense often will alert you to what to look for during the course of the trial.

On a separate page in your notepad, keep track of possible questions to ask the defense or prosecution lawyers, if they are willing to talk to you when the court is in recess. The judge often will order both sides not to talk to reporters. But there are times when he will not. And there is nothing to stop you from trying to get a reaction from the defendant. Because you will not be allowed (in most states) to tape record the testimony in the courtroom, these potential interviews may be the only sound bite in your story.

Many judges will usually call at least one recess during the morning session and another during the afternoon. These breaks are an ideal time for you to file an updated story or to discuss the story with the news desk. When something really significant happens during the testimony, you will have to use your own news judgment as to whether to leave the courtroom and file a new report for the next hourly broadcast. You often will be able to get a fill-in later on from some of the other reporters.

Most of the time you will be summarizing testimony. But there often will be brisk exchanges between the principals which you will want to quote. Try to keep those quotes short, making sure it is clear to the listener who is saying what. Here is an example:

The highlight of the so-called Nob Hill murder trial, now in its third week, was the admission by defendant Barbara Glenn that she killed her millionaire lover, Jackson Turner. But she insisted it was an accident. She said she told Turner she was going to commit suicide and that as he pulled the gun from her hand it went off, killing him. At this point in her testimony, Glenn broke into tears. After a brief recess, the prosecutor began attacking her story. He questioned whether she really would have traveled 500 miles for a rendevous with Turner just to kill herself.

"Isn't it true you were jealous of his other lovers?" asked the prosecutor.

"No! No! No!," Glenn cried out before standing up and finally collapsing into the witness chair.

Later, Jim Johnson, the defense attorney, accused prosecutor Bill Kane of badgering his client.

In cue: "He was doing . . ."
Time: 10
Out cue: ". . . in the end."

And defense attorney Johnson said he would ask the judge tomorrow morning to strike the questions and answers from the record. Prosecutor Kane would not comment to reporters as he left the courtroom.

This is Bill Fowler reporting.

Note that the side willing to talk in the preceding example was the defense. This usually will be the case in a criminal trial. Restrain your use of interviews with the defense to avoid an imbalance in your coverage of the trial. Defense interviews tend to be self-serving. But most of the time they will be the only interviews you will have. The prosecution will be more willing to talk when the verdict is in, particularly if it wins. In civil trials, you will find it is easier to get both sides to talk to you.

One thing you should never do is try to talk to jurors. That could cause a mistrial. However, after a verdict is in, the jury is fair game. How it deliberated often makes an interesting story. Were there holdouts? What was the essence of the disagreement? What led the jury to return the particular verdict? Why did it believe the defendant? This story usually will not be covered on the day of the verdict but makes a good follow-up story the next day. Some members of the jury usually will be willing to answer a few questions if for no other reason than to provide an emotional release from the tension of the trial.

Covering a Disaster

One type of story in which broadcast news excels in informing the public is the disaster, whether it is a plane crash, train wreck, hurricane, or tornado. News broadcasts will report the tragedy quickly and keep the public informed as details develop.

We now are going to show you step-by-step how a radio station might cover a major plane crash. Later in this book we will examine how a TV station might present the same story.

Assume that you are working in a medium-sized radio station in Chicago when a plane crashes at O'Hare International Airport.

It's about 3 A.M., and you—we will call you Ben Francis—are alone in the newsroom. A disc jockey, Bob Thomas, is in the studio nearby. You hear the bulletin bells and rush to the machines. The AP wire is tapping out the words, "A DC–10 has crashed and is burning on the runway at O'Hare International Airport." That's all there is. Within seconds, the same information is moving on the UPI wire.

You snatch the bulletins from the wires and tell the disc jockey that you "want air" immediately. He fades out the music and signals you to go. You read the bulletin, attributing the information to AP and UPI, and tell your listeners there are no details, but they will have them as soon as you do. After Bob has started a record going, you ask him to call the news director at home. You dial the unlisted number for the tower at O'Hare. It probably will be busy, but you may get through. You start a tape machine in the event you get lucky. You are. You learn that the plane is owned by Trans Intercontinental Airlines and it was flight 528 out of San Francisco. Your tape is rolling as the flight controller tells you he has no other details except he can see the aircraft burning at the end of the runway. He tells you to please get off the phone and you do so after thanking him.

As you hang up, you see a button flashing on the phone. Bob has reached the news director at home and told him about the crash. Now you give him the few details you have. He says he will head for the airport and he tells you to get two other reporters out of bed and moving, one to the offices of Trans Intercontinental Airlines, and the second to a hospital, if you discover there are survivors. The disc jockey is hanging over your shoulder now offering to help in any way he can. You ask him to wake up the other reporters. And you remind him to pull any airline commercials that might be scheduled. The policy of most airlines is to cancel commercials for 24 hours following a serious plane crash. Next, you get on the phone to police.

You do not learn much more from police except that apparently there are survivors, and ambulances already are at the scene. You have enough now to repeat the bulletin plus some more information, little as it is. Bob has roused the other two reporters, and both of them are holding on the phone. You fill them in quickly and tell them to get dressed and stand by. Then in the studio again, you cue up the interview with the controller's voice on it and go on the air:

> "Here's a bulletin from the WXXX newsroom. A DC–10 has crashed at O'Hare Airport and is burning at the end of a runway. Police say there are survivors but no details on how many . . . or the number of dead. The plane is owned by Trans Intercontinental Airways. It was flight 528 out of San Francisco. We spoke briefly with flight controller Tim Nelson a few minutes ago.
>
> *In cue:* "It's burning . . ."
> *Time:* 32
> *Out cue:* ". . . all I know."
>
> That was flight controller Tim Nelson.
> To repeat the bulletin . . . a DC–10 has crashed at O'Hare Airport . . . and is reported still burning. There are survivors, but we do not know how many. Our news director, Jack Hand, is now on his way to the airport. Other WXXX reporters also are on this story, so please stay with us for further details which, of course, we'll give you as soon as we get them. I'm Ben Francis.

As you leave the studio, the phone is ringing. It's Jack Hand letting you know that he is now in his car headed for the airport. He wants to know if you have new information. You tell him that police say there are survivors. That is all you have.

It is now 3:30 A.M. and Hand says he will be back with a mobile phone report as soon as he can. You get back on the phone, calling the special numbers you have for the police and fire departments. You learn that ambulances have taken some survivors to Lutheran General and Resurrection Hospitals. Meanwhile, the wires have started to move some new details. The plane broke in two, according to AP, and some of the survivors were able to get out safely through the gaping hole. UPI said that the plane, capable of carrying 264 people, was only about half full.

It is now 3:50 A.M. and you begin thinking of the scheduled 4 A.M. news. You will recap everything you have on the crash and add a few headlines from the radio wire. With luck, you also will hear from the news director.

Five minutes later your hopes are answered. Hand is on the phone. He does not know too much, but he says he has a few details and will do what amounts to a "scene-setter," (a general description of what the disaster area looks like). Jack says he has learned that some of the survivors walked away from the crash. You tell him that the wires say the plane broke in two. The news director says that confirms what he found out.

You put him on hold and return to the studio. The on air light goes on as you get to the microphone and, as you start reading, you reach for the phone by the side of the table. You tell your listeners that there has been a serious plane crash at O'Hare and that News Director Jack Hand is at the scene with the details. You do not reveal the details that you know because that would leave Hand with little to say and might contradict what he has learned.

The news director gives his report and then you ask him a few questions. You know that he probably does not have answers to some of the questions such as, "Jack, do you have information on what may have caused the crash?" But at least it gives the news director an opportunity to point out that "it's much too early to get any details on that right now. Everyone is concentrating on trying to determine if there are any passengers still in the plane . . ."

Hand's report confirms two facts: there are dead, and some passengers walked away from the wreckage. He also says that survivors have been taken to hospitals. He has not mentioned which hospitals, so you ask him. The point is, it is appropriate in such cases for you to try to debrief someone at the scene while you are on the air if you realize that some of the information may have been omitted by the reporter. But do not—and we cannot stress this too strongly—do not toss questions at the reporter that are inappropriate, questions that he could not possibly answer. An example, "Jack, do you know how many other Trans Intercontinental planes have crashed . . . what kind of record do they have?" The chances of Hand knowing the answer to that question is remote.

You thank Jack for the report and advise your listeners that he will be back with another as soon as he has learned anything new. You recap briefly what the news director said and return air to Bill, the disc jockey.

When you get back into the newsroom, all the phone lights are blazing. One call is from a listener. You are polite but get rid of him as soon as you can. On the other lines are Gail Stuart, the reporter you sent to the airline office, and Frank Crawford who is calling to find out if you know where the survivors have been taken. You tell Gail to hang on and inform Frank that he should head for Lutheran General Hospital because it seems most of the survivors are going there. Gail says she is at the airline office but all she knows so far is that there were 159 passengers on the plane and perhaps several children, in addition to a crew of seven. Airline officials are trying to compile a list but that could take an hour or more. So far, Gail says, they have no explanation for the crash. They told reporters that apparently the tower was unaware of any difficulty before the crash.

You tell Gail that you would like her "live" for the 5 A.M. news if she can stay on the phone. She says she will try but the many reporters in the office might protest if she tried to lock up a phone for long. You say, "O.K., do your best." Then you tell her to give you a report now in case she cannot get back for a live spot. You know she could do the live report from the mobile phone in her car, but then she might miss something important in the office. Better not take a chance, you decide.

You give Gail a few minutes to collect her thoughts and you start the tape machine. The spot runs about 1:10. You assume the news director also will report again from the airport on the 5 A.M., and you will use Gail's piece after it. You remind Gail to try to find out how many Chicagoans were on the plane. As you hang up the phone, you hear some more bells from the wire machines. UPI has a new lead, slugged "urgent":

> At least 75 people are believed dead and as many as 50 others injured in the crash of a Trans International Airlines DC–10 at O'Hare International Airport, according to police and airport officials.

This is the first indication that the accident is very bad. As you rip off the top of the story, the teletype continues:

> The plane, flight 528 from San Francisco, was carrying at least 159 passengers and a crew of seven, according to airline officials. At least 25 of the passengers managed to escape the plane after impact when the fuselage split in two.
> "Some of them actually walked away from the wreckage," said a TIA spokesman. He added that it is still not known how many of the survivors are in serious condition, but he said, "many were taken to hospitals."

The machine stops with the promise "more."

As you whip it off the wire, AP comes alive. The lead is basically the same but says the number of dead is more than 50 with another 50 to 60 injured. AP says that around two dozen of the passengers were uninjured.

A problem here is a disagreement on figures. You tear off that copy also and decide it is about time to update the story. You will use it along with reports that you hope to get from your reporters. Of course, there also is the chance that you will not get those calls and then that copy will be essential.

Your lead reads as follows:

A DC–10 has crashed at O'Hare Airport and at least 50 people are dead and the figure may actually be as high as 75 or more.

You write it that way because of the conflict on the wires. Play it safe, you say. Give the lowest and highest figures. Do not try to decide which service is right. The rest of your story reads:

According to Associated Press the number of dead in the crash of the Trans International Airliner is more than 50 . . . but United Press International says the death toll could be 75 or more. The wires also say that between 50 and 60 others are injured, many of them seriously, and that around 25 of the passengers escaped after the plane split in two. Police and airport officials and our reporter at the scene, News Director Jack Hand, confirm that the plane apparently broke in half on impact and many of the passengers escaped through that hole. There's still some confusion about the total number of passengers on the plane. The airline says it believes there were 159 adults on the aircraft along with a crew of seven. It is not known how many were from the Chicago area. The plane originated in San Francisco . . . it was flight 528. Our reporter Gail Stuart is at the airline headquarters, and we hope to have a report from her and Jack Hand shortly.

All this copy, of course, is for standby and to use around the reports that you hope will be coming from those two reporters and from Frank Crawford, who is going to the hospital.

The 5 A.M. news goes well. Jack Hand did a live report from the airport, confirming the wire service stories. He was forced to hedge also on the number of dead because no one really knew the accurate figure. Jack also had a sound bite in the middle of his report with a man at the airport who had seen the plane hit the ground.

While this tape was playing, you noticed that the phone light was flashing. It was Gail. She had found a phone to use and had a report from the airline headquarters. You did a brief Q and A with both Gail and Jack before letting them go.

It is now a little less than two hours since the first bulletin moved and you have not rested for a minute. You get yourself a cup of coffee from the vending machine and get on the phones again.

And so it goes for most of the morning. Little by little, more and more information becomes available. It is almost 10 A.M. before you definitely know that there were 159 adult passengers and three children aboard. There were 69 fatalities and 100 survivors. Frank Crawford does a number of reports from the hospital, including "wraps" with a number of survivors. It was because the survivors were at three hospitals, you discovered later, that it took many hours for a final death count.

Among the excellent sound bites from the airport were Jack Hand's interviews with some of the people who did, indeed, walk through the middle of the cracked fuselage to safety. Gail did a number of live reports from the airline office after making friends with a security guard in a nearby office who pointed to his phone and said, "be my guest."

You finally tumble out of the newsroom at noon, relieved by the only reporter you did not wake up because you knew he would be needed later. You're exhausted. Your emotions are mixed. The story was heart-rending, but at least you had the satisfaction of doing a good journalistic job. It was all in good taste. You were careful to get your figures right. You acted responsibly.

That story would, of course, be the major one for Chicago and your newsroom for days. A number of the injured would die, requiring a frequent update of the fatality figures. Eventually, it was discovered that the plane apparently suffered some structural damage and that was in the news not only that week but for months to come. It also was revealed during the morning of the crash that the passenger list included the names of a popular country music group whose latest record was at the top of the charts. In other words, almost every hour there was some new bit of information that enabled you and others on the staff to update stories.

Let's examine now a log of the leads you used for your hourly newscasts:

4 A.M.   A DC–10 has crashed at O'Hare airport . . . we have no word yet on the number of dead . . . News Director Jack Hand is at the airport with this report.

5 A.M.   A DC–10 has crashed at O'Hare airport. At least 50 people are reported dead and that figure may actually be as high as 75 or more.

6 A.M.   Officials confirm that at least 50 people have died in the crash of a DC–10 at O'Hare Airport. News Director Jack Hand has details.

7 A.M.   The crash of a DC–10 at O'Hare Airport early this morning has taken the lives of at least 50 people, and airline officials warn the toll could be much higher. This report from Gail Stuart at the offices of Trans Intercontinental Airlines.

8 A.M.   The death toll in the crash of a DC–10 at O'Hare Airport early this morning is at least 60. Earlier reports placed the number of dead at around 50, but at least ten of the survivors died in or on the way to hospitals. Our reporter Frank Crawford is at Lutheran General Hospital with this report.

9 A.M.   The death toll in the crash of a DC–10 at O'Hare Airport continues to climb. It now stands at 64. Another 100 or more passengers survived and, remarkably, some escaped injury when they walked through a gaping hole in the fuselage. News Director Jack Hand has that story.

10 A.M.   Airline officials now say the DC–10 crash at O'Hare Airport early this morning took the lives of 69 people, including 23 from the Chicago area. Reporter Gail Stuart has details.

11 A.M.   Among the 69 people who lost their lives in the crash of a DC–10 at O'Hare Airport this morning was a popular country music group, The Nashville Five. News Director Jack Hand has that story.

Noon Officials now say that the number of Chicagoans killed in the crash of a DC–10 early this morning has risen to 28. Frank Crawford has details from Lutheran General Hospital.

As you look over the log, you are pleased. The leads updated the story as warranted, and you were able to bring in reports from one or more of the three reporters in the field for each broadcast. Now you go home and get some sleep. While you are, the staff of your sister TV station is working on the news it will present at 6 P.M. They, too, were up most of the night, and in the TV section you will see how they performed.

Broadcast News Writing

Some Basic Rules

Chapters 4 through 8 will deal with broadcast news writing style. But first let's discuss the physical preparation of the script. There will be differences among the various stations you may work for during your career in broadcasting. But, there are some general rules that apply across the board. They all have one purpose: to make the copy easy to read on the air. The rules include the following:

1. Type your story on one side of a standard size, 8½-by-11-inch piece of paper. Some stations use what are called copy books, several pages of paper bound together with carbon paper between them. They provide all the duplicates needed, especially for television.

2. Triple space between lines. If your typewriter does not have that capability, at least double space. TV stations use large bulletin-size type to make it easier for the anchor person to read off the electronic prompter. For those, always double space between the lines.

3. Most people find it easier to read upper and lower case, and we suggest that you write your copy that way unless instructed oth-

erwise. Upper and lower case also makes it easier to deal with proper names and to emphasize certain words, such as NOT, by putting them in caps.

Example

Mayor Jones says he will NOT go along with the agreement.

Harder to Read

MAYOR JONES SAYS HE WILL NOT GO ALONG WITH THE AGREEMENT.

4. In the upper left-hand corner of the page, type your initials, the date, and the slug of the story. The slug is a one- or two-word description of the story for easy identification, such as Bank Rob; Mideast, or Fatal Fire.
5. When using regular typewriters for radio, set the margins for 65 spaces, for example, from 10 to 75. The average radio newscaster reads about 15 or 16 lines a minute. You then count the number of lines you have written to get an approximate length of time for your script.
6. Indent five spaces for each new paragraph.
7. Do not put more than one story on one sheet of paper. This is important. Once a story is written, your job is not over. There may be major developments just before you go on the air. You may have to rewrite the top of your story or even redo the entire page. Another story on the same page will lead to confusion and extra typing, requiring precious seconds and moments you will not have to spare.
8. Do not carry a paragraph over from one page to another. It is easier to read copy if a paragraph ends on the same page. Do not worry about wasting paper. It is the cheapest item in any newsroom.
9. The same rule applies to sentences. Do not carry them over from one page to another.
10. Do not hyphenate words. It is better for the anchorperson to see the word as a whole.
11. If you need more than one page to write a story, draw an arrow at the bottom of the page pointing toward the lower right-hand corner. This lets the anchorperson know the story goes onto the next page. Although the use of the word *more* at the bottom of a page is newspaper style, some broadcast organizations still use the term on television copy because the arrow does not work too well on the prompter.
12. Keep your editing marks simple. Editing symbols used in print journalism do not work in broadcast copy. What is important is that the newscaster read the script without mistakes or hesitation. He or she has no time to translate symbols on the air. If your copy becomes sloppy with corrections and edits, pull it out of the typewriter and start over.

Accuracy

The best written, most creative copy is meaningless unless it is accurate. Nothing, absolutely nothing, is more important to a journalist than accuracy. Inaccuracy is a grave sin in the professional broadcast newsroom. Check and double check your facts. Be particularly careful with names. Go over each story after you have written it. Do not wait until it is almost broadcast time to check over your copy. You are more likely to catch errors if you correct each story immediately after you have written it, when the details are fresh in your mind. Waiting to the last minute to check your script increases the chance for error. It may be difficult then for you to locate the information you used to write your story and, because of the pressure of a deadline, you may not have as much time as you would like to catch mistakes.

Remember that the wire services are not infallible. Do not accept at face value every wire story. If anything sounds suspicious to you, call the wire service bureau. You will find the editors most cooperative and just as anxious as you are to get the story straight. Many of the corrections that move on the wires are the result of such calls.

If a mistake does get on the air, correct it as soon as possible. Do it while the newscast is still on the air, if possible. If not, make sure the following newscast corrects the mistake. If the error is extremely serious, correct it even if it means interrupting another program to do so. Usually such a decision rests with the news director or station manager. But it is your responsibility to bring such a mistake to their attention.

Libel

Sometimes inaccuracy brings on a legal action. If your mistake exposes someone to hatred, contempt, or ridicule, or causes one to be injured in one's occupation or business, you could be found guilty of libel. The same could be true if your words caused someone to be shunned or avoided by friends or business associates. If something libelous gets on the air, correct it as soon as possible. If you were guilty of libel, the penalty assessed by the court usually will be less severe if a sincere effort has been made to correct the mistake as soon as possible.

As a broadcast writer or reporter, you should know that there are only three defenses against libel: privilege, fair comment, and truth. State laws vary, so you should become familiar with the libel statutes in your state.

Privilege refers to certain records, debates, and hearings that are in the public domain. For example, if you quote from a congressional hearing in which a senator accuses a company of cheating the government, you could not be accused of libel, even if the company were completely innocent.

Fair comment is often a defense against libel if the subject of the comment is a public official, someone who is running for office, or anyone in the public eye who is seeking some sort of publicity or acclaim. This includes authors, actors, singers, and professional athletes. Such people have protection, however, from irresponsible and malicious attacks on their character. A classic example of such a case was the successful six-figure award to performer Carol Burnett who was described by the *National Enquirer* as being drunk in a Washington, D.C. restaurant. The paper claimed a First Amendment right to publish its comments about Miss Burnett. A jury disagreed.

Truth in most states is a complete defense against libel. But some states have ruled that truth is a defense only if the comments were not malicious. Also, proving the truth is not always easy, and the proving must be done by the writer or reporter. If you referred on the air to a labor leader as a racketeer, you had better be prepared to show that he was convicted of such a crime or that you have conclusive evidence of such activity that will stand up in a court of law. Otherwise, you and your station management could lose a lot of money.

Broadcast Writing Style

One of the greatest challenges for broadcast journalism students is learning to write in a *conversational style*. Most students are taught to write very precisely. Traditional grammar and punctuation are always stressed, as they should be, in high school and in college English courses. Every sentence is expected to have a subject and a verb. Contractions are frowned upon. This is the way textbooks are written and this is how English teachers expect compositions to read.

Learning to write well and grammatically is important. However, compositions are written to be silently read, not to be heard. Those in broadcasting must write conversational copy. For most students that is a new means of self-expression.

When we speak to each other, we do not always complete our sentences and we do not always include a verb. Punctuation is rather invisible in our speech patterns. More important is how long we can talk without taking a breath. We tend to end our sentences sooner when we speak than when we write. For example, try reading aloud some of the lead sentences in your local newspaper. You will probably run out of breath before you complete the sentence. Now try rewriting that sentence so you can read it aloud without pausing for breath.

Writing for the Ear

Broadcast writing is different from newspaper style. The radio newswriter must keep the ear in mind when preparing a script. The listener is often doing something else at the same time, most often driving to or from work. Housewives may be listening to radio as they do their work. People can do something else and understand the news on the radio at

Editor Rachel Lawrence and other news staff members in the KCBS newsroom. (KCBS News photo)

the same time if the news is kept simple. Newspaper readers can reread a sentence or paragraph if they wish. Radio listeners cannot.

Simple declarative sentences with short words do the job. It is important to express only one idea or point in a sentence. The TV newswriter has an advantage over writers for radio. In TV, the writer has pictures to work with but must be careful that the words do not fight the pictures. The two elements must support each other.

Short and Simple

Broadcast copy must be clear and concise. You want to communicate information quickly and with as little confusion as possible. A good rule to remember is: never use a long word when you can use a short one that says the same thing, and never use two words if one will do.

Following are some examples of sentences that have too much information along with suggestions for improving them.

Poor

Teachers in Illinois, Michigan, New Jersey and New York refuse to return to the classrooms until they get the pay increases they demand. The teachers' strike has resulted in the closing of schools for more than 80 thousand students.

Good

Teachers in four states refuse to return to the classrooms until they get the pay increases they demand. The strikes have closed schools in Illinois, Michigan, New Jersey and New York. The walkout is affecting 80 thousand students.

Here, you see, we have eliminated the names of the states in the first sentence and just alerted our listeners that four states are involved. Now, if the listeners have any interest in the story, they will expect you to tell them the names of the states. We do that in our next sentence. But to keep any possible confusion to a minimum, we hold the last piece of information, the number of students, for the third sentence. We also improved our copy by eliminating the phrase, "the strike has resulted in the closing." How much better it sounds to say "the strikes have closed schools." The words "has resulted in" are unnecessary and just clutter up our copy.

Another example of "information overload" follows.

Poor

A Smithfield couple, John and Mary Dunn, and their three children were rescued today after being stranded in their car in a heavy snowstorm for ten hours.

Good

A Smithfield family has been rescued after being stranded in heavy snow. John and Mary Dunn and their three children were trapped in their car for ten hours.

Often, it is not a question of too much information but of unnecessary words.

Poor

The president has declared his intention to remain neutral in the congressional fight.

Good

The president says he'll remain neutral in the congressional fight.

"Has declared his intention" really adds nothing to the meaning of the sentence. Here is another example of the same problem.

Poor

The president said the nation would not take a position of support for either side.

Good

The president said the United States would not support either side.

Again, "take a position" is verbose.

Contractions

Conversational style involves more than brevity. We treat words differently when we talk. For example, we tend to contract our words. Usually we say, "We're going to get something to eat," not "We are going to get something to eat." When we greet a friend, it is usually with "It's good to see you again," not "It is good to see you again."

So most of the time contraction of pronouns and verbs is to be encouraged. It is more natural to say:

The lawyer says he'll wind up his case tomorrow and he's confident of winning.

instead of

The lawyer says he will wind up his case tomorrow and he is confident of winning.

Other forms of contractions involve the use of the verb form *to be*.

There's no word about funeral arrangements.

or

The mayor announced he isn't seeking reelection.

A form of contraction that is discouraged joins nouns and verbs. For example:

The mayor's going to Chicago for the convention.

Grammatically, of course, this is not an acceptable contraction. The apostrophe is being used to abbreviate "The mayor is going." That sends a confusing signal because the use of 's with a noun indicates possessiveness.

Contractions should not be used when you wish to emphasize something. For example, it is better to write

The president says he will veto the measure.

than to write

The president says he'll veto the measure.

The key is to read the copy aloud. Your ear will tell you whether or not to use a contraction.

Conjunctions

And and *but* are useful coupling pins in broadcast copy. Many students are reluctant to use these conjunctions because they often were discouraged from doing so in their basic English writing courses. Use them. Also, *but* is preferable to *however* in conversational writing.

That **and** *Which*

Another example of bending the rules is the broadcast use of *that* instead of *which*. In conversation people tend to use *that* rather than *which* although grammatically *which* is often the correct word. Few people are going to question the correct use of these two words in conversation, whether at the dinner table or across a microphone. The point is *which* is a nonconversational word and should be used sparingly, if at all, in broadcast copy.

Although *that* is a comfortable word and should be used more often that *which* there are many times you can eliminate both words from sentences and improve the copy. Do not be concerned with dropping the *that* as you write your news copy. When you read the copy aloud, your ear will pick up the unnecessary use of *that*. Here are some examples:

Mayor Smith says ~~that~~ the strike of teachers will end tomorrow.

A fire department spokesman says ~~that~~ the blaze is suspicious.

The governor says ~~that~~ national guard troops will be sent into the area.

In each case, the copy reads more smoothly without the *that*. But there will be occasions, either for emphasis or because of the pattern of words in a particular sentence, when it is better to leave in the *that*.

The president made it clear to everyone that things are going to change.

The mayor told reporters that once he's elected he'll reduce spending.

Try dropping the *that* in those examples. You will see that in both cases *that* makes the sentence clearer.

Prepositions—Aids to Conversational Writing

Prepositions frequently are helpful in breaking up phrases so they are not only easier to read but also more understandable to the listener. Try both of the following lines and see for yourself which is easier to read and sounds better:

The construction industry's chief negotiator says another round of talks will begin tomorrow.

or

The chief negotiator for the construction industry says another round of talks will begin tomorrow.

You should have found it easier to say "chief negotiator for the construction industry" than the "construction industry's chief negotiator."

The listener can handle "a convention of real estate brokers" better than he can "a real estate brokers' convention."

Pronouns

Pronouns can be confusing to radio and TV listeners, especially if more than one individual is mentioned in your story. Use pronouns only when there can be no possible doubt about the name to which you are referring. The following example is correct:

> Governor Jones says he will run for reelection. The governor made his announcement at a fund-raising dinner for the Democratic party. He said he expects to be reelected without any difficulty.

But avoid this sort of pronoun use:

> Governor Jones has announced that he'll seek reelection. The governor revealed his plans during a meeting with Mayor Smith. He said he was happy about the decision.

The problem with the use of the pronoun *he* in the last sentence is that we really do not know whether it refers to the governor or the mayor. Presumably, both of them were "happy about the decision."

It's a question of clarity and that is always an important concern. If there is any ambiguity about the use of the pronoun in broadcast copy, repeat the name or the title.

Misplaced Modifiers

The meaning of a sentence can be significantly changed when a modifying phrase appears in the wrong place. You can eliminate this problem most of the time by avoiding complex sentences. But it is possible to mix modifiers even in some short sentences.

Here is an example:

> Governor Smith attacked the opposition for its stand on his energy bill in his radio and TV address.

It may seem obvious that the energy bill had nothing to do with the radio and TV address, but it could be confusing to your listeners. Write it this way:

> In his radio and TV address, Governor Smith attacked the opposition for its stand on his energy bill.

Another example:

> The pilot said the two planes almost hit each other during the news conference.

The planes did not almost hit each other during the news conference. That is when the pilot discussed the incident. It should read

> The pilot told the news conference that the two planes almost hit each other.

Dropping Verbs—Sometimes

The use of verbs and the importance they play in broadcast copy will be discussed fully later. But sometimes you can do without them. Why? Because we frequently drop them from our conversation and no one misses them. Editors and anchors in some broadcast newsrooms may insist on a verb in each sentence. But some of our leading newscasters use such lead sentences as "A major snowstorm in Chicago today . . ." It does not disturb us that the verbs *hit, clobbered,* or *blanketed* do not appear in that sentence. Broadcasters tend to overwork such verbs. How many times have you heard that a city has been *hit* by a strike, a tornado, an epidemic, or a power failure?

We are not advocating bad grammar and sloppy writing. But crisp, easy to understand, colorful broadcast writing may stray occasionally from what you learned from Mrs. Smith in English Comp.

Says It All

Strong verbs make important contributions to good broadcast writing, but often, in an effort to manufacture color, young writers pick the wrong verbs. For some reason students have been led to believe that there is something unacceptable about *said*—that it is dull and should be replaced by more dramatic verbs such as *declared, announced, proclaimed,* or *averred.*

Actually, the verb *said* is a splendid word. It can not, and should not, be replaced by other verbs unless they are appropriate. For example, it would be inappropriate to write

The president declared today that he will spend the weekend at Camp David.

It would be better to use the verb *said* in this case and to save *declared* for:

The president declared a moratorium on all punishments for West Point cadets.

You do not always improve your copy or make it more colorful by eliminating the word *said.* The next time you read a novel, count the number of times the author uses *said.* It has become so comfortable that we tend not to notice it. The same is true of broadcast copy. It may bother you to write the word *said* several times in a paragraph, but it should not bother your listener.

There are a few words that we can use, but sparingly, to reduce our use of *said.* When appropriate, you can use *added,* or *told.* For example:

The president told reporters that he would spend the weekend at Camp David. He said he would take a helicopter from the White House on Friday evening. The president added that he would be accompanied by the secretary of state and the chairman of the National Security Council.

Active Verbs

Use active verbs because they *are* more forceful. Passive verbs slow down a newscast. It is more effective to have someone or something creating the action than receiving it. For example, broadcasters prefer to say, "the bandits forced the cashier to turn over the money" instead of "the cashier was forced by the bandits to turn over the money."

Another example: "The mayor called for the resignation of the city attorney" is much better than "The city attorney's resignation was called for by the mayor."

The Present Tense

Immediacy is broadcast journalism's major asset. Whenever possible, report the news as it is happening. By using the present tense in your copy you emphasize that the news is fresh.

Doesn't it sound better to say "the president is flying to Detroit" instead of "the president left Washington for Detroit today"? If the president is in the air during the newscast, it is accurate to use the present tense, and it indicates to your listeners that you are keeping a close watch on the chief executive's activities. Another way to make copy sound fresh is to talk about the near future. You could have said, "The president's plane is scheduled to land in Detroit within the hour."

If you do not know exactly where the president's plane is, you could use the present perfect tense:

The president has left by plane for Detroit.

You also could use the simple past tense:

The president left by plane for Detroit.

Honesty, of course, is essential. You could not say "the president is flying to Detroit" unless you know that to be a fact. Sometimes you will be forced to use the future perfect tense because you have no logical way of saying anything else:

The president was to have left by plane for Detroit. . . .

Some clichés that have crept into the immediacy jargon should not be overused. These are such phrases as "at this moment" the president is on his way, or "just before we went on the air," the president left for Detroit.

Mixing Tenses

There is nothing wrong with mixing tenses in your broadcast copy. For example, it is perfectly acceptable to use the present tense in your lead about the president flying to Detroit and then to switch to the past tense in the second sentence. It would read this way:

The president is flying to Detroit from Washington. Before leaving the capital, the chief executive signed a bill that should help Detroit's financial crisis.

Overuse of Today

Most broadcasters overuse the word *today*. You can delete it in the editing process. An occasional *today* is all right. Sometimes it is essential to pinpoint an event, as in "An earthquake today struck southern California" or "A jetliner crashed today while landing at the Paris airport." In both examples, it is important to indicate when the event took place. But it is a mark of the amateur to use *today* in every story you write. Your listeners assume that your stories deal with events that are taking place today without your reminding them every 20 seconds.

If you use *today* or any time element in your story, make sure to place it as close as possible to the subject of your sentence. For example,

The Senate today passed an energy bill that could ease the nation's reliance on foreign oil,

instead of

The Senate passed an emergency bill today that could ease the nation's reliance on foreign oil,

or worse,

The Senate passed an energy bill that could ease the nation's reliance on foreign oil today.

The word *yesterday* should never be used in a lead sentence in broadcast copy. If you cannot think of a way to eliminate the word from your lead, then perhaps the story should not be used. The reason is obvious: you are writing for a medium that stresses immediacy. You should update the story whenever possible. That technique will be discussed later.

The problem of getting rid of *yesterday* is particularly troublesome for TV anchors of early morning or noon newscasts for which most of the video was shot the day before. If you must use a story that occurred yesterday but cannot be updated, at least move the word *yesterday* into the second sentence. Here's an example of a story that broke on a Monday and how it might be used Tuesday morning.

On Monday:

The City Council voted today to raise tolls from 50 to 75 cents on all the city's bridges.

Tuesday Morning

Tolls on all the city's bridges are going up. The City Council voted yesterday to raise tolls on the bridges from 50 to 75 cents.

Use of Tonight

At many local TV stations you will be encouraged to use the word *tonight* in almost every lead sentence. If the event is taking place in the evening, this is a good way of letting your viewers know they are not getting a rehash of what was on earlier newscasts. If, however, *tonight* is being used as a device to mislead the viewer, that practice should be avoided.

More Style Rules

Punctuation

Punctuation is greatly simplified in broadcast copy. We need periods so that the newscaster knows when to end a sentence. Broadcast writers should use commas in their copy, less as a grammatical consideration than as a means to indicate a brief pause. Dashes or dots may be used to indicate a longer pause. Colons and semicolons should be avoided.

It is a good idea to capitalize some words, particularly *NOT*, so your newscaster does not miss them. Dropping a *not* from a sentence changes its meaning completely, so if you use it, try to warn the newscaster.

Following is an example of punctuation in a typical paragraph of broadcast copy:

```
   A warning of economic troubles ahead from the Jonesville
Chamber of Commerce. Executive Director John Smith--
talking to the Rotary Club--said the tourist business in
Jonesville dropped seriously during the past year. He said
many people are NOT vacationing in Jonesville because of
the increase in crime. In Smith's words, Jonesville is NO
longer a nice place to visit.
```

Use of Quotes

The best way to deal with quotes is to paraphase them. If the words are extremely dramatic or urgent, you may want to use short, direct quotes, but you should avoid using the expression "quote . . . unquote." The newscaster can help by adding emphasis to the words that he wishes to stress. But to eliminate possible confusion, it is necessary to add phrases such as:

> in the president's own words . . .
> as the president put it . . .
> and these are the president's exact words . . .
> the president said, and we quote him . . .

Some newscasters use a combination of such phrases during a report on an important speech. And for clarity they may add at the conclusion of the quoted material:

> and that's the end of the president's statement.

As for quote marks, some broadcasters find them helpful in interpreting their copy but remember that quotes alone in broadcast copy are not sufficient.

Following are examples of how quotation marks might be used in a newspaper or wire service story and how the broadcast writer would deal with the same information.

Newspaper Style

"The nation must remain strong economically if we are to provide for the needs of our people," said Senator John Smith in a speech to the Lions Club in Hometown. "Now more than ever, the business community must adopt a responsible position in the fight against inflation," said the senator.

Broadcast Style

Senator John Smith says the nation must remain strong economically if it's to provide for the needs of Americans. Speaking to the Lions Club in Hometown, Smith said it's more important now than ever that the business community adopt what the senator described as a responsible position in the fight against inflation.

The broadcast version paraphrased the senator's first quote, eliminating the personal pronouns *we* and *our* and substituting *it's* and *Americans* so there is no doubt in the listener's mind about whom the senator is speaking. The senator's second quote also is paraphrased, but it is important that the listener realize the last part of the sentence, referring to "a responsible position in the fight against inflation," are the senator's words, not the newscaster's. So include the phrase, "what the senator described as."

It is important to identify immediately the source of a quote so that listeners do not think the newscaster is expressing his or her own comment or viewpoint. Delayed attribution should be used sparingly, if at all, and never when the quote is inflammatory or provocative. Applying delayed attribution to the example we just used, we could end up with something like

> Now more than ever the business community must adopt a responsible position in the fight against inflation. These words today from Senator John Smith, speaking to the Lions Club in Hometown.

It does provide a different, catchy lead into a story, but confusion could arise in the minds of the listeners, at least initially, about whether the newscaster is making a comment of his own. Sure, the confusion is cleared up in the second sentence, but is it worth the risk?

The problem becomes more serious when the tone of the quote is inflamatory or provocative. For example:

> Secretary of State Smith has lead the nation to the brink of nuclear war. This charge today in an editorial in the Hometown News.

It is important here, we believe, to let the listeners know right away who is making the charge against Secretary Smith. Even more unforgivable would be this delayed attribution:

> The fight for equality being waged by blacks is largely responsible for the nation's economic problems. This charge was made today at a Ku Klux Klan rally in . . .

It is essential here that the Klan be identified immediately, at the top of the sentence, so that no one could possibly think, even for a few seconds, that such words represent the thoughts of the newscaster.

Skipping Initials

Let us again contrast newspaper and broadcast copy. Newspaper reporters are taught to include a person's middle initial or middle name in a story to ensure proper identification.

Broadcasters, however, always seek to save time. If stories are kept concise, more of them get on the air. And one way to save time is to drop middle initials or middle names.

There are exceptions, of course. The late President Kennedy was known as John F. Kennedy. His name in a broadcast story would have sounded strange without the middle initial.

The same is true of middle names. For some newsmakers, a middle name is so much a part of their image that to omit it would confuse the listener. Consider, for instance, a reference to the Reverend Martin King.

Addresses

In a small town, exact addresses are important because everyone can relate to a specific location. If you say there was a fire in a house at 123 Main Street, most people in a small town will know where that is.

In larger cities, however, the exact street address is less important. You can say there was a fire in the First National Bank at River Avenue and Main Street. Or you could say a fire broke out at the First National Bank on River Avenue in the Crestwood section of the city.

A broadcast should give the listener the general location of an event. In television, the specific street address—420 River Ave., Crestwood—probably would be shown on the screen superimposed over pictures of the fire.

Titles Before Names

If a title is an essential part of one's identification, always put it before the name, not after it. The title will alert listeners to expect a name. They are more likely to remember it when they hear it. If the name is followed by a title, as it is in newspapers, the listener may miss the name and catch only the title.

A title sometimes can be used alone in the first sentence and the name delayed until the second sentence. For example, you could write

> The Delaware County Sheriff says the speed limit will be strictly enforced this holiday. Sheriff Peter Smith also says he will have extra men on duty.

If an individual is well known, the title and last name often are sufficient. You could say, "President Reagan is flying to New York." It would not be necessary to write, "President Ronald Reagan is flying to New York."

Broadcasters should never begin a story with a person's name unless the person is well known. You could, for example, write, "Jacqueline Kennedy Onassis arrived in Paris today on a shopping tour." It would not be necessary to say in the first line, "the widow of the late shipping magnate, Aristotle Onassis, arrived in Paris" because she is so well known. On the other hand, you would not begin a broadcast report with the name of an accident victim unless he or she was famous or a public figure.

Mr., Mrs., Ms., and Miss

At most radio and TV stations, the policy is to use *Mr.* only in reference to the president of the United States. You should follow the policy of your station.

Most stations use *Miss, Mrs.,* or *Ms.* to distinguish between men and women. Because of objections from feminists, however, some stations use only a woman's last name.

In reference to a husband and wife, it is necessary to use both titles, *Mr.* and *Mrs.,* the first time their names are given. After the first mention, only the title *Mrs.* is used. For example:

> A California couple has been voted parents of the year. Mr. and Mrs. John Jones accepted the award at a Los Angeles ceremony. Jones is an electrician and Mrs. Jones is a housewife.

Age

Age is mentioned in broadcast copy only if it is a significant part of the story. If a four-year-old is killed by a car or attacked by a dog, the victim's age is of interest. It probably would not be vital to a story to cite the age of a newly appointed school principal, unless he was so extremely young as to make the news story unusual. Age was important in the story about former Cleveland Mayor Dennis Kucinick, who at 32 was the city's youngest mayor. If you believe it is important to give someone's age, it always precedes the name, instead of following it. *Example:* "A tenement fire killed a two-year-old boy and his 96-year-old grandfather."

Race, Shapes, and Sizes

As with age, race should be mentioned in broadcast copy only if it is an important part of the story. If a black man is elected mayor of a city, his race should be reported. If police describe the suspects wanted in a murder case as black or Chinese, reporting such information could help in their capture. If three black or Hispanic men are arrested for the robbery of a gas station, their race or nationality is irrelevant.

The same principle applies to shapes, sizes, and hair color. In writing about the newly elected Miss Virginia it would be appropriate to identify her blonde hair and blue eyes, and perhaps to mention some other statistics, but there is no need to describe the defendant in a murder trial as an attractive, shapely woman with flaming red hair.

People, not *Persons*

The use of *people* when speaking of more than one individual is preferred because it is more conversational, more natural. You would ask a friend, "How many people are going to the game?" not "How many persons are going to the game?"

The Associated Press (AP) specifies

> Use *person* when speaking of an individual: One person waited for the bus.
> The word *people* is preferred to *persons* in all plural uses. For example: Thou-

WRVA desk editor-reporter Tom Calmeyer preparing his newscast.

sands of people attended the fair. Some rich people pay few taxes. What will people say? There were 17 people in the room.

AP also points out that *people* is a collective noun that takes a plural verb when referring to a single race or nation: The American people are united. "In this sense," the AP Stylebook says, "the plural is *peoples: The peoples of Africa speak many languages.*"

Clichés

Eventually, everything can become a cliché.

It is probably not possible to completely eliminate clichés from broadcast copy and perhaps not even desirable because clichés are common in everyday speech. But try to avoid the well-worn cliché.

Some examples to be avoided include "white stuff" as a description for snow, "hail of gunfire," "campaign trail," and "the stage is set."

Others that should be banished are "prisoners on a rampage," (they rioted or created a disturbance), "rumors running rampant," "wild pandemonium," "tensions continue to mount," and "grizzly scene."

Poor use of words, as well as clichés, creep into broadcast copy too often. Don't call an event a "miracle" or "near-miracle." For example, a

TV newscaster reading about the birth of a child to a comatose woman, referred to it as a "miracle." Doctors say the chances of such successful deliveries are about one in 5,000 or less. That information speaks for itself. Give the information and let the audience reach its own conclusions about "miracles."

Transitions

Few transitions work in broadcast copy. It is better to take a quick pause between stories than to concoct some strained transition.

For example, it would make no sense to talk about a "battle" going on between certain labor unions and then use that as a transition to the report of a "battle" in the Middle East. A snowstorm in Buffalo has nothing to do with a "storm" or protest at a housing complex in Connecticut. But some broadcasters refer to a "battle of another kind" or a "storm of another kind" in mistaken attempts to create bridges between stories.

The best kind of transitions take listeners naturally and smoothly from one story to another. Frequently they involve a change of locations or a similarity of topics. For example, it would be perfectly natural to talk about a congressional hearing on energy and then to move on to a story about the increase in solar homes.

> Another day of congressional hearings on the nation's energy problems. Today the lawmakers took testimony from government officials and tomorrow they will question officials of the nuclear power industry.
>
> And on the subject of energy, a home building association reports an increase of ten percent in solar home construction.

Here's another good approach:

> A fire spread quickly through more than ten thousand acres of timberland in parts of Oregon . . . and in the southwest, a fire in an oil rig in the Gulf of Mexico has been burning out of control for several hours.

If there are several fire stories of consequence in the news it makes good sense to tie them together. Or instead of the transition, "and in the southwest," it could have been written: "another fire—this one on an oil rig in the Gulf of Mexico—has been burning out of control for several hours."

Another acceptable example:

> A hurricane watch has been issued for residents along the coast of Florida, between Miami and Palm Beach . . . and in Chicago they're watching the thermometers . . . hoping the week of almost 100-degree temperatures in that city will finally start to taper off. The weatherman is not optimistic.

Attribution

One of the traditional practices of journalism is attribution—naming the source of one's information. Attribution in broadcast copy is always at the beginning, never at the end, of a sentence. A typical newspaper story would read

> Federal income tax returns are going to be examined more closely this year, according to IRS officials.

Broadcast copy might read

> IRS officials say federal income tax returns are going to be examined more closely this year.

But often it is not necessary to use attribution when you are writing for broadcast. Sometimes it only clutters up copy. For example, it's verbose to say

> The White House announced today that the President will leave Washington for New York tomorrow.

You can eliminate the White House attribution:

> The President is going to New York tomorrow.

If the White House announced it, we can assume that the President will make the trip.

Sometimes, rather than eliminate the attribution, broadcasters delay it. If unemployment climbs, you can report that fact in the lead:

> Unemployment rose again this month—jumping to a new record high.

Then you can quote the Bureau of Labor Statistics for the details. You want to catch the listener's attention. You can better accomplish that if you avoid identifying the government agency in the first sentence.

Poor

The Bureau of Labor Statistics in Washington reported today that unemployment rose to ten percent, an increase of four tenths of one percent from last month.

Good

More people were out of work last month. The Bureau of Labor Statistics says unemployment reached ten percent—an increase of four tenths of one percent over the previous month.

Attribution Sometimes Is Essential

Attribution sometimes just clutters up copy, as in the case of the White House illustration. But very often attribution is essential and should come high in your copy. Important announcements from the government or political leaders should be clearly identified, and, of course, any controversial or inflamatory statements should be attributed. In stories about crime, attribution is essential to protect those involved. If police identify a suspect in a criminal case, then you must attribute that identity and the charges to police. If police say a man confessed to a holdup, then you must attribute the confession to police. The reason for attribution is that the suspect could have been mistakenly identified, or his alleged confession could have been obtained illegally.

It would be unfair and perhaps difficult to get a fair trial if the media accepted as fact every allegation made by authorities against a suspect. Although most police officers are sincere and dedicated, they can make mistakes. Journalists must avoid convicting someone in the headlines. Some radio and TV stations will not report confessions of any kind, even when the claim comes from police, because often the confession becomes a matter of dispute during the trial.

Another important and practical reason for extreme caution in reports dealing with crimes is the possibility of legal suits. Even if you quote police, that is no guarantee that your station will not be sued if you identified someone as the rape-killer of a young woman when, later, the accused proved he was in another part of the country at the time of the crime. If you attribute such charges to police, your defense may be somewhat stronger.

This same sort of logic introduced the words *alleged* and *accused* to news copy even before radio and TV. The habit was adopted by broadcast journalists. The consensus seems to be, "it's not a solution, but it's the best we have." Saying *alleged* or *accused* in relation to the name of someone who has been arrested does not guarantee immunity against a libel suit if the person is not guilty. A reporter or newscaster might think he is protecting himself with such phrases, and often there is no suit even if the "accused" is released by police. But there is always the possibility of legal action.

Numbers and Statistics

Many news stories depend on numbers and statistics. A story on unemployment, the stock market, the government budget, or the cost of living would be meaningless without numbers.

If numbers are not used properly in broadcast copy, they can be confusing to listeners. It is difficult enough for the radio and TV audience to digest all of the information that is broadcast without having to interpret a mass of complicated numbers or statistics. So keep your numerical information as simple as possible. One way to do this is to keep asking yourself: What do these figures really mean? How can I tell the viewer or listener about these figures in as plain and simple a way as possible?

A press release from the Bureau of Labor Statistics may tell you the following: The cost of living rose 0.5 percent last month to a new Consumer Price Index of 175.89. This is the highest level for the CPI since two years ago when it was at 165.75. The cost of food rose 1.35 percent; the cost of gasoline rose 2.77 percent; the cost of medical services rose 2.24 percent, and the cost of mortgages rose 1.89 percent.

How would you translate all this for your audience?

Here's one example:

> Your pocketbook was pinched again last month—but this time it was the tightest pinch in two years.
>
> Today, the government released figures that show it cost us one-half of one percent more to live last month. Gasoline and medical costs rose the most. The fill-up at the pump took nearly three percent more out of your pocket than last month and medical costs shot up almost two and a quarter percent. The price of mortgages and food also rose.

Simplifying numbers for the viewer or listener is not the only problem the broadcast journalist has with figures. He must make the numbers easy for the anchorperson or reporter to read on air. Following are some rules for writing numbers in broadcast journalism style.

Spell out any numbers that might be confusing and use figures for the rest. For example, the numbers one and eleven always should be spelled out. Some writers and newscasters also like to spell out all numbers below eleven. It is easier to read larger figures. For numbers more than 999, you must use a combination of words and figures. Here are some examples:

Avoid	*Use*
1	one
11	eleven
seventy	70
eight hundred	800
1,000	one thousand
15,000,000	15 million

Decimals

Many figures released in Washington and by various scientific organizations contain decimals. In broadcast copy you never use the decimal point; you spell it out. Whenever possible, try to eliminate the decimal point reference completely. For example, in citing a cost of living increase of .06, you would eliminate the decimal point in your copy and write instead that it "jumped six tenths of one percent." Some writers convert 2.2 into "two point two percent." We prefer "slightly more than two percent."

When dealing with statistics such as the cost of living, it is difficult sometimes to round them off. But you should eliminate the decimals completely when dealing with complicated budgets and reports concerning such things as birth and death rates and the Dow Jones Averages. Instead of telling your audience that "one point nine percent more people" recovered this year from some disease, write that "almost two percent more people recovered . . ."

Unless you are writing a sophisticated business report, it is best to round off the Dow Jones Industrial Average. If stocks go down 1.13, tell your listeners that they are off a little more than one point. If the number of shares traded was 23 million, 300 thousand, write "more than 23 million shares were traded."

Never use *a* before numbers in place of *one*. It should read "one million dollars" or "one dozen roses," not "a million dollars" or "a dozen roses." The reason for this is that the word *a* often sounds like *eight* to the listener.

In copy, spell out all fractions; never use figures. It should be three quarters, not ¾. It's easier for the anchorperson to read.

Hyphenate important numbers so the newscaster will read each number separately. A telephone number should look like this: 7-4-5–5-6-1-2.

Never use percentage or dollar signs. Always spell them out:

50 percent	*not* 50%
50 dollars	*not* $50.00
50 cents	*not* 50¢

Symbols and decimal points are easily missed when reading copy live on the air.

Pronunciation and Phonetics

You would think only a fool would go into a studio with a script that included words he could not pronounce. But all of us have heard newscasters tripping over words. Often the newscaster did not take the time to go over the copy before air time. Sometimes copy was completed just before the newscaster entered the studio.

If the newscaster does not find the time to read his script carefully before reading it to thousands—maybe millions—of people, he has only himself to blame for mistakes. But you can be sure that he will transfer some of the guilt to you, the writer, if you did not give him enough time to read the script.

Both of you may be at fault if the newscast turns out badly. If you, as writer, included difficult words, phrases, or proper nouns in your script without alerting your newscaster, you were loading the gun. The newscaster pulled the trigger by failing to go over the script to find the troublesome words that you had included.

There is less justification, of course, when a writer/newscaster mispronounces words. If you are writing your own copy, you should be familiar enough with it to read it professionally in the studio.

Observe two basic rules:

1. Always phoneticize any words and names that are strange and difficult to pronounce.
2. Always read your copy aloud. The ears are a much more reliable censor than the eyes because you are writing copy for ears—not eyes.

The ears will detect poorly constructed phrases and sentences and sound combinations that are confusing. They often will alert you to redundancy in your copy.

In most of the nation's newsrooms, newscasters read their own copy. Only news organizations in the top markets can afford the luxury of newswriters. Even network radio has been replacing newswriters with newscasters who can turn out their own copy. So when mistakes are made on the air, the majority of them are made by newscasters who prepare their own material.

If you are going to read news copy on the air, it is not enough to phoneticize only the difficult words. You should practice those difficult-to-pronounce words until you can read them properly and without hesitation.

Too many on-air blunders are the result of the "rip and read" approach. AP and UPI would be the first to admonish newscasters who tear off the latest five-minute summary and try to "wing it" without any preparation.

If you are uncertain about how to pronounce a word, check the dictionary or the reference books that should be in every newsroom. Some words and names, however, will not be in books. Sometimes you will need to get help from other sources, such as professional organizations, associations, libraries, and museums. In New York, the United Nations is a great help when you must deal with a diplomatic name. So is the Voice of America in Washington. And consulates in various parts of the nation may be of assistance. Your local medical association is a logical place to check out the pronunciation of a new, strange-sounding drug.

Regional Words

Pronouncing regional proper nouns will pose a particular problem for you if you are working as an anchor away from home, and you probably will be.

If you join a responsible, thorough news operation, there may be a list of names that newcomers to the area have difficulty pronouncing. Learn them. If you are with a less professional organization, you will not get such help. If you mispronounce names on the air, you invite viewer ridicule.

Let us offer some suggestions for keeping such mistakes to a minimum. Read all the local stories in your newspaper and mark the names you have questions about. Unfortunately, this will not solve all your problems, because those names will sometimes be in the paper a day after you need them. Some names look innocent enough in print but can be an anchor's nightmare. For example, in San Antonio, Bexar County is pronounced "Bayer" County; in Louisiana, the family name Herbert is generally pronounced "A-bear"; and in Virginia, Henrico County is pronounced "Hen-rye-co." If you can find a native in the newsroom, ask for advice on pronouncing any unfamiliar names before you go on the air. If you are reporting from the field, make sure that you know how to pronounce the names of everyone involved in your story. If you are uncertain, phone the people in question when you return to the newsroom. They would rather that you call them at home or at the office to find out how to pronounce their names than to hear a mangled version on the air.

The wire services issue pronunciation guides periodically. They will list many of the most troublesome names in the news that particular day, but they are by no means complete. Keep the guides in the drawer of your desk for future reference. Following is an example.

AP PRONUNCIATION GUIDE

    NEWS

JAMES DOZIER – DOH'–ZHUR

HANS DIETRICH GENSCHER – GEN'SHUR

GINNAY – GIN–NAY'

ANGEL ANIBAL GUEVARA – AHN'HEWL AHN–EE'–BAHL
   GAY–VEHR'–AH

CHARLES HAUGHEY – HAW'–HEE

GERALDO RIVERA – HEH–RAHL'–DOH

ELIAS SARKIS – EE'–LEE–AHS SAHR–KEES'

WALTER STOESSEL – STEH'–SUL

TYRE, LEBANON – TY'–UR

LECH WALESA – LEHK VAH–WEN'–SAH

    SPORTS

GUY LAPOINTE – GEE LAH–POYNT'

LINZ, AUSTRIA – LINTS

JEAN–CHRISTOPHE SIMOND – ZHAHN KREE–STAWF' SEE–MOHN'

BALAZS TAROCZY – BAH'–LAHSH TAH–ROH'–CHEE

If the wires have not supplied the pronunciation that you need, they usually will do their best to help if you call them on the phone. A local or regional bureau probably will have the pronunciation of newsmakers in your area, but you may have to call the main phoneticization desk if you need a pronunciation for a national or international story.

Two ways of showing the phonetic spelling in your script are to leave space after the difficult word so you can type in the phonetic spelling, or to print the phonetic spelling above the name or word. The latter is less confusing for the newscaster and easier for the writer.

If the name is extremely difficult, try to avoid its repetition. A foreign diplomat, for example, can be described by his rank or title after the first mention of his name. If you must re-establish his name later in the story, you should repeat the phonetic spelling in your copy. You cannot assume that the newscaster will be able to pick up the phonetic spelling from the earlier copy without losing his place or stumbling on the word.

Here is a guide to phonetic spelling used by United Press International.

Vowels

A *Use AY for long A as in mate.*
  Use A for short A as in cat.
  Use AI for nasal A as in air.
  Use AH for short A as in father.
  Use AW for broad A as in talk.

E *Use EE for long E as in meet.*
  Use EH for short E as in get.
  Use UH for hollow E as in the or le (French prefix).
  Use AY for French long E with accent as in pathé.
  Use IH for E as in pretty.
  Use EW for EW as in few.

I *Use EYE for long I as in time.*
  Use EE for French long I as in machine.
  Use IH for short I as in pity.

O *Use OH for long O as in note, or ough as in though.*
  Use AH for short O as in hot.
  Use AW for broad O as in fought.
  Use OO for O as in fool, or ough as in through.
  Use U for O as in foot.
  Use UH for ough as in trough.
  Use OW for O as in how, or ough as in plough.

U *Use EW for long U as in mule.*
  Use OO for long U as in rule.
  Use U for middle U as in put.
  Use UH for short U as in shut, or hurt.

Consonants

Use K for hard C as in cat.
Use S for soft C as in cease.
Use SH for soft CH as in machine.
Use CH for hard CH or TCH as in catch.
Use Z for hard S as in disease.
Use S for soft S as in sun.
Use G for hard G as in gang.
Use J for soft G as in general.

Sometimes proper pronunciation is difficult for even the most professional broadcasters. Correspondents working for the same network have used different pronunciations. One example that persisted for some time was the pronunciation of the capital of Iran. Some correspondents pronounced it Teh-ran and some said Teh-her-ran. President Franklin Roosevelt's name was and still is mispronounced by many people on and off the air. The proper pronunciation is Rohz-vehlt, not Rooz-vehlt.

Originality and Color

Importance of Rewriting

One of the most difficult habits for a young writer to break is copying the same phrases and construction that appear in wire service stories. Wire stories (except for the broadcast wires) are written for newspapers, not for broadcasters. It is your job to digest the information in those wire stories and to express them in your own words. Be original.

Here are suggestions to help you convert that wire service or newspaper story to good broadcast style:

1. Whatever your source of information, read it through carefully at least once, more often if you have the time. Make sure you understand what the story is all about. Your understanding is the key. You will not be able to write a simple and clear story if you do not understand it.
2. Now ask yourself: "What are the major points or facts of this story?" Underline them in the wire copy or newspaper clip. You will pick up speed in recognizing major points or facts as you acquire more classroom writing experience.
3. Before you put a single word on paper, pretend you are talking to a friend. In your own words, tell him what the story is all about.

Then, speak the words aloud. In many broadcast newsrooms, writers can be heard saying a phrase or reading their copy to themselves in a low voice.

4. Now, put those words you have said to yourself on paper. It will be difficult at first, but try this rewriting without referring back to the original wire copy every few seconds. Learn to digest that information.

5. Now that your story is on paper, read it over, catch your typos, tighten your phrases, and check your facts.

Try this method with several stories from newspapers or wire services. The more practice you get, the faster you will be able to write them. And don't forget these key steps:

1. Read and understand the facts.
2. Identify the major points.
3. Pretend you are talking to a friend.
4. Say it aloud.
5. Put it on paper.
6. Polish and edit your story.

Story Length

There is no set formula for determining the length of a radio or TV news story. But, of course, the broadcast story must be a great deal shorter than a newspaper version. If it is a particularly busy news day, a newspaper, in theory, can add extra pages—although most papers will not do so because of the additional cost. Broadcasters cannot add extra hours to the broadcast day. Of course, during an emergency or national crisis most stations will cancel regular programming. But changing the length of radio and TV newscasts frequently to comply with the flow of news would create chaos with programming. For the most part, radio and TV stations are locked into schedules that are planned weeks and months in advance. The only answer when there is an unusually heavy news day is to write tighter. A newspaper may devote 20 or more paragraphs to a major news development that will be covered in eight lines in a radio newscast. Later we will discuss in detail the desired lengths of TV news stories. For now let's just say that the average TV news story by a reporter runs between one and a half and two and a half minutes and is as short as 10 or 20 seconds when read by an anchor.

In radio, news broadcasts run only about five or six minutes and quite often much less. If you subtract the time for the routine opening and close on a five-minute newscast, take away an additional minute or so for commercials or public service breaks, and deduct still more time for weather and possibly a Wall Street report, little time remains to report the news, perhaps less than three minutes. If you have ten stories you consider important enough to share with your listeners, you can devote approximately 20 seconds to each news story. That is about five type-written lines of copy for each story—quite a difference from the 20 paragraph stories in the newspaper.

This emphasizes the importance of identifying the major facts. Often, you have a number of points that you want to report, but because of time limitations you must narrow your choice to two or three facts. This is where news judgment becomes a decisive factor. Your time to write is short and your time on air is even shorter.

Color

Because broadcast newswriters are constantly challenged to capture and hold the attention of their listeners, they are expected to develop a flair for colorful writing. But that doesn't mean broadcast writing must contain an element of showmanship. Unfortunately, some news directors insist every news story ooze with color. Such a mandate usually produces purple prose. Such phrases as "rain-drenched streets" and "winging his way" are not colorful but trite.

You should work color into your writing more subtly. A well-chosen verb or adjective may do the trick. An occasional pun is okay but do not overdo them.

Because broadcast copy is conversational, it is more relaxed than newspaper copy, and that in itself should make it more colorful. It helps also to look for interesting comments from the people you are writing about. The people often provide the color. All the writer must do is faithfully record the language and emotions.

Color should never be strained. It should flow naturally from the facts of the story. And there are times when it is not appropriate—when the stories involve death, serious injury, crime, or natural disaster.

An excellent example of colorful writing is the work of CBS News Correspondent Charles Osgood. His special talent for bright, witty writing (he'll even use verse on occasion) has made him a favorite of the executive producers whenever there is a story that calls for special treatment. Usually, they are humorous, offbeat stories. Osgood often sees the humor in stories when it isn't obvious. But he stresses that "if you start off saying you are going to make a story funny, you are in big trouble."

Osgood said many journalists tend to write only the factual side of a story that deals only with numbers and statistics. "You need to have a little heart and guts in what you write," he said, citing a story about a building collapse as an example. "The impressions can be very strong when you are there. It's a horrendous scene. But," he added, "it's almost as if we filter out these things. We get bogged down in the number killed and injured, the size of the building, and the number of rescue workers. The truth of the story lies not so much in the numbers but in the things you see and feel and hear and sense."

Osgood said he tries to "write talk"—constructing sentences that are

CBS News correspondent Charles Osgood. (CBS News photo)

natural to the spoken rather than the written language. He said he also uses some "vocal tricks . . . things you do naturally with your voice . . . to hold and engage the audience in the story process."

Osgood grabs the audience's attention with lines such as, "I've got something I've got to tell you . . ." or "You're gonna like this . . ." or "You'll hate this next story. . . ." The point, said Osgood, is that we talk that way when we meet a friend on the street or in the elevator. Those are the kind of lines we might use to begin a story.

Osgood said to engage an audience you have to be engaging. "Sometimes you turn on the radio and hear a stream of words about the weather . . . and you miss what the guy said. Although you're very interested in knowing what the weather is, he didn't hold your attention long enough to give you the information. He wasn't involved in what he was talking about and when this happens," said Osgood, "the listener doesn't have a chance of getting the message."

The broadcast studio is "very sterile," Osgood said, "and sometimes it seems you're talking to a wall. But you're not . . . you're talking to a man in a car . . . someone getting dressed in a bedroom . . . they are really there and you have to talk to them as if you are holding a conversation." Osgood said we naturally pause a lot when we talk to each other, and he makes sure he pauses appropriately on the air.

Stressing the importance of being natural, Osgood pointed to his colleague Charles Kuralt who, he said, does not sound any different in private conversation than he does on the air. "His cadence and choice of words don't change. He doesn't shift into another gear when he sits down to write. His style is the same as when he's talking to you. That's why he's effective."

As we mentioned, Osgood enjoys using rhyme in some of his reports. In the following CBS "Newsbreak" he rhymed his own words and much of the actuality that was recorded over the phone with a congressman.

Newsbreak

Charles Osgood: *Newsbreak. I'm Charles Osgood reporting on the CBS Radio Network.*

Congressman Jim Jeffords, Republican, Vermont,
Will have the very best commute that anyone could want.
He's moving to his office, to his office on the Hill,
And it's there that he'll be living, or at least he says he will

The story in just a moment.

(Announcements)

Osgood: Jim Jeffords is a congressman who says he isn't giving in
To the condominium they're making of the

Representative James M. Jeffords
(R., Vermont): Building I was living in.

Osgood: Of the change in building status, he's not at all approving,
So he's not about to take it; count him out

Representative Jeffords: Yes, I am moving.

Osgood: It would be a bit expensive to stay, without a doubt.
He realized that, of course,

Representative Jeffords: So I decided to move out,

Osgood: Which meant he had to look around for someplace else that he could be,
And he wanted to be close,

Representative Jeffords: So I checked the rents around D.C.

Osgood: The rental costs are up in Washington, as you may know.

Representative
Jeffords: It would cost so much that it would put me into a negative cash flow.

Osgood: Negative cash flow, if you don't know what that's about,
Is when what's coming in is less than what is going
out.
Now congressmen are salaried.

Representative
Jeffords: We make $60,000 a year.

Osgood: But Jeffords has two residences—

Representative
Jeffords: There's one up home and then one down here and—

Osgood: To sell the one up home is something Jeffords doesn't
want.

Representative
Jeffords: Because I have my family up in Vermont.

Osgood: And recently, you see, he's been somewhat financially
troubled.

Representative
Jeffords: Up home my fuel bill's doubled.

Osgood: Ah, he has found what the rest of us also now find.

Representative
Jeffords: That's what kinda puts you in a bind.

Osgood: On a congressman's time there is so much demand.

Representative
Jeffords: If you add commuting on top of that, it gets a little bit
outa hand.

Osgood: So, commuting turns him off, and so what doesn't turn
him off is
A practical alternative.

Representative
Jeffords: So the thing would be to move into the office.

Osgood: Whatever'd be the hardship there, he thinks that he
can take it.

Representative
Jeffords: They have enough of the essentials there to make it.

Osgood: It's comfortable, Jeffords says, comfortable, if not great,

Representative
Jeffords: Why, it's— of course there's a bathroom in each of the

	offices, and there is a refrigerator, and there's a hot plate.
Osgood:	And congressmen enjoy some special privileges of power.

Representative
Jeffords: So over in the gym, I have a locker and a shower.

Osgood: He will move some furniture, the congressman said.

Representative
Jeffords: More to move my sofa, which changes into a bed.

Osgood: As to what he'll do with other stuff, he'll work that out somehow.

Representative
Jeffords: Well, I was tryin' to figure that one out right now.

Osgood: One of Jeffords' colleagues from the other side of the aisle
Tried living in his office on the Hill there for a while,
But whatever the convenience and the savings it entailed,
He doesn't live there anymore; for him the idea failed.
But Jim Jeffords thinks it's worth a try,
And so a try he'll give.

Representative
Jeffords: Oh, I don't know, I'm not one that's very choosy where I live.

Osgood: So, from now on, where he spends the day is where he'll spend the night
And he thinks that will be okay.

Representative
Jeffords: I think I'll do all right.

Osgood: And now, this message.

(Announcement)

Osgood: Newsbreak. Thursday, the 26th of March, 1981. I'm Charles Osgood, CBS News.

Osgood said CBS executives have never complained about his use of verse in his reports. They encourage individualism, he said; "there really is no one set style at CBS."

Emphasis on Writing

Some broadcast executives are concerned that not enough emphasis is placed on good writing.

Sam Zelman, vice-president for the Cable News Network, told us that CNN's "most serious" journalistic problem is writing. Most of the organization's writers have little experience, and some are learning on the job. CNN Vice-President Ted Kavanau said, "We're running a school as well as a network."

One of the difficulties, Zelman said, is that the schooling young writers get before joining CNN is inadequate. He was not as critical of college education as he was of elementary schools. "Apparently, somewhere along the line, they forgot to learn spelling, syntax, how to use the declarative sentence—the simple narrative style of telling a story," he said.

Zelman added, "A lot of kids come to TV news feeling that no one is going to see their words so why do they have to know how to spell. It's a question of discipline. If you're sloppy about spelling, you're sloppy about sentence construction—you're sloppy in everything you do."

Another CNN vice-president, Ed Turner, said students must learn the basics, "How to get the information into a story accurately before worrying about the bells, whistles, and flourishes that too often find their way into a young writer's copy. After you've learned how to deal with the fundamentals," he said, "you can start being clever."

Turner said young writers should develop a "clean and lean" approach to broadcast newswriting. According to Turner, Ernest Hemingway would have been a good broadcast newswriter because he "didn't waste words and used the adjective judiciously."

Turner also cited ABC News commentator Paul Harvey who, he said, "writes the best copy for radio." Turner said Harvey is the "master of the tease line—knowing how to get you into a story that you couldn't care less about." Following is an example of Paul Harvey's copy.

Paul Harvey News

```
    While you slept last night . . . .
A Yugoslavian jetliner was in fog . . . on final . . .
over the Mediterranean Island of Corsica . . .
when instead the DC-9 hit a mountain.
More than a hundred aboard, probably no survivors.

    And they've caught John Simonis of Lake Charles,
Louisiana. He is the ski-mask rapist . . . . he has
raped 130 women in nine states.

    A blizzard in Nebraska is moving east.

Washington: Budget Director Stockman proposes phasing
out most urban development. Thus to save taxpayers 4.2
billion.* HUD boss Sam Pierce will resist cuts.
```

---

*The authors would have rounded off 4.2 billion to *more than four billion dollars*.

ABC News commentator Paul Harvey. (Photo courtesy of Paul Harvey News, ABC Radio)

Update on the death of actress Natalie Wood.
Coroner says "accidental drowning."
She had been drinking . . .
Blood level alchohol generally considered enough to
intoxicate . . . .
To escape a shipboard argument between her husband and
her leading man she tried to leave the yacht in a
rubber dinghy . . .
But going over the side she slipped, hit her head on
something, fell into the water, drowned and floated
ashore.
There will be further toxocological tests on the body.
A quantity of prescription drugs found on the yacht
included sleeping pills and Darvon and Dalomine.
MGM has twelve million dollars in the dead-end
movie . . . which she would have completed . . . in
three more days.

The <u>Seattle Times</u> reports from Vancouver. . . .
welfare demonstrators in the Hyatt Regency Hotel
resisted police.

Says one woman was cut in the fracas . . .
Oh, no--we're not going to start THAT again!

Midwest Americans live longer says University of
Missouri research. But in the north-central
Midwest. . . . that's Nebraska and Minnesota, South
Dakota and Colorado, Iowa and Kansas. . . . the
mortality rates are FIFTY PERCENT lower than our
national average.
Lots of minerals in the Midwest water.

Spotlight: In college football, Clemson's unbeaten
Tigers are number one.
At tonight's basketball game between DePaul and
Illinois . . . . father and son--Ray and Tom Meyer--
will be coaching the opposing teams.

Upturn in the construction industry?
It's too early to be certain but. . . . building
activity, after months of decline, held steady last
month. (October)

Shop talk: Backlash.
BRICKS of Wichita, Kansas . . . . bought a large ad
in the Eagle Beacon . . . accusing prime time news on
all three networks of negativism, pessimism, cynicism
. . . . of trying to talk us into a recession.

The inventor of Rubik's Cube . . . . Dr. Erno Rubik
. . . . now has another puzzle on the market. Called
THE SNAKE . . . . 24 five-sided pyramids to reassemble
23 trillion possible combinations.

How do you figure this:
Man and woman in custody in Baltimore kidnapped eight
people in four states during the last ten days . . . .
yet made no demand of any of them . . . did not harm
any of them . . . .

One thing more:
B.J. Chandler is school superintendent in Dardanelle,
Arkansas . . . reports the junior high girl came to
school wearing one red sock and one blue sock . . .
When Mr. Chandler asked her the significance she said
she was an "individualist."
She said, "I have a right to be different if I want
to . . ."
Then she added, "Besides, all the kids are doing it!"

Lead Sentences and Lead Stories

Writing the Lead Sentence

The most important element in any news story, whether for print or broadcast, is the lead sentence. The lead is the bait that draws fish to the hook. Then you can begin reeling them in. The lead sets the tone of the story. Without a good lead, the listener's mind will probably begin to wander.

We are fond of the expression, "take one bite at a time." Remember it and you will have cleared the first hurdle of good broadcast newswriting. But what kind of a bite should we take first—a soft one or a hard one?

Hard and Soft Leads

The hard lead goes right to the heart of the story. The writer decides which piece of information in the story is most important and then deals with it in his first sentence. An example:

Governor Smith says he will sign a death penalty bill if the state legislature passes it. The lawmakers are expected to do so next week.

Using the same information, a broadcast newswriter might decide to use a soft lead, such as this:

> Supporters of a death penalty bill got some encouragement today from Governor Smith.

The soft lead is less direct. The writer has alerted listeners that they will be hearing something about the death penalty bill but delays saying that the governor will sign the bill if it is approved. That information would come in the second sentence.

Which of the two leads is better? Some argue that soft leads are more desirable because they "warm up" the audience. Such leads are designed to grab the listener's attention. The theory is that the broadcast audience can be distracted by a variety of things. Traffic jams or an accident will demand more attention from the motorist than his radio, and a mother will have difficulty concentrating on the news on her kitchen radio if her two youngsters are battling over the last piece of cake. Soft lead proponents would say that the motorist and mother are more likely to hear the most important part of the story—the governor's decision to sign the bill—if they hear the warm-up line first.

Soft leads are fine if not overused. A newscast that had nothing but soft leads would be tedious and wasteful. Remember that those warm-up lines take extra time. If you have only three minutes for news, you cannot devote a third or more to warm-up sentences. It is advisable to keep soft leads to a minimum in short newscasts. You will have more time to experiment with them in a 30- or 60-minute TV newscast or if your radio station is doing all news.

Most of your lead sentences, especially in late-breaking stories, should go right to the point. Keep them short and free of long names and titles. If you must use numbers, make them as simple as possible and avoid starting the sentence with them.

Leads come in all shapes and forms. A professional broadcast writer should be able to produce several different leads that will be acceptable to a newscaster or copy editor. If you are reading someone else's copy, always remember that few people think exactly alike. Be objective. Learn to accept that there is more than one approach to a story. Tell yourself, "It's not the way I would have written the story, but it works."

Following are examples of six possible leads for the same story, all of them acceptable:

> The Labor Department says unemployment jumped again in October, reaching a new high of ten point four percent. That's an increase of three tenths of one percent over September . . . and the highest unemployment in more than 40 years.

> The nation's unemployment soared to a record ten point four percent in October . . . the highest it has been in more than 40 years. The increase was three tenths of one percent higher than the previous month.

The administration has suffered another setback in its efforts to curb unemployment. Figures released today reveal that unemployment in October was the worst since 1940. It now stands at ten point four percent . . . a jump of three tenths of one percent in just 30 days.

The number of people out of work in this country is higher than it has been in more than 40 years. This bad news coming today from the Labor Department . . . saying that unemployment soared to ten point four percent in October . . . three tenths of one percent more than the previous month. You have to go back to 1940 to find unemployment that bad.

The worst unemployment statistics in more than 40 years were released today by the Labor Department. Ten point four percent of the work force unemployed in October . . . up three tenths of one percent since last month. That's the highest number of Americans out of work since 1940.

The nation's unemployment picture continues to darken . . . with more Americans out of work in October than at any time since 1940. It soared to ten point four percent . . . a jump of three tenths of one percent over the September figures. Another serious blow to the administration's hopes of bringing unemployment down.

Suspense Leads

Sometimes a hard news story can be told effectively by delaying the most important details to the end. Here is an example:

John Farrell walks to work every day down Main Street, passes the First National Bank, and says "Good Morning" to Dick Lovett, the security guard. This morning as Farrell walked by the bank, he saw Lovett going in the door with three men. Farrell shouted out his usual warm "Good morning," but Lovett did not respond.
Farrell at first was upset by the behavior of his friend. Then he began thinking that it was unusual. By the time Farrell walked one more block, he was looking for the nearest phone . . . to call the police.
When police arrived, they caught the three men fleeing from the bank, guns in one hand and bags of cash in the other.
John Farrell is the hero of the day.

This lead is effective because it creates suspense. But be careful not to drag it out needlessly. Broadcast news listeners are accustomed to getting their stories quickly and to the point. This kind of change of pace can be a pleasant break, especially if not overworked.

Shotgun Leads

Leads that deal with two or more related stories are called *shotgun leads*. They also are known as *umbrella* leads. For example, if a series of tornadoes strikes Nebraska, Iowa, and South Dakota, a shotgun lead might be as follows:

Tornadoes slammed into three midwestern states, killing ten people and causing millions of dollars in damage. The twisters tore into Iowa, Nebraska, and South Dakota over a four-hour period. In Nebraska, six people were killed and more than 50 homes were destroyed. Three others died in Iowa, and one person was killed in South Dakota. More than 60 homes were damaged or destroyed in these two states.

The newswriter combined three related tornado stories into one lead sentence before going on to give details about what happened in each state. That is much better than writing three separate stories about what happened in each state and tying them together with transitions.

Another example of the shotgun lead:

As school reopened today in most parts of the country, teachers in six states decided to stay home. In the East, more than 15 thousand teachers struck schools in New York, New Jersey, and Connecticut, and another eight thousand walked out of classrooms in Illinois, Michigan, and California. Hardest hit was New York, where some 50 thousand students were affected.

You might end the story there or, perhaps, add another line or two of detail about the strikes in the other five states. Combining information in related stories often makes more sense than talking about such events separately.

Shotgun leads, however, are not always appropriate. They work especially well for network newscasts that are aimed at a large, dispersed audience. But if you are writing a newscast in New York, your lead on the teacher strike story would focus on the walkout in New York or, perhaps, deal with the tristate area of New York, New Jersey, and Connecticut. The strikes in California, Illinois, and Michigan probably would be covered in a sentence or two at the end of the story.

Of course, if you are in a state where teachers showed up for work without incident on the first day of school, that might very well be part of your lead. Example:

Schools opened today in Virginia without incident, but 25 thousand teachers struck schools in six other states.

Negative Leads

Try to keep the word *not* out of your first sentence. It is better, for example, to say

The governor says he'll veto a mass transit bill.

Avoid

The governor says he will not sign a mass transit bill.

Both say the same thing, but the positive lead is stronger and easier to understand. There should be no confusion about the word *veto*, but if the listener missed the word *not*, he might think the governor is planning to sign the measure.

Non-news Lead

Make sure that your hard news leads include at least some element of news. Otherwise you will end up with what is called a "non-news lead." Here's an example of such a lead:

> A 10-year-old boy is in critical condition today in Hometown Hospital.

That is not news. But the reason the boy is in critical condition, might be news. In this particular case, the child had thrown a snowball at a motorist's car and the driver got so angry he allegedly ran the boy down. The lead should have said:

> A 10 year-old-boy who tossed a snowball at a car is in critical condition after the driver of the car allegedly ran the boy down.

Updating the Lead

Some stories just will not go away, and you must carry reports on the same story throughout the day. A plane crash with numerous fatalities is an example. You cannot ignore a story about the death of 70 people in a plane crash just because you carried the story in previous newscasts. You must find some new angle—some new information—that will let the audience know you are not merely repeating the same facts.

In covering a plane crash, you should keep checking with the authorities to see if the death toll rises or if there is any change in the number of survivors. You can update the story by adding any new information about the cause of the crash. Interviews with eyewitnesses may provide new information or human interest angles.

You should do your best to include new information about the crash each time you broadcast the story. If you run out of ideas to update the story, you should at least rewrite the information so it sounds different from earlier reports.

Naturally, you will be dealing with many stories each day that are less dramatic than a plane disaster. The challenge to find new angles for these stories will be greater.

Choosing the Newscast Lead

Deciding which story should lead a newscast for radio and TV is much more complex than writing a lead sentence. And the process for radio is very different from the television approach. Selection of the lead story for television will be discussed later.

WRC Radio newsroom in Washington, D.C. (WRC photo)

A radio newswriter must weigh a number of factors before selecting a lead story for a newscast. Obviously, the major consideration is the relative importance of the available news stories. But there are other questions one must ask. Who is our prime audience? What time of day is it?

Prime Audience

Who are you writing for? Are you turning out news for a local station or a network? Does the station's signal go ten miles or 75 miles? The answers will have a bearing not only on the story you choose to lead your newscast but also on the rest of the stories you include in the report.

If your station has only 1,000-watt power, you will pay special attention to what is happening in your community. A tractor-trailer overturning and exploding in flames on Main Street could be more important than the governor announcing he will sign a death penalty bill. But if your station has a 10-thousand-watt signal out of the state capital, the governor's statement may be a bigger news story and the tractor-trailer accident of lesser interest.

If your typewriter is in a network newsroom, you will not even be aware of the overturned truck and your interest in the governor's comments may depend on the size of his state or his national reputation. The network is looking for stories of more general nationwide appeal because it is serving millions of listeners throughout the country. A network writer will be more aware of the Washington stories and the latest developments in the Middle East than in a power failure that affected 2,000 people in New Hampshire. The assumption is that more listeners across the country are interested in the Middle East crisis than they are in the New

Hampshire power failure. Naturally, if your station were in New Hampshire, the power failure would be your major story.

Local News Priority

Broadcast audiences, for the most part, are more interested in what is happening in their own backyard than in another country. So you must pay more attention to that yard.

If your station is in New York City, the derailment of a commuter train that delays thousands of people on their way to work would be more important than 100 people losing their homes in a mud slide in California. But a Los Angeles radio station would not even mention the train derailment. Its full attention would be on that mud slide.

Time of Day

Prime time in radio is from 7 to 9 A.M. and from 5 to 7 P.M. Those periods also are referred to as *drive time*. This is when many commuters are getting up, dressing, driving to work, or driving home from work.

For most listeners, it will be the first news they have heard since going to bed or since leaving work. They will be anxious to hear the local, national, and international developments. But more important, they will be looking for news about the weather, traffic, and anything else that may mean delays in getting to work or home. On stormy days they will be listening for advice on school closings and the effects of the storm.

That derailment of a commuter train previously mentioned becomes much more important if it occurred just before or during the rush hours. A derailment at 10 o'clock in the morning or at night has limited news interest because few people would be affected. But if the trouble could not be corrected before the next rush hour, it could become a major story.

The time of day, then, is often critical in determining how important a story is to your listeners. A storm that dusts the area with an inch of snow is important mostly to the weather forecaster if it occurs around noontime. If the snow melts and does not affect the homebound highway traffic, the story has limited news value. Add another two or three inches of snow about 5 P.M., along with some freezing temperatures, and you have a major story.

For the broadcast journalist, prime time radio is almost synonymous with public service. Audiences depend on broadcasters for information that affects their lives in even the slightest manner. A good newsroom has a well-organized system for checking on traffic conditions and train and airline operations. If the staff is small, it may be the responsibility of the writer or the newscaster to run through the list of various city organizations and transportation companies responsible for providing services and keeping the roads clear. In larger newsrooms, this chore is assigned to desk assistants.

The time of day also influences news judgment, to a lesser degree, when it comes to selecting stories that might be of interest to certain groups. Last night's sports scores are more interesting to the morning drive audience than later on in the day. On the weekends, let the listeners know how all the teams are doing in the afternoon. Stock market reports are popular in the early evening hours because listeners returning to their homes presumably are anxious to discover how their investments performed.

During these prime time radio periods, do not worry about searching for updated leads to a story that has been around for a few hours. You can correctly assume that the majority of your listeners are hearing the story for the first time. Give them as many details as time will allow.

And during both drive time periods, do not forget frequent time checks. Most of your audience has a bus or train to catch or a car pool to make.

Daytime Radio

Following the morning drive time, most of the radio audience consists of women or, in the afternoon, teenagers coming home from school. This doesn't mean that your newscasts should contain stories of interest only to those two audiences, but it's a good idea to keep an eye out for such material. Late morning and early afternoon is a good time for consumer news items or helpful household or gardening tips, but not for an extended interview with a coach talking about last night's big game. Save it for the 5 P.M. homeward drive.

Hourly financial reports also are a good idea. Many women own stocks—or share them with their husbands—and the noontime average is just as important for some of them as the best buys at the supermarket.

If your programming is geared to the younger generation—rock or disco music—your news also should be. Quick, fast-paced news wrap-ups with stories about celebrities and entertainers are more likely to hold teenagers' interest than a lengthy report on a U.N. debate.

Nighttime Radio

The size of the radio audience declines in the evening as television audiences increase. But if you are writing and reporting news on the evening shift, do it as expertly as possible despite the small size of the audience.

Many enterprising news directors—if they have adequate staffs—try to cover town meetings and other evening events that might produce news for not only that night but also for the morning newscasts. If you are the only newsperson working at the station, your boss probably will expect you to cover some of those night events, which usually means overtime work.

The traditional time for wrapping up the news, on radio as well as

TV, is 11 P.M. Before you say goodnight, try to give your listeners a good look at the day's news events both at home and abroad. And do not forget the sports scores. Recap the results of any afternoon games and report the progress of the night games. A detailed look at the weather also is appropriate so your listeners will know what to expect when they head for work in the morning.

Weather

Commuters are not the only people who care about the weather. Boat owners are interested in the winds and how rough the waters are. Skiers want information that will help them plan weekend trips. Tornadoes, hurricanes, floods, and droughts can result in death and destruction, so storm alerts are important. Weather information is probably the most popular subject for most radio listeners.

Most stations provide a brief weather forecast at the end of each newscast. Usually, the report will give the temperature, chances of precipitation, the wind conditions, and sometimes the barometer reading. If the weather is a major story, treat it as you would any other news story. Talk to the experts to find out what caused the storm and when it is expected to end; speak with the police and emergency workers about casualties and damage; and, of course, interview people who were affected by the storm.

The Stock Market

To some viewers and listeners, stock reports are as important, and often more important, than weather reports. A weekend of rain is unpleasant but a 30-point drop in the Dow Jones industrial average could be catastrophic for many investors. Do not for a moment think that only the rich are interested in the ups and downs of the market. Millions of Americans, in one way or another, have some interest in the fortunes of Wall Street. Many corporations have employee stock-sharing programs, and many brokerage firms offer plans that allow the small investor to buy securities a little at a time. Also, the new relaxation of federal regulations concerning tax shelter pension plans offers new incentives for additional Americans to invest in stocks.

Unfortunately, most journalism students seem to have trouble understanding how Wall Street operates. You should know at least enough about how the stock market functions to report it intelligently to your audiences.

You will be mostly concerned with what happens on two exchanges: the New York and the American. Activity on the New York Exchange is the most widely reported.

The Dow Jones industrial average is computed on the basis of the price of 30 stocks listed on the New York Exchange. Many Wall Street experts say the Dow Jones average is not really an accurate barometer of how the market performs, because the 30 stocks used to determine the average are not randomly selected and have a built-in bias. Nevertheless, the Dow Jones is the most commonly quoted average.

Most radio stations give the Dow Jones figures each hour as they are reported by the wire services, along with the volume (number of shares traded.) Some stations also report the activity on the American Exchange.

Financial reports are most commonly broadcast in this manner:

> On Wall Street today, the Dow Jones industrial average was up more than two points in light trading.

Some stations will give a little more detail:

> On Wall Street today, the Dow Jones industrial average was up more than two points, closing at around 910. The volume was heavy—more than 80 million shares. Stocks were slightly higher on the American Exchange.

Broadcasters should avoid citing exact figures. Round off all figures so they are less difficult to understand, easier to deliver, and take fewer precious seconds in your newscast. Television newscasters frequently round off the figures while the exact numbers are shown on the screen.

Headlines

Many news broadcasts begin with an abbreviated summary of the major stories. These headlines tell each story in a few words, which should be delivered with some urgency but without theatrics. The present tense works best. Here are some examples:

> Mayor Smith fires two of his aides for allegedly taking kickbacks. . . .
>
> Fifteen people are injured when a roof collapses at the Majestic Theatre . . .
>
> City Hospital faces an emergency unless it gets a supply of blood . . .
>
> And the Atlas Furniture Company says it will lay off 30 workers next week . . .

Openings and Teases

Many stations have a policy establishing the way newscasts should open and close. Others may permit you to begin and end your news in a manner that is comfortable for you.

A common method of beginning a newscast is to give a headline and a promise of some details before identifying yourself. A commercial may follow or you may go right to the details. Here are some examples:

Mayor Smith fires two of his aides for allegedly taking kickbacks. I'm John Jones . . . details on that story right after this. (commercial)

or

Mayor Smith fires two of his aides for allegedly taking kickbacks. Good morning, I'm John Jones. The mayor announced the firings about 30 minutes ago at a press conference . . .

Your station may prefer a more traditional approach, such as

Good morning. I'm John Jones with the WXXX news. The mayor has fired two of his aides for allegedly taking kickbacks. The mayor announced the firings . . .

Some newscasts will provide several headlines at the top, promise some details, and then go to a commercial.

Closes and Kickers

After you have given the major news stories, the last part of your broadcast usually will include stocks, weather, and sometimes sports.

A typical close might be as follows:

On Wall Street this afternoon, stocks were up about three points in active trading. The weatherman says we can expect some rain this evening and clear skies tomorrow. The temperature right now is 52 degrees. That's the WXXX 3 o'clock news. I'm John Jones. Next news at four.

Many newscasters also will include a light or humorous story to end the broadcast. These stories are called kickers. The idea is to leave the listener with a good feeling after giving him the grim news. If a story lends itself to humor, try it by all means. But do not strain, because humor should come naturally.

Good Taste

Radio and TV are like guests in a home. Once invited, they should not offend the host.

A newspaper reader decides which stories to read. But in broadcasting the viewer or listener has less choice. Sometimes stories that offend good taste are presented before people can decide not to listen or watch. Often these stories concern violent crimes such as murder or rape, or sensitive issues such as abortion. Broadcasters should not ignore legitimate news stories. But they should be careful about how they report such stories and how much graphic detail they give. Consideration should be given to the time of day and to the age of those who might be listening.

Obviously, broadcasters do not use offensive language in their scripts.

But sometimes profanity is a significant part of a quote that you want to use on the air. A classic example was President Truman's use of the term *S.O.B.* to describe a music critic who had panned his daughter's singing performance. Debates took place in many newsrooms as to whether to repeat the term. Some stations did not use the quote. Today, most broadcasters probably would.

At times you will have to deal with the question of good taste, both in choosing stories or in selecting quotes. When in doubt, get a decision from your superior.

Commercial Placement

You also can offend people by placing commercials carelessly in your broadcast. A funny or singing commercial is inappropriate following a story about death. Often, if alerted to a problem, your sales department can switch to a more low-keyed commercial. Better still, try to place another less-disturbing story between the one about death and the commercial. Many TV stations will try to make the transition less jarring by fading to black before a commercial. If you do go to black, make sure it lasts several seconds.

Commercial placement presents other problems. Would you follow a review of a new movie with a commercial for that movie? Suppose your consumer affairs reporter did a story saying all aspirin are equally effective. Would you follow that report with an aspirin commercial?

Among all your other newsroom duties, if you are in charge of the broadcast, do not forget to check the commercial log for possible placement problems.

10

Keeping Up with the Copy

Organizing Your Copy

No two writers or editors organize their copy in the same way. You may devise a system of your own that works best for you. Let us offer some suggestions, starting with wire service copy. When you rip copy from the wire machine, roll it so the printed side is concealed. This will allow you to read the copy in a chronological order when you return to your desk. If the desk has a middle drawer, you may want to open it slightly so the copy will rest there as you begin to read. You are now ready to select and separate your stories. Use a ruler to cut them apart. And as you do, put a word or two (*slug*) in one corner to identify it. Use a thick-point pen or pencil so you will be able to spot the copy you need quickly.

If you have more than one story dealing with the same subject, keep them together. If it is a day when you have a number of Supreme Court decisions, scribble a slug on the first story that moves on the wires and attach the rest of them to it as they come in.

When you have finished reading all your copy, you will probably have a dozen or more stories on your desk. All should be folded in half so they take up less room. Organization and neatness seem to go hand in hand, so keep your desk tidy. There is nothing more frustrating than not being able to find the source copy when the editor or newscaster questions something that was written.

CBS News correspondent Reid Collins writing a network radio newscast. (CBS News photo)

If your newscast includes sports, keep all that copy together, and do the same with potential kickers and features.

If you have more than one wire service (some newsrooms have AP, UPI, and Reuters), keep all versions of the same story together. Some writers make jackets for their copy by folding sheets of paper in half and writing the slugs on the jackets instead of on the stories.

The most difficult task is still to come. While you were getting organized, the wires continued to tap away. There probably will be a few yards of additional copy hanging from the machines by now, and 30 minutes later you will have another roll to deal with. Keeping up with the wires does not end until your shift does. And frequent trips to the machines to clear the copy are vital.

Because the wire services are constantly updating stories, you must make the necessary adjustments in your copy. Otherwise, you run the risk of going on the air with outdated or incorrect information.

The wire services offer two types of teletype machines: the high-speed wire, which turns out more than 1,000 words a minute; and the slow-speed, conventional wire that serves most radio and TV newsrooms.

The wires continue to move new leads, tops, inserts, and corrections in stories when necessary on the slow-speed wire. But high-speed customers receive a complete, updated, and corrected version of a story each time a change is required.

A Lineup of Stories

Once you have organized your copy, you should start to think about which stories you may want to include in your newscast. Some newswriters make a list of all the stories they think they may include in their newscast. This can be only a tentative list because a number of new stories will undoubtedly move on the wires while you are writing your newscast. This may force you to rearrange the order of the stories. But if you have some sort of basic list, minor adjustments can be made without much trouble. Another reason for preparing a list is that you are not as likely to forget a story that may be buried under copy on your desk.

Writing from the Back

After you have organized your copy and have a tentative list of stories to write, you should try to decide which stories are not likely to change and start writing them first. Leave the breaking stories—those that are likely to change—until the very end. Write the features and sports, if the games are over, and get rid of the kicker and anything else that will not require a rewrite.

If your lead story is about a plane crash, there could be a number of new developments between the time you start writing and air time. A lot of valuable time could be wasted if you rewrite your copy every time a new story moves on the wires. For this reason, broadcasters always write the news from the back. The most important stories are done last if there is any possibility of a new development.

If you are waiting until the last minute to write about the airline disaster, you can get some of the details that will not change out of the way. All you will have to do then is put a top on the story just before air time. You could write the following information an hour before the broadcast:

> The aircraft was trying to land in a thick fog. Officials said there was no advance warning from the pilot that he was having any difficulty. The plane was on its way from Dallas to JFK. It made a stop in Washington to pick up additional passengers.

None of that information is likely to change, so you can type it on a separate piece of paper and have it ready to go. This will save valuable minutes before air time and allow you to concentrate on the new material that you know you must write in the final moments before the broadcast.

Costly Decisions

If you stare at blank paper in your typewriter for very long, you are in trouble. The best solution for such paralysis is to write anything to get started. If it is no good, throw it away and start over. An old maxim that predates radio and television says the best-written story in the world isn't any good if you miss the deadline.

So, turn your copy out as fast and as professionally as you can. Do not agonize over one story so long that you neglect the rest of the script.

Dangerous Assumptions

Much of your precious time will be devoted to checking facts. If you must choose between accuracy and writing style, you should choose accuracy every time. The best-written story is not worth much if its information is wrong. As was stressed earlier, get your facts straight.

If the President was scheduled to depart from Washington for Europe at noon, make sure that his plane has actually left the ground before you say so. Do not rely on the wire service advances for such information. Much of the time, Presidential schedules run late and the same is true of marriages, ship launchings, and ground-breakings. Obituaries also must be checked to verify a death and to be sure names and other facts are accurate.

Do not assume anything. If you are dealing with a plane disaster, check and double check constantly with airline officials and authorities. Get as many facts and figures as possible before writing your story. Do not assume that because nothing has moved on the wires the story has not changed. It takes time for the wires to gather and transmit information. Check the same sources they are using and you will save valuable minutes. If you depend on the wires to protect you—to update their stories just before your air time—you will be disappointed more often than not. Keep in mind that the news services' A wires are keyed to less-frequent newspaper deadlines, not those of radio and TV.

Hold for Release

Some reports that you receive on the wires and in the mail will be marked at the top, "Hold for Release." You must exercise caution with these. Do not take for granted that an event or a speech will occur at the time specified in the release. Check with the wire service or those who mailed you the release to make sure the event really took place.

Some wire stories move with "automatic release" times. But these often are times established to achieve the maximum publicity for those releasing the information. For example, a politician, scheduled to make a speech at 11 P.M., will agree to its publication at 6 P.M. This allows the early morning editions of newspapers and the 6 P.M. radio and TV newscasts to use the story ahead of time. The politician does not want to miss the early editions of the papers and the prime time broadcasts.

You may use the material in advance, but you should use the phrase "in a speech to be delivered later tonight." It would not be accurate or honest to use either the present or past tense in reporting the speech at 6 P.M.

Protecting the Newscast

After a long stint at the typewriter writing and rewriting a newscast, you may be tempted to step out for a coffee break, but don't do it. It is your responsibility to watch the wires until the newscast is over. A new top could move on your lead story or a completely new story may start moving seconds after the newscaster begins reading his script. New copy is often fed to newscasters while they are on the air. If you want to jeopardize a budding career in broadcasting, there is no surer way to do so than by walking away from a newscast before it is over.

11

Editing and Timing Newscasts

Cleaning Up Your Copy

If you have had a course in print journalism or worked for a high school or college newspaper, you probably are accustomed to using a variety of editing symbols in your copy. But those symbols will not work in broadcast copy. You are preparing copy that must be read without mistakes or hesitation. You will have no time to translate symbols on the air. If your copy is sloppy, retype it, because too many edit marks on the script will increase the chances of a reading error.

If you must make changes in the copy, do so neatly. If you triple space copy, you will have plenty of room between the lines to make changes.

If you must correct a word, cross it out completely with a dark pencil or felt-tip pen and write the new word directly above it. Never try to correct a letter in a word. Rewrite the entire word.

```
WMY 1/1/83
Bank Rob

          Three gunmen were seized this morning while
                           FIRST
     fleeing from the Firsts National Bank of Smithtown.
                                        GETAWAY
     The bandits were racing for their gateway car when

     police arrived at the scene.  The police were

     A Smithtown resident alerted police to the robbery.
                                   A GROUP
     He became suspicious when he saw some of customers

     standing in one corner of the bank.  The bank Manager,

     Fran Bank Manager Frank Mann said he feared someone
                            THE
     would be shot during holdup because the gunmen were

     very nervous.
```

An example of how a story might look after it has been written and edited.

Timing Copy

No two newscasters read exactly the same way or at the same speed. Newscasters tend to read a well-written script a bit faster than a poor one. If they have sufficient time to go over the script before air time, they will be more comfortable with the words. The result usually is a smoother and faster reading. How, then, do you determine the number of lines of news to write for a broadcast? If you are writing for yourself, it should not take too long to discover how many lines you read a minute. Just count them up at the end of the broadcast. If you are preparing news for other newscasters, you should make sure they have extra copy until you determine their reading speed. It is a good idea to write more copy than you will need, in any case, as will be discussed in the next section.

CBS News correspondent Douglas Edwards. (CBS News photo)

The average radio newscaster reads about 16 lines a minute if the copy is written within the standard 65 spaces. That means it will take 30 seconds to read an eight-line story and 15 seconds to read a four-line story.

Now, let's examine a typical newscast. Suppose that your station has a five-minute news summary on the hour. Is it really five minutes of news? Not likely. If your sales department has been doing its job, you may find two commercials have been sold, one running 30 seconds and the other one minute. You also have a standard 10-second opening and close for the newscast, which consumes another 20 seconds. And you will include stocks and a brief weather report just before the close. That eats up another 30 seconds.

As you can see, you no longer have a five-minute newscast, although that is the way it is sold and described to listeners. If your newscast really was five minutes long and your newscaster reads 16 lines a minute, it would mean that you would have to write 80 lines of news copy. But your job actually is much easier. Take a look:

5:00 of news at 16 lines a minute	80	lines
Less 1:30 for commercials, or 24 lines	−24	
	56	
Less :20 for opening and close, or 5 lines	− 5	
	51	
Less :15 for stocks, or 4 lines	− 4	
	47	

Less :15 for weather, or 4 lines $\underline{-\;4}$

                                                       43

Your five-minute newscast has shrunk to 43 lines—about two minutes and 40 seconds of actual news. Now you can see why it is so important to write your stories as briefly as possible. If you try to include about seven or eight stories in your newscast, you have only about five lines, or approximately 20 seconds, for each story.

Extra Copy

If you are a newscaster, one of the most frightening things that can happen to you is to run out of copy while you are on the air. If you are lucky enough to have someone else in the newsroom, you may be able to signal your problem. Otherwise, you are in real trouble, for which there is no excuse.

Writers—or newscasters who prepare their own scripts—should always go into the studio with extra, or so-called pad, copy. These are stories that are relatively unimportant. No one will be concerned if they are not included in the newscast. But they may come in handy if a newscast is mistimed or an audio news or commercial tape malfunctions, suddenly producing extra time in the broadcast. Such extra or pad copy should not be confused with padding or stretching out any news story. Each story should be concise.

Backtiming

The best way to guarantee that a newscast ends on time is to use a system known as backtiming.

Because most newscasts have a standard close—perhaps a stock market report or sports and some weather before the sign-off—you know each time how the last section of the news report will end. It is essential that the newscaster read these final items, except in an emergency, because many listeners will be waiting for them. It also is important to end the newscast on time so that the rest of the program schedule is not disrupted.

The newscaster can guarantee all this by timing the final pages of his newscast and deducting that time from the total length of the broadcast. To understand how backtiming works, let's examine the five-minute newscast cited earlier.

In addition to sports, weather, and a standard close at the end of a newscast, you also have 1:30 in commercials, so let us assume that the 30-second spot goes just before the weather and right after the sports. The end of the broadcast looks like this:

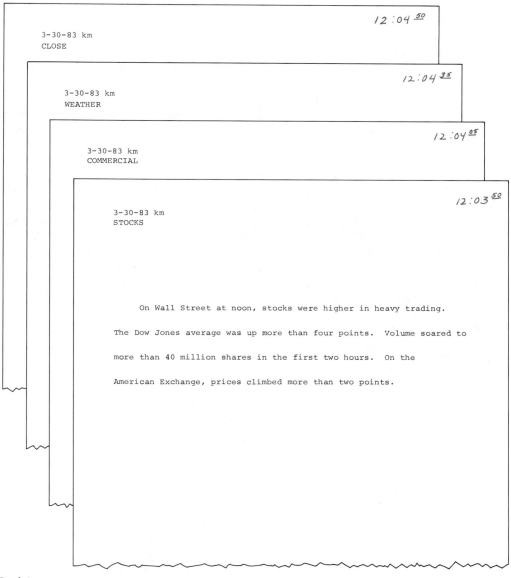

12:04 50

3-30-83 km
CLOSE

12:04 35

3-30-83 km
WEATHER

12:04 05

3-30-83 km
COMMERCIAL

12:03 50

3-30-83 km
STOCKS

On Wall Street at noon, stocks were higher in heavy trading.

The Dow Jones average was up more than four points. Volume soared to

more than 40 million shares in the first two hours. On the

American Exchange, prices climbed more than two points.

Backtime copy.

```
:15 stocks
:30 commercial
:15 weather
:10 close
1:10 total
```

If you add up the four items, you know that your newscaster must go into the last commercial 1:10 before signing off. In other words, the final news item must be concluded one minute and 10 seconds before the end of the broadcast.

Let's say that the newscast runs from noon to 12:05 P.M. If it takes ten seconds for the close, the newscaster must begin reading it at 12:04.50. To determine when to start reading the weather, deduct another 15 seconds, which puts you at 12:04.35. If the commercial before the weather is 30 seconds, deduct that and you find that the newscaster must begin the commercial at 12:04.05. The stocks consume another 15 seconds, so the backtime package begins at 12:03.50.

After indicating the backtime in the upper right-hand corner of the script the newscaster places the backtime copy in a separate pile on the studio desk, within easy reach.

The newscaster should always use a stopwatch to determine backtime. Do not be afraid to read the copy aloud. If you do not, you are likely to read more quickly when you are rehearsing than when you are on the air. That would cause you to run over your allotted time. Many stations are run by computer switching systems, and your microphone could be cut off before you finish the newscast.

Audiotape Inserts

Telephone interviews, the questions and answers from the news conferences, along with the reports from correspondents and eyewitnesses at the scene of an event all serve one purpose—to liven up the newscast and make the listener almost feel he was there. Nothing is duller than the sound of a single voice reading one story after another. Audiotape inserts offer variety, pace, and excitement to the broadcast. Let's examine the various types of audiotape inserts that you will be using in your broadcasts.

Actualities

A young boy slips and slides his way down the side of a snow-covered mountain after his father is killed in a plane crash. He tells newsmen, "Dad taught me never to give up."

A newscaster could have told the story without the sound of the boy's voice. But the impact would not have been the same without the actuality—the boy's voice—describing the crash and allowing the listener to hear the love and admiration of a young child for his dead father.

Actuality, sometimes called sound or a sound bite, is as important to radio news as videotape is to television news. A TV audience wants to see and hear the president of the United States describing plans to solve the energy crisis. A radio audience expects to hear the president's voice.

Much of a radio news staff's time is devoted to collecting actualities. The telephone can be a major asset to an aggressive news team. Within minutes, a reporter can be speaking with an eyewitness to an explosion or bank robbery or recording an interview with the winner of a Pulitzer Prize.

Going to the Scene

There rarely is an excuse for recording local news actualities or interviews on the phone, although many radio reporters do. A small news staff may not be able to cover as many stories as it would like unless it relies on the telephone. But if there are enough people in the newsroom, local telephone interviews should be kept to a minimum. When listeners hear a telephone interview with a mayor, they wonder why the reporter did not take the time to go to the mayor's office.

Voice Reports

A recorded report from a reporter at the scene of a story that does not include actuality is called a voice report or voicer. In other words, all you have is the voice of the reporter. Sometimes you must accept this because actualities will not always be available. For example, if the mayor is meeting with other city officials at city hall on some emergency, it is better to have a reporter tell the story from the press room than to listen to a newscaster reading copy. You hope that when the meeting ends the mayor and other officials would talk to reporters and the next newscast would include the actuality.

It usually is a good idea to hold voice reports to a minute or less. A variety of well-paced, different voices is what makes a radio news broadcast lively.

Wraparounds

Frequently broadcast news reporters are required to voice "wraparound" reports, which sandwich a piece of actuality between an opening and close. Your opening should be brief, perhaps two or three sentences. Describe the news event and prepare the listener for the upcoming actuality. The close of the report, following the actuality, also should be brief, a sentence or two containing additional details and identifying you and your station. Here's an example:

Reporter: Mayor Jones met with reporters a few minutes ago and said he would run for reelection. The mayor refused to discuss reports that he has lost some support among his fellow Democratic Party leaders. But he did comment on his Republican opponent's charges of corruption.

Actuality of Mayor's Voice: There's absolutely no truth to the vicious attack on me and my administration. The people of this city are better provided for than ever before, and my enemies have failed to prove their malicious charges.

Reporter: Those charges include alleged kickbacks to some city officials by companies doing business with the city. The mayor said he has complete confidence in every member of his administration. This is Len Tierney, WXXX News, at City Hall.

Wraparounds usually run a minute or less. If the story is particularly important or a major breaking event, it can run longer. Sometimes you will need a transition—a narrative bridge—within a wraparound when you have more than one actuality. Here's an expanded version of the example you have just read, which illustrates how narration might be used within a wraparound:

Reporter: Mayor Jones met with reporters a few minutes ago and said he would run for reelection. The mayor refused to discuss reports that he has lost some support among his fellow Democratic Party leaders. But he did comment on Republican Party charges of corruption.

Actuality of Mayor's Voice: There's absolutely no truth to the vicious attack on me and my administration. The people of this city are better provided for than ever before, and my enemies have failed to prove their malicious charges.

Reporter: One of those charges the mayor was referring to came from Republican City Councilwoman Fran Stone.

Fran Stone Actuality: The mayor and his administration have grown fat while the people of our city have seen taxes soar and industry move away. It's time for a change . . .

Reporter: Stone accused some members of the mayor's staff of taking kickbacks from companies doing business with the city . . . but the mayor denied that charge, saying he has complete confidence in every member of his administration. This is Len Tierney, WXXX News, at City Hall.

In this example, the reporter used the line "One of those charges the mayor was referring to came from Republican City Councilwoman Fran Stone" as his bridge to join the two sound bites.

Often, wraparounds and voice reports are more effective when they begin with a "cold open." That means that before you hear the reporter's voice you hear some actuality or natural sound at the top of the report. A cold open might go like this:

Cold open
of mayor: I have complete confidence in every member of my adminis-
                  tration . . .

Reporter: That's the way Mayor Jones reacted a few minutes ago to cor-
                  ruption charges against some members of his administration.
                  In announcing that he would run for reelection, the mayor
                  said there was absolutely no truth to the corruption charges
                  made by Republican Party leaders.

Mayor's
Voice: The people of this city are better provided for than ever be-
                  fore, and my enemies have failed to prove their malicious
                  charges.

Reporter: Those charges include alleged kickbacks to some city officials
                  by companies doing business with the city. This is Len Tier-
                  ney, WXXX News, City Hall.

Feeding from the Field

Most of the time you will return to the studio with the tape recording you make in the mayor's office, but often the information will be so important that you want to feed it from the scene to get it on the next newscast. Good news operations will have well-equipped mobile units that will allow you to report and feed actuality from the field. You also should know how to feed voice reports and actuality to the newsroom on the telephone. The simplest way is to feed the actuality from the tape recorder through a cable and alligator clips attached to the contact points of the telephone mouthpiece. This assumes that you can find a telephone and that the mouthpiece of the phone can be removed. It may be a pay telephone with a mouthpiece that has been sealed with epoxy glue. You may have to persuade someone in a nearby office to let you make a local or collect long distance call.

If you are doing a voice report directly into the phone mouthpiece, you often will find that your voice has a fuzzy, unsatisfactory quality. If you are told that the quality is poor, it sometimes helps to bang the mouthpiece. This can reduce noise during the transmission and enhance the frequency response. Also, it sometimes helps to back away from the mouthpiece.

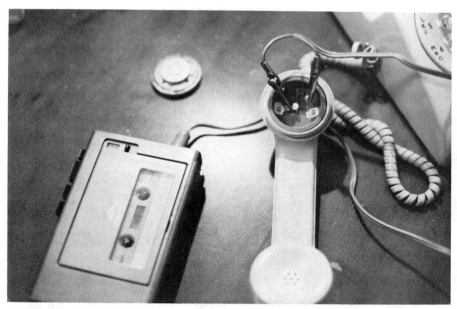

Using alligator clips to feed material from tape recorder into telephone.

A second method of feeding tape to a broadcast station uses a telephone but does not require removal of the mouthpiece. A device that makes this possible is called an inductive coupler. It fits snuggly around the front and side of the telephone mouthpiece and connects the output of the tape recorder to the microphone through an electronic magnetic link. The advantage of inductive couplers is that you can feed tape on phones that have epoxy-sealed mouthpieces.

A third way to feed material to a broadcast station from the site of a news conference or other news event involves the use of a broadcast line. This is not a regular telephone circuit. It must be ordered hours or often days in advance of intended use. Broadcast audio lines are usually available in several different degrees of quality, that is, offering more or less frequency response or high fidelity. The best (class A equalized) broadcast line sounds as lifelike as a direct studio transmission.

Importance of Editing

A good actuality can be ruined by poor editing. Learn to use a razor blade, grease pencil, and editing block early in your broadcast career. You must know how to edit tape properly when you get that first job at a radio station. In the largest markets, union engineers sometimes will physically cut the tape. But you will tell them what to cut and where to achieve the most effective results.

Following are suggestions for cutting audiotape:

Editing audio tape on the "Edit all" block.

1. When working with tape, always look for a natural place to make your edit. You can cut out portions of a person's comments as long as you do not distort the meaning. But it will sound awkward if you fail to maintain continuity when you edit someone's remarks. Do not chop your tape indiscriminately just to achieve a desired length.

2. Remember that your audience will probably detect your editing if the voice sounds unnatural. You cannot, for example, cut a person's remarks in the middle of a phrase unless the inflection of the voice is going down. If you edit the person's voice as it is going up, it will sound abrupt. It may cause a listener to think something has been withheld. To make an edit sound natural, always look for a pause, a long breath, or even an "er" when cutting your tape.

3. Don't cut your tape so short that the actuality becomes meaningless. If your newsmaker is interesting, he probably deserves more than ten seconds to make his point. If your actualities are not good enough to run more than ten seconds, you should consider whether they are worth using at all, unless in the middle of a wraparound.

4. You can improve your actuality by removing long pauses and a series of "ers" from tape. You need not remove every pause and every stammer. But often you can increase the impact of audiotape and make it more interesting by cutting out silent gaps or complex clauses that slow down your actuality. Any editing that does not

distort or destroy the meaning or mood of the actuality is permissible and desirable.

Mixing Voice and Sound

Always try to use natural sound when it is part of the story. If you are feeding a report back to the station from a fire scene, listeners should hear the noise of sirens and firefighters in the background.

Often you can record the natural sound separately and feed it back to the studio along with a voice report from the mobile unit or telephone. The engineer at the studio will mix the two. The sound will be established at the top of the report, faded under the narration, and brought up again when the reporter is signing off.

Obviously, this practice is permissible only if the natural sound was recorded while the reporter was at the scene covering the story. For example, a war hero is buried with full military honors. You record the rifle shots and taps. When the services are over, you feed your report on the ceremony back to the station from your mobile unit. You also feed some of the taps and rifle salute. Your engineer at the studio will do the rest. When the report goes on the air it probably would start out with the taps and rifle shots fading out as you begin your report, "One of the nation's best-known war heroes was laid to rest today . . ." When your story is almost complete, the engineer will fade in the taps and hold them under while you identify yourself. After your sign off, the engineer will bring up the taps for a second or two and fade them out.

Of course, that is not the way it happened at the location. It is conceivable that you could have recorded your report with the natural sound of the taps and the rifle shots in the background. But that might have been in bad taste if done at graveside during the actual ceremony. Ethics really is not an issue here. The edited version put together at the studio honestly reconstructed the mood at the time the event took place.

Ethical Concerns

Editing and mixing sometimes raise questions of ethics. It would be dishonest to add applause following a candidate's remarks if there was no such applause. It does not matter that the candidate received applause at some other time during the speech. The applause, if used, must have occurred at that moment. A similar distortion would occur if applause for the candidate was edited out, or if heckling or boos were eliminated. Omission of sound can distort just as much as the misuse of sound.

What do you do then if you have a minute or two of loud applause at the end of an important speech? It is all right to establish the applause and then fade it out rather quickly. You cannot run a minute, or even 15 seconds, of applause. But the newscaster may comment that the applause continued for several minutes if that is what happened.

Taboo Practices

Radio broadcasters should never employ dishonest practices intended to deceive listeners. Such taboo practices include the dubbing in of sound effects and the recording of voice reports by staff members who are not covering the story.

Only the natural sound of an event is permissible. If you missed the sound of police or fire sirens at the scene of a disaster, do *not* try to fool the public or your news director by using sound effects from the record library. Such deception could and should be grounds for your dismissal.

Similarly, there is no justification for "manufacturing" voice reports by staff members not involved in covering a story. Such attempts to "impress" listeners with a variety of voices are dishonest use of tape for tape's sake. An uninvolved staff member reading from wire copy or fact sheets can contribute nothing to a newscast.

Tape Cues and Sheets

Whether you are writing broadcast copy for yourself or a newscaster, you must include in your script some vital information about the actualities and other tapes in your newscast. You must indicate the exact length of the tape and provide cues. The first few words at the beginning of the tape are called the "in cue" and the last few words of the tape are the "out cue."

If your radio station employs studio engineers, they will expect the writer or editor to provide a cue sheet, which usually is a carbon copy of the newscaster's script. The cue sheet will tell the engineer when to play the tape. By comparing the "in cue" on the sheet with the starting words on the tape, the engineer can be sure he has the right tape. This is particularly important in a busy newsroom which may be turning out several dozen actualities and other tape inserts each day.

If you are running your own control board, it is equally important that you know the length of each tape and the cues. The "out cue" will tell you that the actuality or voice report is over and that you should continue reading your script. If you do not know when the tape ends, your confusion probably will create a pause. Nothing slows down a newscast more than dead air.

Some newscasters record two or more sound bites on the same cartridge. This can be dangerous if the person on the board does not have a cue sheet.

Here is an example of what your script should look like:

```
     The president met with congressional leaders on the
  energy crisis for two hours, and when he left the
  meeting he told reporters he was pleased with the
  talks.
```

In cue: "The meeting was very fruitful. . . ."
Time: :16
Out cue: ". . . a good year ahead."

One of the congressional leaders, Gloria Smith of Kansas, also was optimistic about the future.

In cue: "There's no doubt in my mind. . . ."
Time: :14
Out cue: ". . . of this great country."

It always is a good idea to have with you in the studio at least a brief summary of what is on the tape. Then if the tape breaks or the machine malfunctions you will not sound tongue-tied. Both problems occur regularly and when they do you should explain,

> "We're experiencing some mechanical difficulty . . . but the President said that he had a fruitful meeting with congressional leaders on energy problems and is optimistic about the future."

You might want to add a line about Congresswoman Smith's comments but that would not be necessary. Your audience probably was unaware that you planned to use her voice as well as the president's.

Sound Bite Tags

It is a good idea to identify the voice a second time at the end of an actuality. This is particularly true if the tape runs more than 15 or 20 seconds, increasing the possibility that the listener did not hear or has forgotten the identity at the beginning of the tape.

The repetition of the name at the end of the sound bite also can be used to give a line or two of additional information about the story.

Example

One of the congressional leaders, Gloria Smith of Kansas, was optimistic about the future:

Cue in: "There's no doubt in my mind. . . ."
Time: :14
Out cue: ". . . of this great country."

Congresswoman Smith added that it would take serious sacrifice on the part of the American people, if the nation is to win the fight against inflation. The Kansas Republican said Congress and the president cannot do it alone.

In addition to identifying the congresswoman in the tag to your sound bite, you gave your listeners additional information about what she had to say. This is much stronger than just saying, "and that was Congresswoman Gloria Smith of Kansas."

Lead-in to Tape

Every piece of audiotape actuality, voice report, or wraparound must be properly established with a lead-in sentence or two. The lead-in must contain enough information about the story so you do not confuse the listener. But there is nothing more amateurish than a lead-in to an audiotape giving virtually the same information that is on the tape. Following are examples of what to do and what to avoid:

Good Lead-in: The president told reporters after the meeting with congressional leaders that he's optimistic about the economy.

Tape: "I think the worst is over and that industrial production will increase and the cost of living will drop in the coming months."

That lead-in is fine, but let's take another look at it when the tape is cut differently:

Bad Lead-in: The president told reporters after the meeting with congressional leaders that he's optimistic about the economy.

Tape: "I'm optimistic about the economy. I think the worst is over and that industrial production will increase and the cost of living will drop in the coming months."

The lead-in no longer works because it is redundant. You must either cut the tape to eliminate the president's first few words or rewrite the lead-in. It could go something like this:

The president told reporters after the meeting with congressional leaders that he believes the nation's economy is headed for better days . . .

The change in the lead-in is slight, but the redundancy has been eliminated.

Bad lead-ins are almost always the result of carelessness or laziness. No one bothered to listen to the actuality.

Lazy is the only word to describe this type of lead-in:

The president spoke with reporters and had this to say.

It is bad because it doesn't give the listener any indication of what the president is going to say. If the actuality is short, only an alert listener will understand its full meaning. The actuality should be a natural continuation of the lead-in.

Also remember if you are working in the newsroom to check lead-ins with the reporters at the scene. If they are reporting live, they will want to know if they are to do a "hard" or "soft" open to avoid redundancy. It usually is best that the reporter at the scene uses a "soft" lead and the anchorperson gives the "hard" news. Here are some examples.

Anchor: Ten people were killed this morning when a DC–8 crashed in a thick fog at Logan Airport. Our reporter Dick Jones is at the scene and has this live report:

Reporter: Officials at the airport still do not know whether it was the fog or some malfunction that caused the crash.

If there had been no consultation between the newsman at the scene and the editor or newscaster in the studio, the reporter might have started his report with the number of dead. If the newscaster or anchor did the same thing, the result would have been very unprofessional.

At times, the reporter at the scene should begin with a "hard" lead. This is especially true when the story is changing rapidly and the reporter has new details, as in the following:

Anchor: A tragic plane crash at Logan Airport this morning, and our reporter Dick Jones is at the scene now to give us this report.

Reporter: The death toll is at least ten, but only moments ago the man in charge of rescue operations told me that there are more bodies still inside the wreckage.

In this case it was agreed that the anchor would make no mention of the death toll, which would be included in the "hard" lead from the reporter at the scene.

Of the many variations of live switches and lead-ins, one that always makes listeners cringe is the sequence, "We're now switching live to Logan Airport for this report from Dick Jones," followed by, "This is Dick Jones at Logan Airport."

The Blind Lead-in

The blind lead-in is a way of introducing a sound bite when you do not know at the time you are writing exactly what the newsmaker or reporter will be saying. Here are some examples:

- "The mayor was asked to comment today on the school situation."
- "John Arvank is manager of the brokerage house that bears his name."
- "Trish Darvey has a live report now from outside Lincoln Junior High School."
- "The former president met reporters after signing a contract for his new book."

Leads such as these get on the air much too often. But they may be necessary if someone else, some place else, is deciding what the sound cut will be or has no time to tell you. Blind lead-ins are tip-offs that the reporter is not on top of the situation about which he is writing. Consider these possible alternatives to the preceding examples:

- "Mayor Smith said he would seek a court injunction against the striking teachers."

- "John Arvank thinks the price of gold is sinking because of lack of confidence in the U.S. dollar."

- "Police are now said to be holding a suspect in that fire bombing of Lincoln Junior High, as Trish Darvey reports now from the scene."

- "The former president brushed aside questions concerning whether a snub by the Australian government caused him to postpone his planned trip around the world."

These lead-in lines obviously work better because they are more specific. They do a better job of preparing the listener for what is to come next.

13

TV News Overview

Introduction

Television is the single most dominant medium in the life of the Western world. With television playing such an important role in our lives, it is not surprising that polls show most Americans get their news from the TV set. Radio comes next, followed by newspapers and weekly newsmagazines.* What this means is that about two-thirds or more of the American people get their news *only* from television and radio.

With such a vast audience, it is not surprising that television killed many daily newspapers in this country and drove radio listening into the morning and evening drive times mentioned earlier in this book. Television has taken advertising money away from most of its competitors. Advertisers want to reach the most people for each dollar they spend. And they have found that because of its huge audience, television is the best value. This means that billions of dollars a year flow into the networks and local TV stations.

In the beginning days of television—the late 1940s and the early 1950s—news was a headache for television executives. It was something that the FCC required all broadcasters to present. Network evening news broad-

*It should be noted that the newspaper industry challenged these polls.

125

Cable News Network (CNN): Turner Broadcasting System's satellite communications complex of eight satellite earth stations located at the headquarters building in Atlanta. (Photo courtesy of CNN)

casts were only 15 minutes long and not much better than those weekly newsreels that used to play in movie theaters. Local TV news often was little more than brief stories read over slides.

By the late 1950s and the early 1960s, television was no longer an infant. And TV news was also growing. The audiences were larger and commercial revenue was increasing. The networks had expanded their evening newscasts to a half-hour. In many major cities, local news broadcasts were given an equal amount of time, and by the mid 1960s some TV stations had expanded to one-hour newscasts.

Television station managers suddenly realized that more people were tuning in for the news and more advertisers were calling to place ads.

Television news today is a fast-growing, fiercely competitive multimillion dollar business. This fight for dollars has had a major impact on the way local television news is presented and who is chosen to present it.

Television news is surrounded by entertainment programming. Entertainment considerations have a major effect on television news—even to the use of entertainment jargon in the daily language of the newsroom. Most station managers and owners are businessmen who have no professional background in journalism. They are interested in the financial report.

It is not surprising that when television news consultants began selling their advice on how to improve ratings they found willing ears. And TV managers who listened often found that their stations became number one in their markets. It was not long before two of the major consulting firms—Frank Magid and McHugh and Hoffman—had nationwide reputations and all the business they could handle.

What were these news consultants telling the station managers and news directors to do? They were advising them to use more film and videotape, to make stories shorter, to get more stories into the broadcast, to use more graphic techniques, and to hire on-camera broadcasters with appealing personalities.

They were telling the executives that broadcasters must relate to each other on the set and engage in what became known as "happy talk." The viewer, the consultants preached, will respond more to a happy team—a team that smiles and jokes a lot. One such personality is sportscaster Warner Wolf in New York City. When Wolf switched from Channel 7 to Channel 2, the first night he appeared on the air, Channel 2 jumped from second to first place in the ratings. As far as station management was concerned, Wolf certainly was worth his reported $450,000-a-year salary. The higher commercial fees that could be charged for being number one are several times that amount.

Such influences account for some anchor people getting six-figure salaries and for the fashion of two-member anchor teams. TV news is trying to appeal to as many different people in the audience as possible. Two, then, can be better than one. And two anchor people meshing together as a team on the air help to promote that feeling of reporters all working together.

In their desire for personalities to attract a wide audience, station managers and news directors buy frequent market studies. Some of these tests, such as the so-called skin tests that use electronic devices to determine a person's emotional reaction to a newscaster, are often criticized.

WCBS–TV anchor team in New York. (Photo by Lionel Phillips)

As unhappy as many broadcasters are about such tests and the show business approach, there is little young journalists can do about the entertainmentlike state of news at most local stations. If they want the jobs, they will have to go along. If they do not conform, they probably will be fired. But presenting the news in an entertainment format does not mean you cannot give the viewer important news of the day along with some intelligent explanation.

The Spillover to Networks

Network news organizations have been affected by what is happening on the local level. They have adopted flashier production and graphic techniques and begun to place more emphasis on personality and appearance. When CBS chose Dan Rather over Roger Mudd to replace Walter Cronkite, it reportedly was because the network believed that Rather had more sex appeal.

The Cosmetic Set

Both networks and local stations will pay a great deal of attention and spend a lot of money on a broadcast news set. The set will not make or break a broadcast's ratings, but the visual appearance is one more factor

NBC News correspondent Tom Brokaw, New York anchor of the NBC Nightly News. (NBC News photo)

NBC News correspondent Roger Mudd. (NBC News photo)

in the overall appeal. Also, a comfortable set usually will make the on-air people more relaxed and help them to react better with each other.

Appraising TV's Performance

The most frequently heard complaint about TV news is that it just scratches the surface and never really goes into depth on any one subject. Unfortunately, the criticism is valid. With few exceptions, TV news operations are geared to covering breaking news. Most of the time they are more concerned with getting on the air first with the news. Broadcast news operations, for the most part, are designed to react to events. Television has become good at covering news conferences, chasing fire engines, and getting to the scene of a murder, but its record is poor in exploring the intricacies and shortcomings of our cities' health care delivery system and corruption in local unions and government. Television news too often leaves those stories for newspapers to develop, preferring most of the time to react to the headlines.

This is not meant as a blanket indictment of broadcast news. Some stations make a determined effort to dig for stories and many try to look beyond the headlines, but they are far too few.

Walter Cronkite. (CBS News photo)

Walter Cronkite's Disappointment

Not long before his retirement from the "Evening News," CBS correspondent Walter Cronkite said it was his "great and continuing disap-
pointment" that the news program he anchored for 19 years had not been
expanded to at least an hour. "I truly believe," he said, "the growing
responsibilities placed upon us demand that." He cited the political campaign of 1980. "There is no way," Cronkite said, "in a half-hour that we
could do the story justice. There is no way we could adequately explore
the issues, detail the candidates' positions on those issues—except in the
most superficial way—and report the other news of the nation and the
world."

Cronkite added, "I keep thinking there must be some better way of
using the marvelous communications medium that television is, to play
a more constructive and enlightening role in the American political process." He gave the MacNeil/Lehrer report a pat on the back, saying the
30-minute examination of a single story or topic in the news is "something the networks could emulate. With their much greater resources,"
he said, "they could add a whole new dimension to the picture of the
world Americans receive."

Cronkite also was critical of television's failure to tell the local story.

He said the major newspapers and radio and TV concentrate on what is going on in the cities while the "real communities, the neighborhoods are left, effectively, without a voice." He called TV a major cause of the problem because "it has driven many smaller newspapers out of business and because of its emphasis on the widest possible audience." Cronkite offered cable technology as a possible solution to the dilemma.

He said he looked forward to "growing numbers of young journalists covering the neighborhoods with highly local news programs, using the leased facilities of common carrier channels. I can see the day," he said, "when the young journalist will look forward to 'owning' a community cable telecast just as my generation dreamed of owning a country paper."

The CBS news correspondent also had a warning for young people. Cronkite said too many are coming out of schools of communication "more committed to being instant successes, stars in show business, than in being journalists. Their ambitions," he said, "are fed in some degree by the excesses in our business, not the least of which are the hiring practices at too many local stations that put the highest premium not on reporting but on the ability to giggle."

Cronkite added, "the fault, of course, is not with the people themselves but the manager who hired them and the so-called news consultants whose advice the managers buy. The result too often is sickening trivialization and sensationalizing and a total abdication of news responsibility on the local level." [1]

Cronkite said a person who wants to be a newsman or newswoman should "concentrate on reporting, learning sources, where to find them, how to deal with them, and how to organize and write what they've acquired. And the presentation of that by means of television should be the last consideration." [2]

Cronkite also was critical of the print media, noting that while it often faults television news for yielding to show biz values, the trend at many newspapers is toward less news and more entertainment. [3]

Jeff Greenfield, who reviews television for CBS's "Sunday Morning" agrees that TV should not get all the blame. "The sins that beset television," he says, "are sometimes true not just of television but also of the mass culture and of the mass media in general."

Greenfield—like Cronkite—noted that it is common to critize TV news because a transcript of a half-hour news program would fill barely two thirds of one page of the *New York Times.* But, he added, if you look at 95 percent of the newspapers in the country, you would find little hard news after the first page. "You'd find comics, the horoscope, how to turn your tablecloth into a bedspread, gossip, sports, and a lot of other material not exactly in the category of hard news or thoughtful commentary." Greenfield noted that 60 percent of most newspapers are made up of advertisements.

On the other hand, Greenfield said that if you look at TV in the broader sense—beyond the half-hour newscast—you can find a good deal of substance. Like Cronkite, he cited the "MacNeil/Lehrer Report," as well as

PBS's "Firing Line" and commercial news programs such as "60 Minutes" and "Nightline." "All of these programs," said Greenfield, "go beyond the headlines."

But does this mean that the evening newscasts do an adequate job of informing Americans? "No," said Greenfield, "it means, however, that television is a house in which there are many mansions."[4]

Cable News Network (CNN)

For viewers who want more than a headline service, a major breakthrough occurred in 1980. There is no doubt that the Cable News Network was the most significant development in broadcast journalism in 20 years. It is embarrassing to look back for other milestones and to discover nothing of any consequence from the time the networks expanded news from 15 to 30 minutes.

If CNN's 24-hour news service is the most exciting thing to happen in broadcast news in two decades, then the flamboyant entrepreneur Ted Turner has to be the most important innovator in broadcasting since William S. Paley parlayed a cigar business into one of the most powerful and influential communications empires in the world.

The chairman of another media giant—Edward N. Ney of Young and Rubicam—summed up the feelings of many when he said, "you expect an idea like this (an all-news TV network) to come out of New York or

Ted Turner, president of Turner Broadcasting System and founder of the Cable News Network (CNN). (Photo courtesy of CNN)

Los Angeles, but all of a sudden here's 'the Mouth of the South' leaping in where the others are being conservative. He's got courage, style, and—most important—he's shooting the dice. I give him A-plus for pushing the state of the art." [5]

The future of CNN is still to be decided, a similar venture by ABC and Westinghouse.* Turner also has a second all-news TV network, an all-news radio network, and an overseas news service.

When Turner launched CNN in June of 1980, there were many skeptics. Some of the experts said people really did not want so much news. But Turner was confident, boasting he was going to do news "like the world has never seen before." He said that CNN would be "the most significant achievement in the annals of journalism." [6]

That brought some amused responses from the executives at the three major networks who noted that Turner's budget for his whole operation was a fraction of what they spend to do 30 minutes of news. But Turner charged that the networks had grown too rich and bureaucratic. They go first class and "I go tourist," he said. [7]

The tourist class is exemplified by the CNN staff. There are no unions at CNN and among the approximately 1,200 people employed by CNN is a large percentage of young people fresh out of college. They are called "video journalists" and are trained to operate cameras, videotape editing equipment and most of the other hardware housed in the CNN headquarters in Atlanta.

Video journalists who demonstrate editorial skills also are given an opportunity to write news and, occasionally, to cover a story. With the exception of the copy editors, directors, and producers who for the most part have been recruited from the networks and large-market TV stations, most of the editorial and technical staff at CNN has worked less than five years in broadcast news, and much of the staff has only a year or two of experience. A nucleus of experienced professionals holds the operation together.

Scratching Potential

One of the criticisms of CNN is that it really is not making the best use of its round-the-clock news. "They're just doing a 6 o'clock news every hour," is a common complaint. And there is some justification for that view. CNN was handicapped by a comparatively small budget and not as large a staff of reporters as it would like. CNN turns out a typical evening newscast each hour with the traditional two-minute news stories on floods, medicine, the economy, and other routine stories. It also offers a variety of talk and discussion programs throughout the day and night and frequent analysis from Washington, but not much in-depth coverage in the newscasts. CNN executives are aware of the problem.

CNN Vice-President Sam Zelman said, "We should be spending more time exploring things like the quality of education." He was referring to

*ABC/Westinghouse venture ended in 1983 with the sale of the satellite news channel to CNN.

CNN newsroom in Atlanta is part of the set.

all news media, not just CNN. "If we're going to look at violence, it should be a long look," he added. "Spot news stories do not inform the public about what is going on in our society as well as do stories dealing with societal changes and trends."

Most competitors acknowledge some envy of the all-news networks. They can go live at any time of day or night and do not have to worry about breaking into regular programming, as do the other networks. The only thing they interrupt with news is news.

However, CNN does have many problems; the most serious is its failure to attract a large audience except during a crisis.

During the TWA hostage crisis in 1985, CNN enjoyed a good share of the TV audience. But most of the time, CNN's audience is comparatively small. This means that CNN is unable to demand the kind of fees for its commercials that are necessary for it to improve its news coverage, pay its workers competitive salaries and still show a profit.

The result is that CNN relies too much on affiliate stations for coverage of news. This creates an inconsistency. When a story breaks in a city where CNN has a strong news affiliate, the coverage can be quite good. But in markets where the CNN affiliate provides inadequate news coverage, CNN suffers badly.

Because of its budget restraints, it seems unlikely that CNN ever will be able to provide the kind of consistent, professional coverage of breaking stories that we have come to expect from the other three networks.

14

The TV Assignment Desk

The assignment desk is the heart of a television news operation. It is a central command post that coordinates the coverage of news. Its many duties include developing story ideas; assigning stories to reporters and crews; keeping them abreast of breaking developments, and getting stories back home in time for broadcast.

A TV assignment desk can be as elaborate as the 24-hour, seven-day-a-week operation found in all network and some large market operations. It can be as small as a futures file on a news director's desk in a small market.

In many smaller TV newsrooms, the assignment editor's work is frequently the responsibility of the news director, who also may be the broadcast producer and anchorperson. When the late night news is over, the lights in the newsroom will dim and operations will cease.

Many smaller newsrooms find the morning's biggest headache is trying to catch up—trying to find follow-ups and updates on stories that broke during the night. Sometimes a small station has a tipster arrangement with the police or fire departments. The story must be a major one to summon a reporter and cameraperson from their beds in the middle of

CNN assignment desk in Atlanta.

the night. This also is true of the very largest markets where almost everyone involved in the production of news carries a union card. The penalties for calling crews back to work are too costly for it to become a habit.

This chapter will examine how assignments are made in a variety of TV newsrooms—in markets as small as 70,000, in cities of a half million or more, and in a major metropolis like New York. First, let's look at the most elaborate assignment desks, which are staffed around the clock.

The Overnight Assignment Editor

The news day usually starts at midnight with the arrival of the overnight assignment editor. He relieves the editor who had been in charge of the desk from around 4 P.M. A third editor will take over the desk about 8 A.M.

The overnight editor quickly reviews with the homeward-bound editor what occurred during the previous shift. They also discuss any particular problems that are expected to develop during the night. A reporter and crew may still be out on a story and, if so, the overnight editor will need to know all the details. It will be the new editor's responsibility to decide how long the crew should stay with a story. There are always two factors at play: money and morale. Keeping a camera crew and reporter on a story all night is expensive. If the story is important enough, management usually will not second-guess the editor. But more important is the physical well-being and emotional state of the reporter and crew. They may have been dashing around the city for eight or nine hours, frequently grabbing a bite to eat on the run. Also to be considered is the time of their next shift. If the reporter and crew are kept in the field, will it play havoc with assignments later in the day?

Scheduling Story Possibilities

The major concern of the overnight assignment editor, in addition to protecting the news operation during the dark hours, is to provide a battle plan for the upcoming day. After sending the evening editor home, the overnight editor will look over the typewritten log for the previous 16 hours. Each assignment editor must maintain a log that tells at a glance how every reporter and crew was deployed throughout the day. The log also contains various housekeeping notes: everything from broken camera gear to wake-up calls for reporters who sleep through alarm clocks.

After reading and digesting the log, the overnight editor reads the wire copy and culls the early editions of the morning newspapers. This is in preparation for the major overnight duty, preparing a four- or five-page document that lists all the major stories to be considered for coverage during the day. At some stations these are called "scheds" or "in-

Assignment/producers desk at KSL–TV in Salt Lake City. (KSL–TV photo)

sights.'' When the stories can be determined in advance, it also will list the time the reporters are to report to work and their assignments. This listing will be duplicated during the night ready for distribution to reporters, producers, and executives when they start arriving in the newsroom at 7 A.M. The overnight editor should demonstrate a talent for suggesting stories that might otherwise be missed. Some of those suggestions may be developed into interesting reports on the evening news.

The overnight assignment editor has an important role in determining how those first reporters and crews to arrive in the newsroom will be utilized. Decisions must be made about which reporter is best equipped to handle a particular story. Reporters must be briefed before they leave the newsroom. It also is the assignment editor's job to provide detailed traveling instructions for the crews. Poor information can delay a crew's arrival at the scene and sometimes means a story cannot make the broadcast.

The Dayside Editor

The day assignment editor arrives at about 7:30 or 8 A.M., is briefed, and checks the insights for early assignments. Naturally, any breaking story will be given priority over the suggestions that appear on the insights.

KSL–TV News assignment editor Cary Larsen discusses story idea with a reporter. (KSL–TV photo)

Crews assigned to a feature story or a soft news story can be, and frequently are, pulled off such stories when a breaking story develops. Many assignments and suggestions made on the overnight insights fall by the wayside in the effort to cover new stories that break during the day. The major burden of making sure the new events are covered falls on the daytime assignment editor who is constantly under pressure.

The day is filled with excitement, frustration, decision making, second-guessing, and fights. Assignment editors must have thick skins and a constant rein on their tempers because when things go wrong many angry voices are directed at them. "Where's my tape?" the producer wants to know. The traffic manager snarls that a courier is lost and blames the assignment editor for giving the wrong directions. The executive producer wants to know why the desk did not assign a reporter instead of only a camera crew to a fire. The camera crew complains about having had no lunch. And reporters grumble about their assignments. While the editor talks on the phone to a disgruntled politician who wants to know why no one turned up at his news conference, the news director complains that all the telephones are ringing. The news director and the producers want quick reflexes, sound news judgment, and cool heads at the dayside assignment desk.

The Evening Assignment Editor

After being briefed by the departing daytime editor, the evening editor has three major responsibilities:

1. Cleaning up whatever loose ends still remain for the evening news broadcast. This includes keeping tabs on the reporters and crews who are still shooting stories and will be returning late to base.
2. Making sure that the news assignments for the late night news are being worked on and will come back in time.
3. Setting the wheels in motion for any coverage that can be set up in advance for the next day. This will help the overnight editor who will be reluctant to wake up people in the middle of the night.

Assignment Desk Assistants

Many TV stations provide assignment editors with researchers and desk assistants. Researchers help dig up background information and also make preliminary telephone calls to set up a story for the reporter and camera crews.

Desk assistants rip wire copy, answer the phones, do clerical chores, and sometimes help out with telephone calls on major breaking stories. In middle-size markets, these jobs are excellent training for reporter positions. In the major markets, this entry-level position sometimes can lead to a researcher's job and even to an assignment editor's position.

KSL–TV News desk assistant Allison Barlow types the script of a story to be fed later by a reporter at the station's Washington bureau. (KSL–TV photo)

The Smaller TV Assignment Desk

At a TV station in Binghamton, New York—population of about 70,000—the assignment editor also is the news director. And that is an improvement over the way it was. Before Ken Srpan arrived at WBNG–TV, the former news director anchored the news as well. In smaller markets—Binghamton is the 110th—it still is not unusual for the news director to make the assignments, produce the newscasts, and anchor them. Srpan recalls that's the way it was in his first TV news job in Zanesville, Ohio. "There were only two of us," he recalled, "and we did everything . . . including shooting our own film and sweeping up at night. It was great experience."

Srpan, who is now news director at WPTF in Raleigh, N.C., says that when he was in Binghamton, despite its size, there were only a "handful of days" when he was hurting for news. "We had a good variety of news: health problems, ground water contamination, the city council constantly fighting with the mayor, and the county legislature battling the county executive." There were lots of good stories when I was there," he said.

Srpan had only five reporters. "They all had beats," he said, "but were available for general assignment as well." One reporter covered the courts; another watched city hall; a third kept an eye on county government; the fourth looked after the suburbs; and the fifth handled health and medicine.

Srpan said that when he arrived in the morning he went over the daybook and newspaper to see if he missed anything and to get possible story leads. "The reporters suggested ideas of their own," he added.

WWBT–TV in Richmond, Virginia (55th market) has a considerably larger news staff. The news manager, Ron Miller*, has ten reporters and an assignment editor. He also employs student interns in a number of capacities, including desk assistants who help the assignment editor and fill in on the weekends and evenings. As in most TV stations, no one minds the shop from midnight to 5 A.M. Miller said he is somewhat uneasy about this but relies heavily on a former truck driver who roams the city each night in a vehicle equipped with scanners and an ENG camera. "Donnie Neblett would rather stay up all night listening to scanners than sleep," said Miller. "When he tipped us about a story one night, it occurred to me that he could be useful to us." Miller and his staff trained Neblett to use a camera and to edit tape, and "we taught him something about news judgment," Miller recalled. Neblett continues

WWBT–TV cameraman Donnie Neblett. (WWBT photo)

---

*Miller is now news director of WBTV in Charlotte, NC.

WWBT–TV news staff at morning conference. (Photo courtesy of WWBT–TV)

to roam the streets of Richmond looking for stories during the night and fills in for other staff members on the weekends.

At 5 A.M. an intern arrives at WWBT-TV, rips the wires, and is joined by a morning news anchor an hour later. The intern checks with police and fire departments and makes some other calls so he can fill in the assignment editor who arrives around 8:15. The assignment editor has about 45 minutes to go over the wires before the reporters start arriving at 9 A.M. Miller meets with his staff soon after 9. The assignment editor reads the budget and runs over other ideas.

"I insist that our reporters suggest ideas at these meetings," Miller said. "I like to get a dialogue going so we can talk about what we might do that day. We bounce ideas off each other." Miller said the rap sessions also help him to keep track of who is contributing and who isn't. Miller said he tries for ten stories that involve his reporters each day. "Sometimes we make it; sometimes we don't," he added.

Each reporter at WWBT-TV has a beat or concentrates on certain subjects such as medicine, community affairs, or business. The reporters also are available for general assignment work.

Miller said the assignment editor makes the hour-to-hour decisions on what breaking stories to cover, "but, of course, is free to check with me and frequently does on some stories." All of the staff tries to monitor the scanners "so that we don't miss anything," Miller said, "and a reporter will take over the desk when the assignment editor goes to lunch."

Staying in Touch

The assignment desk and reporters and crews in the field must constantly exchange information. Those out covering the news must communicate on a regular basis with the assignment editor. They should feed each other information that will help determine the way a story is covered and presented on the air.

The reporters in the field must give the desk a clear appraisal of the stories to which they have been assigned. When the assignment is made, stories sometimes are perceived as being stronger than they really are.

Staying in touch also is essential because news stories are constantly developing and the assignment desk may need to move reporters from one story to another. As soon as a reporter arrives at the scene of a story, he or she should notify the desk by phone or two-way radio.

The assignment desk should have a telephone number at which to reach the reporter at the story site if possible. Some stations provide beeper devices for reporters that will let them know they should call the desk. When the reporter completes a story, he or she should contact the assignment editor to find out whether to return to base or to move on to another story.

Picking Your Own Story

In some markets, usually small ones, reporters are given almost complete control over the stories they pick. It may be a good learning experience, but because most reporters in small markets are young and inexperienced, the quality of news often suffers when no one has a firm grip on assignments.

A problem usually develops when the news director at a TV station is no more than a figurehead. Frequently, he or she must also produce and anchor the news and write much of the anchor copy. Chances are the news director may not even see the reporters in the morning before they grab their own story ideas.

If you work at one of these training stations, you will have an excellent opportunity to test your news judgment. Select your stories for their news merit and not because they're quick and easy and fill your time quota for the day. The freedom of not having an assignment editor carries added responsibility.

The Traffic Desk

A traffic desk is found only at the networks and in the largest markets.

A traffic manager has nothing to do with the selection and covering of stories. The traffic desk makes sure that reporters and camera crews have functioning cars or vans to get to and from the scene of a story. It also arranges air charters for out-of-town stories.

CBS News traffic desk. (Photo by Lionel Phillips)

The traffic desk often has several couriers who are regularly dispatched to bring cassettes back from reporters in the field when they are sent off to cover another story.

The Spec People

In some cities camera people on a speculation basis will shoot videotape on a breaking story for news organizations. The stations are under no obligation to buy it. These "spec" photographers will work through the night, using their own gear. They know that this is the time when most TV newsroom operations have closed down. They listen to the police and fire radios. When something breaks, they rush to the scene to shoot the flames or a criminal being booked at the local police station. When the TV news desk starts its day, the spec people will be there with their stories or will have dropped the tape off during the night. If the news director or producer likes it, the spec people make a sale.

Although most spec photographers are moving from film to electronic news gathering (ENG), many in smaller cities continue to work with film. Some reporters string for stations in suburban or rural areas, usually doing voice-over narration of film they have shot themselves. For example, although the Binghamton, New York, station, WBNG, is completely ENG, it still processes film sent in by these stringer photographer-reporters.

15

TV News Reporting

Developing Skills

Most TV reporters begin their careers in markets too small to support more than one or two broadcast stations. The young reporter is likely to be one of six or fewer staff members. This means that most days will be spent on the run—covering several different stories.

A typical day might begin with telephone rounds of the police departments in the station's area to check for any crime news of importance. You also will call area hospitals for unusual medical emergencies or good human interest stories. You might even make calls to the local governments to see what is happening there. Take advantage of these phone calls to build friendly relations with the many sources of information. And keep a personal list of their business and home telephone numbers where you can reach them on breaking stories and other times you need information fast. This may help you beat the competition on a news story.

At larger stations, many of these chores will be done by the assignment desk. But you still must keep up to date on the news. Read the wires every chance you get. Go through the local newspapers. And also subscribe to the nearest newspaper with a solid national reputation—

such as the *New York Times, Washington Post, Los Angeles Times, Des Moines Register,* and *Miami Herald,* to name a few.

If you can obtain it, you should also read the *Wall Street Journal.* Although chiefly known as a business and financial newspaper, it has the best daily summary of national and international stories and publishes many articles that will give you useful background.

The national newsmagazines provide a weekly summary of the world's major events and they frequently run stories that go into depth. These sources should provide you with lots of information to store in your memory. Back issues of each publication in a desk drawer or file cabinet can make a good instant library when you are under deadline pressure.

Tools to Carry in the Field

Almost every TV reporter leaves the newsroom with a camera person or crew who will make sure pictures are taken and sound is recorded. In some small markets you may have to use the gear yourself. Every reporter, of course, carries a note pad and pen, for jotting down important facts while covering a story. Such notes make it easier to write a script under deadline pressure in the field or back in the newsroom. It is important to write the correct spelling of a newsmaker's name and his title, because this information probably will be displayed on the screen when your story airs.

Also carry an audiotape recorder. Use it to record people interviewed in the field. The quality of the recording is not important because it will not be played back on the air. By using that audiotape along with your written notes, you can began organizing your on-air report before you come back to the station. If you have time, you will want to see the tape that was shot in the field before you start writing. That audiotape can help you decide quickly what sound bites to use and the length of the sound cut.

The best way to use your audio cassette player is to take the sound directly from the videocassette recorder (VCR). If you patch from the VCR output to the audio cassette input, your audiotape recording will give you an exact duplicate of the sound that is on your video cassette (with blank stretches, of course, on the audio cassette which continues to run while the VCR does not.) This would be a great advantage, for example, at a news conference or long interview.

Observation is an especially useful tool on initial assignments in the field. In addition to observing the facts of a story, watch how more experienced reporters are covering the event: who are they interviewing? what are they photographing? where are they doing portions of their narration on camera? You will learn from the choices and decisions they make as you try to gain confidence in covering a wide range of story assignments.

NBC News correspondent John Chancellor doing a commentary from Beirut. (NBC News photo)

Types of TV Stories

Spot News

A spot news story can be something that develops suddenly, such as a fire or bank robbery, or it can be a planned event, such as a protest demonstration or an Easter egg roll. Its origin may be an advance tip, such as a press release or a listing on the wire service schedule, or a transmission over the police or fire radio. At any rate, your job as a reporter will be to explain clearly what has happened. You must strive to be accurate, fast, comprehensive, and vivid as you work under deadline pressure and perhaps sift through conflicting or incomplete information.

Let's consider coverage of a fire. You are sent out at 2 P.M. to do a story for the "Six O'Clock News." In the two or three hours you will have at the scene, you will, of course, find out the basic facts: the location of the fire in the building; the time it broke out; the number of injured and dead; who they are; and when the blaze was brought under control. Most important are the human angles. Were any firemen killed or injured? Were any of those in the building recent victims of another fire? Are any of the victims related?

You also will find out about the people made homeless by the fire; the amount of damage suffered by the businesses involved; and whether they will be able to reopen and when.

Don't get so caught up in numbers and statistics about fire equipment and alarms that you lose sight of the effect of the fire on people.

The Enterprise Story

A fire story can be advanced the next day into what is called the enterprise story. Let's look at the possibilities. During yesterday's fire several tenants blamed their landlord for setting the fire. That allegation was not broadcast because it could not be substantiated at that time. Now, with a full day ahead of you, there is time to check police and fire department records. Have there been other fires at properties owned by the same landlord? Do fire officials suspect arson? Do the tenants making the charges have any axe to grind?

These are not the only questions to ask in following up on a fire; frequently, there are unanswered questions following a spot news story. Asking them and following your instincts may lead to new and significant information. Such enterprise reporting will distinguish you and your news operation from the others. Some news organizations take enterprise reporting a step further. They have on their staffs an individual or a team that initiates investigations on their own. These will be discussed in depth in Chapter 23, "Investigative Reporting."

The best enterprise stories usually will suggest themselves. Frequently you will get an idea on the way to work. Was that strange-looking garbage truck that you saw a new purchase by the city? If so, how many are there? Why the change? What do the new ones cost? Who benefits from the sale?

Trend Story

Reporting that recognizes cultural and technological changes produces trend stories.

In the early 1970s, there was a trend story on one network about the use of pocket calculators in elementary schools. Was it a good idea to let youngsters do basic math with them? Would they forget the basic principles of math? Or, as advocates claimed, would the calculators free children from mental drudgery and make them more creative?

A young teenager wearing earphones and racing down the street on skates led to another trend story. This story examined the popularity of the new, tiny stereo systems that appear to be replacing the booming portable radios so offensive to many pedestrians.

The reporter checked stores that sell audio equipment to obtain figures on the sales of the ministereos. He interviewed store owners and some of the teenagers who were using the new headsets. The reporter also interviewed city officials to see if there were fewer complaints about noise pollution since the headsets became so popular.

Sometimes, a trend story can develop into significant news. An example is a story about tanning tablets taken internally to get a tan from the inside out. These pills contain coloring agents. The people who take them are literally dyeing themselves. Is this legal? Is it healthy? Is it sane?

A reporter noticed these pills on sale one day at a drug counter. After asking questions, he discovered that the Food and Drug Administration (FDA) had not approved the tablets and therefore they were being sold illegally. The reporter also learned that the active chemical ingredients were being obtained on the black market by the American distributor. What started out as a simple trend story about a social quirk soon became more important. The major issue seemed to be the FDA's ability or inability to cope with thousands of new substances brought to its attention each year.

Police Sting the FBI

This is the anatomy of a story, how the decision was made to cover it, problems that arose in the field, what happened after the reporter and videotape returned to the office, and the final form it took on the air. This true story provides an especially good case study because it proved to be of local, national, and international interest. The following account includes some general observations that can be applied to any news assignment.

The FBI in New Haven, Connecticut suspected that Police Chief Joseph Walsh in nearby Bridgeport was guilty of corruption. He already was under investigation by a grand jury. To prove the allegation, the FBI collaborated with a convicted car thief, Thomas Mara, who was told to offer the police chief a bribe. The FBI operative was fitted with a hidden tape recorder and also a wireless microphone. The FBI planned to monitor the bribe and if it was accepted, the police chief would be arrested.

Without the knowledge of the FBI, the police chief, who was suspicious, also wore a wireless microphone. When the FBI collaborator offered the bribe, the chief arrested the man and confiscated his equipment and bribe money.

This story about one law enforcement agency ensnaring another occurred at a time of national concern about the propriety of investigating techniques used to develop evidence against politicians. The FBI had been under considerable criticism for setting traps in the Abscam case in which agents posed as rich Arabs offering bribes in return for political favors.

CBS and other electronic news organizations were trying to catch up on the Bridgeport story. *The New York Times* had the story in its early editions that were printed before midnight. It was 12:15 P.M. when a CBS reporter and camera crew reached Bridgeport police headquarters. Five other television reporters and crews, along with a number of print reporters, were already on the scene trying to interview the police chief.

The CBS reporter, Steve Young, started talking to one of the detectives who took part in the reverse sting. During the interview, Young asked the detective, "How would you describe the FBI operation?" It took the detective a few seconds to reply, "It was Mickey Mouse." This is a good example of earlier advice that silence can be golden. Give interviewees time to react. If necessary, pauses can be closed up later in editing.

Young also was trying to figure out what parts of the story could not be illustrated pictorially and would have to be told on camera. Any concern about picture possibilities quickly faded when Young entered the police chief's office. On his desk were the wireless microphone and tape recorder confiscated from the FBI collaborator by the Bridgeport police, the chief's wireless transmitter, and the $5,000 in bribe money.

Unfortunately the chief turned out to be a relatively dull interview. In addition the interview had to be repeated due to equipment problems. First there was a short-circuit in a microphone cable. Then, when that was fixed, the battery powering the tape recorder failed and had to be replaced. Equipment often fails at the worst times. Try not to get rattled. You will upset not only yourself, but also the person you are interviewing and the crew with which you are working.

The availability of the police recording of the bribe offer and subsequent arrest increased the possibility that the Bridgeport sting story could be turned into an interesting TV news story. It also reduced the importance of the interview with the police chief.

While Young was speaking briefly with his office to inquire about the possibility of extra photographs (some had been located in the hands of a photo stringer, and arrangements to bring them to New York were being worked out), the crew was shooting a few exterior scenes of the police station. It was approximately 2:15 P.M. when Young and the crew left the police station to locate the fire station that had been the listening post for the police during the double sting operation.

They shot an exterior of the fire station as well as several shots of the parking lot across the street in which the bribe attempt and resulting arrest had been made. To add visual interest and drama, Young also wanted a high shot of the parking lot from inside the fire station.

The problem was that the fire station was not in use and all the doors were locked. It was now 2:30 P.M. and time was running out for Young. Shopkeepers in the neighborhood said that a key was kept by the Department of Public Works two blocks away. The crew stayed in place. Young ran the distance and obtained the key from a public works employee who had to clear the request with the Mayor's office. It then took ten minutes to make the high shots and another five minutes to shoot an on-camera close in which Young discussed what might happen to the bribe money.

At about 4 P.M. the helicopter lifted off with Young and the pilot, heading for New York. The helicopter touched down at a small heliport on the eastside of Manhattan about 35 minutes later. A waiting courier took Young and the videotape to the newsroom.

On the way, Young wrote a script in longhand. His rough notes would help him and the tape editor locate various scenes. Both the pictures and interviews had been recorded on just over one videocassette. A conscious effort had been made to hold down the amount of material shot in anticipation of a late return time.

At 4:50 P.M. when Young reached the CBS office, a videotape editor was waiting to screen the material. The photos already moved by the wire services had been transferred to videocasette. The producer also had some graphics prepared for the story. They showed a map of the state of Connecticut, locating Bridgeport where the sting occurred, as well as New Haven, the FBI state headquarters. Another graphic showed the approximate locations of the parking lot where the attempted bribe occurred and the separate FBI and police listening posts. An audio recording of the bribe offer had been obtained by the producer earlier in the day. But the technical quality of the tape recording was not very good; to make sure it could be understood and to keep the story more interesting when the tape was played, the producer had the sections likely to be used typed out so they could be shown on the screen. It was agreed that the most effective and dramatic way to tell the story would be to let the people involved tell their own story with a minimum of reporter narration.

Both the correspondent and producer decided that there should be a reference in the script to the pending grand jury investigation of the police chief. Young chose a sound bite in which the police chief himself drew a connection between the grand jury investigation and the FBI sting attempt.

By now it was approximately 5:30 P.M. The broadcast was an hour away. The length of the Bridgeport story was determined by having Young time his narration and add to that time the rough times of the desired sound cuts. The executive producer was told the piece would take about two minutes and might not be ready for screening before it was broadcast.

The story was ready for air less than 30 seconds before anchorman Dan Rather began to read the lead-in to it. Following is a complete transcript of what the television audience heard and saw.

You will notice that the script is divided into two columns with the *video* on the left and the *audio* on the right. This is called the "split page" and all of the material that you will write for television will use this format. Details on the split page and definitions of the terms shown in the video column will be explained in Chapter 19, "Scripting Television News."*

---

*The abbreviations V/O, SOT, and O/C have been spelled out in parenthesis for your clarification. Only the abbreviations would be shown in actual TV news scripts. (See Chapter 19 for an explanation of other abbreviations used in TV news scripts.)

Video	Audio
Video	*Audio*

Joseph Walsh
  Bridgeport Police
  Chief	

Walsh full-frame	
SOT (Sound on Tape)	"I think it was vicious, I really do."
Young V/O (voice-over)	Bridgeport Police Superintendent Joseph Walsh, talking about the FBI's attempt to bribe him with five thousand dollars in hundred dollar bills. The FBI used a convicted car thief, Thomas Mara,

Black-and-White wire
  picture--
  Mara highlighted
	as a confederate. It wired him with

Mara's tape recorder	a tape recorder strapped to his leg
Mara's transmitter	and a transmitter hidden in a pack
Street-level shot parking lot	of cigarettes. Mara lured Walsh to a meeting in this parking lot, told

(Graphics section--
  Walsh/Mara pictures
  and text of
  conversation)
	Walsh he would give him a lot of money if the police superintendent returned a lucrative city car-towing contract to Mara's uncle.

SOT (sound on tape)
  Walsh (<u>recording from
  police hidden mike</u>)
	"I trust you, you trust me."

Mara (from police hidden mike recording)	"You know, I gotta do what I gotta do to get it back. You just let me know what's gotta be done."
Walsh	"You tell me" (<u>laughter</u>).

Young V/O (voice-over)
Walsh exiting
  courthouse day of
  grand jury session
  (fed by affiliate)
Walsh's hidden
  transmitter
High shot from
  firehouse
 	
Cut to close-up
  parking lot
	What Mara and the FBI didn't realize was that Walsh, subject of a grand jury corruption probe, was suspicious, had had himself wired with a hidden transmitter, and police were watching and recording the conversation in a building across the street.

(Graphics section)
SOT (sound on tape)
Walsh (hidden mike
    recording)

"Well, what are you offering?"

Mara (hidden mike
    recording)

"I can come up with about thirty grand."

Walsh

"Thirty grand!"

Anthony Fabrizi (full-
frame) Bridgeport
Police Inspector:
(On-camera
interview)

"Tom Mara got out of the superintendent's car, walked up Main Street to his own car, opened the trunk of the car, and removed an envelope from same."

Walsh (<u>hidden mike</u>
<u>recording</u>)

"How much is there?"

Mara (<u>hidden mike</u>
<u>recording</u>)

"Should be five in there, Joe."

Walsh (<u>hidden mike</u>
<u>recording</u>)

"I'll trust you."

Mara (<u>hidden mike</u>
<u>recording</u>)

"No, why don't you count it."

Walsh (<u>hidden mike</u>
<u>recording</u>)

"I trust you."

Mara (<u>hidden mike</u>
<u>recording</u>)

"You sure?"

Walsh (<u>hidden mike</u>
<u>recording</u>)

"Now, put your hands on the dashboard. You're under arrest for attempted bribery. Put your hands on the dashboard!"

Young V/O (Voice-over)

And that was it. The FBI was caught flat-footed, stung by its own sting. There was a tussle when FBI agents moved in. Police refused to return the FBI's surveillance gear, arrested Mara, and held on to the five thousand dollars as evidence.

Black-and-white
pictures——Wire
service plus
stringer

SOT (sound on tape)
Mayor Mandanici

(<u>On telephone</u>) "That's why I'm calling for a congressional investigation."

Video	Audio
Young V/O (voice-over) (over interview set-up shot)	The mayor of Bridgeport, John Mandanici, is hopping mad.
SOT (sound on tape) Mayor Mandanici (from interview)	"We've caught them doing something illegal. And as a matter of fact, I think they're arrestable. They should be in jail."
Police Superintendent Walsh (from interview)	"I've been under investigation for a year, and I think this was their last desperate chance to embarrass me."
Young (interviewing Fabrizzi)	"How would you characterize this FBI operation?''
Inspector Fabrizzi	(<u>pause--smiles</u>) "Mickey Mouse."
Young O/C (on camera)	The FBI office in New Haven issued a terse one-line statement. "The undercover operation was approved and monitored by the U.S. Department of Justice." The police chief says if the courts approve, he'll turn the FBI's five-thousand-dollar bribe money over to charity. Steve Young, CBS News, Bridgeport, Connecticut.

Cutoff and Its Consequences

Each time you cover a story, you must always keep in mind your deadline. Your story must be ready to air in the spot where it is scheduled in the broadcast. Otherwise, the producer must reshuffle the entire broadcast. If this happens often with your stories, it will not only destroy the flow of the broadcast but will make you unpopular with the producer and the news director. While you are out in the field covering a story, you must work out what is known as a cutoff time. This is the time you must leave the scene of a story or send the tape back to the newsroom so enough time remains to put together a finished story before it is to go on the air.

Do not forget that traffic may be heavy when you try to return to the newsroom. Allow at least one hour for editing the story. If you alert the

Reporter-anchor David Margulies of WFAA–TV reporting from scene of tornado. (WFAA News photo)

desk, others will be able to get any late-breaking information you need to write your script when you get back to the newsroom.

The new technology can make it easier to cover a story. In the days of film, the cutoff for spot news was earlier because the film had to be processed before it could be edited. Tape is instantly ready for editing, so you can stay longer at the scene of a story. With breaking news, you can do a live remote while the pictures, interviews, and narration are transmitted (microwaved) back to the newsroom for editing.

Plan ahead, carefully analyze your cutoff time, and be realistic. Change your story concept to conform with reality and aim only for what can be achieved.

Making Every Minute Count

Covering a late afternoon story that is to lead off a 6 P.M. TV news broadcast often is a struggle against time. The answer to such stressful circumstances is to continue working on the way back to the newsroom. The reporter who arrives back at the newsroom with no clear idea of the most important points of a story or where they are located in the video material creates a nightmare for everyone.

When you're returning in the news van, review your picture notes and the editorial points of the story. Try to finish as much of the script as possible. Many reporters complete at least a rough version in longhand. At those points in the script where you plan to use sound cuts, write in

ENG editing station at WCBS–TV News. (Photo by Lionel Phillips)

the content verbatim, if possible, from your notes or review the audio-tape recording you made at the scene.

These preparations will help you make a close estimate on the total length of your story so the producer can plan the broadcast. A producer can make adjustments if a few stories are slightly longer or shorter. But one-and-a-half minute stories that unexpectedly run to two minutes can cause serious problems.

It is helpful to "talk through" your story with the broadcast producer, who may suggest a slight restructuring so that dramatic file footage can be placed at the top of the story. You then incorporate changes in a type-written script. The most pressure now is on the video tape editors. They will not resent suggestions from you; the piece may not get completed unless you pitch in. Spend most of the remaining time with the editor. You should know where the establishing shots are on the cassette and in what order the interviews were done.

Usually, videotape editors like to pick their own shots after screening all available material. They should be allowed to do that, especially when you are working on a feature or special story over the course of more than one day. Under such circumstances, you may tactfully suggest why you think a particular choice of shots is appropriate or effective, or explain what may not be readily evident to the editor who has not been to the scene. In late-breaking stories, especially when the editor did not shoot the story, he may have to edit without having looked at all the tape. You may need to work more carefully with the editor to help him find the pictures and interviews. In many markets, the tape editor has actually shot the story in the field. And at some stations reporters shoot and edit their own videotape.

Time Coding

If your station has some of the tape editing equipment that incorporates time code, you are very fortunate. This electronic system can put the time of day on the tape along with the television picture, sound, and control signals. If gear is so equipped, a reporter can be of great assistance to the editor.

If you have your technician in the field adjust the time code to the time on your watch, all you need to do is jot down the clock times of important statements or shots. Armed with accurate time codes, you should be able to help an editor quickly find necessary shots. And if the trip back to base is a long one, it may be possible for you to review some of the material by playing the tape back, listening to the audio through earphones, and watching the picture in the camera's viewfinder.

Covering the News Conference for TV

Advice given in the radio reporting portion about covering news conferences also applies to television. It is especially important for TV that you arrive at a news conference early. Camera positions may be at a premium for latecomers. Try to sit in plain sight of your camera operator. You will not want to shoot everything, so the camera operator has to know when to start and stop. If an advance text of a statement is available, you might underline the portions that interest you as a guide to the camera operator.

Those who call a news conference may provide a plug-in point to a house public address system, but most often you will set up your own microphone. Check the audio system in advance to make sure voice level and technical quality are good.

Try to find out in advance what kind of lighting problems you can expect. Electronic cameras must be adjusted for color balance before the news conference. This involves aiming the camera at some white object and pushing the "white balance" control. More on that later.

Manners

Good manners mean you do not trample on the rights of those who called the news conference or other reporters covering it. If you are videotaped on camera (a stand-up) while the event is still taking place, do so quietly. Few things alienate newsmakers and other reporters more than a reporter who thoughtlessly turns everybody else into a prop. Locate yourself in such a position that your spoken narration will not interfere with others. If that is not possible, find some other suitable location, perhaps outside the conference room or outside the building.

At a news conference, an unacceptable technique is the fake or counterfeit question. This is the practice of repeating another reporter's question for your own camera after the news conference ends. The purpose of the deception is to make it appear that you asked the hard questions.

A cub reporter might consider the counterfeit question a good way to impress a news director. Take heed: many in management consider such behavior sufficient grounds for dismissal. If a news director urges this shabby practice, it might be a good idea to start looking for another job.

Reporter Involvement

Reporter involvement often is recommended by the TV news consultants who are paid to tell station managers and news directors how to market the news to attract the largest number of viewers. This means that, in some way, the reporter will make himself or herself part of the story.

Acceptable forms include a reporter seen in a cutaway shot at a news conference, shown on camera as the news event takes place in the background, and walking with someone during an interview. The purpose is to impress on the viewer that the reporter was at the event. This is part of the meaning behind those terms "Eyewitness News" and "Action News." These examples of reporter involvement present no ethical problems and often make the video portion of the news story more interesting. But when a TV news reporter actually takes part in an event to achieve reporter involvement, this presents an ethical dilemma.

The traditional philosophy is that the reporter is an objective observer, relaying information to the viewer without becoming part of the story. In some TV newsrooms reporters are encouraged to become involved in their stories for no legitimate reason. The danger with this is that the reporter may appear to be less objective in the eyes of the viewer, an advocate for a cause, and not a reliable source of information.

Every reporter at one time or another faces the problem of involvement. A heavy snowstorm closes schools and to illustrate the fun the kids are having, you might slide down a hill on a sled. Or you are doing a story on folk dancing and before you know it, you are out on the dance floor showing how it is done. Or your news director might ask when you return from the opening of a new ice cream parlor, "Why didn't you eat one of those five dollar sundaes at the counter for your close?"

If that sort of reporter involvement makes you cringe, your choice is clear-cut. Go along or look for a job elsewhere. Some news directors share your concern. Ron Miller, of WBTV in Charlotte, North Carolina, said he believes audiences like to see reporters only when their roles serve some purpose. He cited an example of a reporter who is shown on camera giving blood while covering a story on the opening of a Red Cross drive. Such participation demonstrates to the public that the procedure is quick and painless.

What troubles Miller—and others—is when reporters inject themselves into a story for no good reason. "Many of them," he said, "are just on an ego trip."

Certainly there are many legitimate cases in which the reporter should get involved. For example, a common acceptable technique for a reporter at the scene of a crime would be to reenact where a killer apparently stood in the shadows of a house waiting for his victim. The reporter might then walk his way through some of the story, showing the audience where the bullets lodged in the side of the house. The purpose, of course, is to help the viewer understand better what actually took place at the crime scene. One word of caution, though. Do not overuse the walking technique. Also avoid pointing too much. Some reporters insist on turning around and pointing to almost every object they are describing. Do this sparingly.

Appearance

Nothing is as distracting to a TV viewer as a male broadcaster's askew collar or the glare and jingle of a woman reporter's jewelry. Appearances matter in television news, even though the reporter should not be the message but the conveyor of the message.

In general, your choice of clothing should be conservative and simple. Neither the cut of a man's jacket nor the plunge of a woman's neckline should be too extreme. Clothing should be suited to the task. Inappropriate dress not only diverts the viewer's attention but also detracts from your credibility.

Increasingly, local TV news reporters dress informally in sport jackets,

CNN anchors Marcia Ladendorff and Lou Dobbs. (Photo by Robert D. Kaplan, CNN)

slacks, shirts, and ties. Jeans and sports shirts, however, are not suitable for covering city hall or the board of education.

You should consider not only the kind of clothing you wear but also the colors. Loud colors are to be avoided. For in-studio work, there also are technical considerations. Sometimes a color may be banned on the news set because of the way video graphics are generated. One of the basic systems is called chromakey. If you wear a tie or dress in the forbidden color, technicians will have difficulty keeping the video graphics from being superimposed onto your clothing. Check with the executive producer or director to determine if any color is a problem.

Another consideration in choosing what color clothing to wear is the overall color of the news set. If it is beige or tan or some other light color, it probably would be a good idea to wear darker colors to set you off from the background. And if the set background color is dark, a better choice would be light-colored clothing.

Makeup

There seldom is time to worry about makeup in the field. But many of the nation's major market stations and the networks have makeup experts for broadcasters working in a studio. They try to get five or ten minutes of your time to apply makeup. If you are doing your own makeup, make sure you use a flat, nonshiny type. In the field you can use a twist-stick version of TV pancake makeup which resembles a fat lipstick. A qualified makeup person can suggest the right shade for your complexion.

Prompting Techniques

Some TV reporters in the field find it difficult to deliver the on-camera portions of a script without constantly looking down. Occasional downward glances are realistic and helpful in the reading of a script. But breaking that eye contact with the viewer for most of your on-camera time gives the impression you do not know the story.

One remedy is partial memorization. Do not try to learn several hundred words at once. Break the material into blocks of ideas, keeping in mind the logical flow of what you have written. Even though you have written the copy, you must analyze it for content before you can effectively read it without constantly looking down. The key is to understand the relationship of ideas.

You need not be concerned with memorizing your on-camera script on a late-breaking story or live report from the scene. The news story will telegraph a sense of urgency to the viewer and an over-slick presentation can be counterproductive. Your delivery should appear appropriate to the situation. Bolting out of a labor negotiation session to report a settlement live makes an informal, ad lib situation right. Doing a wrap-up several hours later requires a more polished approach.

CNN anchor Beverly Williams reads over scripts before VJ distributes copies to producer, director, Videfont and prompter operators.

News script being fed past the small prompter camera. (Photo by Robert D. Kaplan, CNN)

Anchor reading script from the prompter screen.

In a studio the solution to delivering on-camera narratives is different and easier. The most common studio prompting system involves a black-and-white TV camera, TV monitors, and mirror devices. To prepare prompter copy for the system, the reporters (or writer, producer, or anchor) type their copy onto a multipart carbon set or copy book. Copies go to many people, including the director, anchors, producer, and font operator.* One copy, usually a white copy, must go to the prompter operator who will feed the pages in numerical order across a small, lighted stand. Peering down at the copy is a small, fixed-focus TV camera. The image of the copy is fed electronically to monitors fixed above or below the studio cameras' lenses. Through a system of reflective mirrors, the image of the TV screen is reflected so you can read the script while looking at the broadcast camera lens. The operator of the prompting system usually has a headset in order to clearly hear the person reading the copy. The operator can adjust the rate of the scroll to match the reading rate of the broadcaster. In many of the nation's TV newsrooms, the prompters are handled by student interns. In larger markets, they are often operated by full-time employees or people working for the prompter company. The prompters allow the most natural kind of reporter-audience communication.

*See pages 235–237 for a further discussion of fonts.

Beats and Assignments for Television

City Council

In the radio section, you learned that local legislative bodies are an important source of news to smaller communities and that much of your early career will be spent covering local government news.

The advice offered on covering local government for radio applies to TV reporters as well. But the one big difference and greater challenge for the TV newsperson is pictures.

TV news organizations in major cities are frequently criticized for not paying enough attention to local government. Most large TV newsrooms have an "action" reporter who handles complaints from viewers about government red tape or consumer ripoffs. But many of these same stations have no reporter regularly assigned to a city hall beat. The reason again is pictures. The possibilities for interesting pictures at city council meetings are not great, and such meetings can tie up reporters for hours when they could be out covering stories that are more visually appealing.

In the smaller markets, news directors may rely more on the workings of local government to provide stories. So it is especially important to cover such stories in an interesting fashion. The picture possibilities may seem limited but with some thought they often can be developed.

Ken Srpan, news director of WPTF in Raleigh, N.C., said a reporter covering city council should get the agenda for the meeting early in the day or the day before and decide which item is likely to produce some news. Then, Srpan said, the reporter should try to shoot some footage that deals with that story or get some interviews with people who are affected by the council's deliberations.

In poorly produced city council stories, the camera pans across the council chamber, slowing down occasionally to zoom in on one of the speakers before resuming its sweep of the room. The camera then shows the reporter busily taking notes. As the camera focuses on the councilmen, the reporter comments on the highlights of the session.

Some reporters try without much success to add a second dimension to this dull story by doing a stand-up just inside or outside the chamber.

Let's look at how you might bring alive an otherwise dull city council story.

You check with your contact at city hall and discover that the most interesting item on the council's agenda is a proposal to change a one-way street back to its original two-way traffic flow. Since the street became one-way, accidents increased, business deteriorated, and neighbors complained about increased noise and pollution. Many motorists used the street as an alternate means of getting through town.

At mid-morning you and your camera operator head for the avenue in question. You get lots of cover footage (shots of street and traffic) and station yourself near a traffic light. As motorists stop for the light, you ask, "What do you think about making the street two-way again?" Several drivers are unaware of the proposed change and have not given it much thought. You finally get three or four good responses, mostly against the change because "it's going to mean more time getting to and from work."

Next you visit stores on the street. The owners like the idea. "Traffic moves more slowly on a two-way street . . . people are more likely to check out stores on both sides if they're going slower."

Finally, you interview some homeowners. You find they are unanimously in favor of going back to a two-way street. Some of their comments include "faster traffic means more accidents . . . fewer people sit on their porches these days, and families with kids are avoiding the street."

"That's a wrap," you tell your photographer and you head back to the station. You have plenty of time to cut some tape to go with whatever happens at the city council meeting that night.

Before you and your camera operator go to the city council meeting, you isolate some sound bites with motorists, a shopkeeper, and two homeowners. You also have some cover footage of the one-way street signs and the cars moving quickly down the avenue.

At the meeting, the one-way street controversy proved to be the most interesting and heated discussion. You shoot a cassette of the debate, which finally ended with a motion to table the item pending further discussion. You have plenty of time left to prepare your story for broadcast. It goes like this.

Video	*Audio*
V/O City council spectators	Some 200 Grand Street residents packed the city council chamber demanding their street be made two—way again. The debate lasted two hours and at times became heated.
SOT :22 Font: Councilman Sam Jones	TRACK UP OUT: "fooling anybody." TIME :22
V/O Smith	Councilman Frank Smith represents the district involved.
SOT :18 Font: Councilman Frank Smith	TRACK UP OUT: ". . . never give up." TIME :18
O/C on street	How do motorists feel about the idea?
SOT :23 Montage of motorists	TRACK UP OUT: ". . . can never tell." TIME :23
V/O	We also spoke with several shopkeepers on Grand Street.
SOT :28 Montage of shopkeepers	TRACK UP OUT: ". . . can't really wait." TIME :28

Video	*Audio*
V/O Fast traffic going past homes	Homeowners we spoke to also are looking forward to Grand Street reverting to a two-way street again.

SOT :19 Montage of homeowners	TRACK UP OUT: ". . . sure it will happen." TIME :19

V/O More shots of city council)	Most of the 200 people who jammed the city council chamber seem to support the change back to a two-way street. But the council decided to table the measure for further study. This is Frank Smith in Alexandria.

Political Campaigns

Politicians at every level of government conduct their campaigns to win or hold onto public office with television very much in mind. The camera influences what politicians do, when they do it, and where they do it—with one aim in mind: selling their personalities to the TV audience.

Television and politicians have had a close relationship since the 1950s. One of the first political television advisers to gain prominence was Robert Montgomery, a television producer and former movie actor, who helped President Eisenhower improve the effectiveness of his televised addresses. The debates on television between presidential candidates John F. Kennedy and Richard Nixon helped Kennedy win election in 1960. And the debate between President Carter and challenger Ronald Reagan in the final days of the 1980 campaign is credited with boosting Reagan over the top. Television gave birth to something new—the media consultant. No longer do television advisers limit themselves to technical matters. They advise politicians how to conduct their campaigns, using TV and radio as the main means of communication with the public.

Today, many politicians engage media advisers who help shape entire campaigns and deal with the press. When covering a campaign, whether at the local, state, or national level, reporters must resist being swept up in the atmosphere of enthusiasm. Media advisers often create events that invite superficial coverage while presenting their candidate in the best

CNN White House correspondent John Holliman. (Photo by Robert D. Kaplan, CNN)

possible light. Don't climb on anyone's bandwagon, but at the same time don't board a campaign bus with a chip on your shoulder. Maintain as much objectivity as possible along with a reporter's healthy dose of skepticism. Following are some points to keep in mind as you try to decide what is newsworthy.

1. *Theme:* What did the candidate have to say? What is its significance to the community? Has this candidate said the same thing before? How does it compare and contrast with themes struck by the candidate's opponents?
2. *Setting:* What place did the candidate choose? Is the setting significant, that is, is the candidate courting a certain segment of the electorate? If so, why? Do you believe the candidate has strong or weak support from this group? Why?
3. *Reception:* How did the audience react? What points drew a favorable response? How did the audience perceive the politician?
4. *Accuracy:* Did the candidate misrepresent himself? Were the facts distorted to enhance his own record or to put down the record of his opponent? You must point this out—not shrilly, but objectively.

Covering a mayoral campaign in a large city or a senatorial campaign, you may be assigned regularly to one of the candidates when the campaign enters the homestretch. At that point the following additional factors come into play.

1. *Consistency:* Does the candidate say the same thing to different audiences, or different things to different audiences? Does the candidate believe, or at least say, the same things consistently or does he tell people what they want to hear?

2. *Campaign adjustment:* Is the politician changing his major themes? If so, why? Is he chasing public opinion? Question the candidate and those managing the campaign about this.

3. *Issues versus strategy:* Much has been written criticizing television coverage of political campaigns for not devoting enough time to the issues. Often the criticism is valid. Concentrate on the issues. But also be aware of any sudden change in the candidate's position or strategy.

4. *Who's Who:* There is not likely to be a large entourage surrounding a candidate for mayor or an incumbent in a small city, or even in many larger ones. You will deal most of the time with a press secretary. Campaigns for statewide or national office are managed by a much larger group of people. Advance staffers will go to the next location to try to ensure a good crowd turnout and to solve technical problems before they occur.

5. *Emotional overinvolvement:* It is crucial that you keep your emotional distance from the candidate. That is sometimes difficult to do. Do you find the candidate personally disagreeable or wrong on the issues? Those feelings have no place in your reporting. However, if a large part of the electorate has such opinions, report them.

For the same reason, you must not permit yourself to become a cheerleader for candidates whom you admire. This can be particularly difficult because you will be spending so much time near or with the candidates. Their triumphs may well be yours. A good speech by the candidate may result in good "play" for your story. A victory by the candidate could mean reassignment for you and more visibility at city hall, the state legislature, Congress, or the White House.

Crime

Crimes receive more attention than most other types of news stories at local TV stations. They are easy to cover and have wide appeal. They also provide good pictures and can excite the emotions of viewers. For example, those with children can relate their fears to the stories about youngsters molested or killed. No one who lives in a city of even modest size is completely free from the fear of walking down the street at night and, in many places, even in the daytime.

The important question to ask about a crime story is what makes this one different from the hundreds of others? A mugging on the street is, unfortunately, a common occurrence in large cities. But suppose the mugger is a 14-year-old and the victim a 94-year-old? Suppose a bank robber is an eight-year-old child playing bandit with a toy gun? Both events actually happened. They have a special interest because they are unusual. Some crimes attract media attention because of their viciousness. An example is the story of three CBS employees walking to a parked car when they stumbled upon a mob hit-man killing a woman who was believed to be an informer. When they went to her aid, the killer shot all three men in the head. He later dumped the woman's body elsewhere. This story attracted nationwide attention because of its horror.

TV stations are inclined to give daily crime stories to general assignment reporters. This differs from newspaper practice where the police beat is often an assignment held for many years by the same person. But for some broadcast reporters, like Chris Borgen of WCBS-TV in New York, reporting crime is a specialty. Borgen does not handle the day-to-day routine crime story. WCBS-TV makes extensive use of his experience as a former New York City police officer.

Borgen has built a tremendous number of sources over the years. These sources have helped Borgen obtain exclusives when crime stories break, such as the bungled robbery of a Brinks armored truck by underground radicals in New York's Rockland County. His sources often enable him to give viewers details not available to others in the media.

Borgen says a good police reporter has the ability to build valuable sources on both sides of the fence—"the police and the people they chase." This demands integrity because both sides must learn to trust you. "The policeman," Borgen says, "wants to be sure you will not embarrass him or place him in a negative light. The criminal does not want you to judge him or disagree with his way of life."

Borgen also advises young reporters to learn who does what on the police force. Then, when you arrive at the crime scene with your camera crew, you will be able to "spot the fingerprint guys getting ready to dust, the forensic people looking for the evidence left behind, the ballistics experts trying to find the bullet shells. They all will make good visual shots for the camera."

Borgen also suggests talking off-camera first to the police officers you plan to interview. Often, he said, they will speak to you first in police jargon. Borgen finds that this often gives him background information for good questions when the camera is running. The police officer usually feels more at ease when he talks informally to a reporter he knows without any cameras or notepads in sight. Then you can ask him to talk to you on camera. If an officer talks in jargon terms on camera, ask him to explain what he said to you again. Often this will make the officer speak plainly.

One of Borgen's favorite techniques in reporting a crime story is the reconstruction of the crime at the scene. He begins by finding out all the details he can from the police. Borgen then uses the camera to illustrate the crime step-by-step as the police say it happened. The body may no longer be on the ground, the weapon may be missing, the blood may have been washed away, but Borgen will show the viewer where the victim was when the crime was committed, how the police believe it happened, how the police believe the killer escaped, and what evidence was left behind.

Of course, the police are not the only ones Borgen relies on to get his story. He also looks for the human factor in the crime. He interviews bank tellers who describe how frightened they were while the bandits were robbing the bank, or the friends and neighbors of the victim who can relate what kind of person he was.

The keys to good crime reporting are to try to recreate the excitement and emotion of the event and to always look for some way to illustrate your facts.

Covering the Courts

The TV reporter's problem in the courtroom is how to get pictures. At present, no federal courts permit cameras in the courtroom. Some state and local courts do, and the number is growing. Many courts allow TV cameras in some of the corridors of the courthouse. This will give your camera operator the opportunity to videotape the principals in the trial as they enter and leave the courthouse. Within the guidelines explained in the radio section, there is nothing to stop you from trying to interview these principals. Remember that there are many entrances and exits to a courthouse. If someone wants to avoid the camera or if the authorities want to keep the press away from a defendant, they usually can.

Television has solved the problem of showing what happened in the courtroom by hiring an artist. A good courtroom artist must be fast and have a good memory. Some artists do preliminary sketches which they color later. Be sure the artist makes basic drawings of the whole cast of characters: specifically, the entire jury, the judge, defense and prosecution attorneys, the defendant, the plaintiff in a civil trial, and the witnesses. Do not hesitate to point out good emotional moments for the artist to depict. A good artist will instinctively notice telling visible signs that make for a good sketch—the way witnesses sit, the type of clothes they wear, and their facial expressions. When used with a voice-over report by a correspondent, the artwork makes the story move better visually and helps to hold the viewer's interest.

Testimony in a courtroom or any type of judicial hearing usually concerns a witness's story of what happened. The artist can provide a series of drawings illustrating that testimony. An example was a story of a Coast Guard hearing about a stranded pleasure boat allegedly rammed by a barge under tow in Long Island Sound. All those aboard the pleasure boat drowned except the owner who testified that the tug's crew refused to give assistance. The tug boat captain denied the charge and was later cleared. Fortunately, the Coast Guard allowed newsmen to make audiotapes of the testimony. This was layed over an artist's conception of events, according to the testimony. Together, audiotapes and artwork provided a dramatic account of that day's happenings at the hearing.

Sketch of courtroom scene during the murder trial of Wayne Williams in Atlanta. (Courtesy of artist David Rose and CNN)

Some news organizations frown on such artist conceptions on grounds that they give too much credence to the witnesses' testimony.

Another source of good pictures for the courtroom story is file footage of the original story on the day when it happened. This provides visuals of some events that are being discussed in the courtroom. Properly identified as file footage with a date, this will present no ethical problem.

In major criminal trials, if your station has microwave capability, you probably will be set up to do a live remote if the jury is deliberating while your broadcast is on the air. This often provides an element of suspense to the broadcast, helping to keep the viewer tuned for that possible verdict or to tune in the next broadcast to see if the jury has returned. Your remote will often be in areas far from the courtroom. You will need an aide to let you know if something is happening. In the beginning, you may be able to spice up your live remotes with interviews, especially from the defense. But the longer the jury is out, the more nervous the principals become and the less willing they will be to talk.

There are three other types of stories you will be assigned frequently: demonstrations, disasters, and features. Some news directors prefer to assign certain reporters to these stories, depending on the reporter's personality and reporting skills. For example, a reporter with a light touch is more likely to be assigned to feature stories. But in most newsrooms, you will be required to demonstrate your ability to cover all these assignments.

Demonstrations

One of the easiest ways to get news coverage for a cause is to stage a demonstration. Often with an almost knee-jerk reaction, the cameras will appear at the scene. The visuals of people marching around, carrying placards, and shouting slogans is a natural for the home screen. But does a demonstration by 10, 20, or even 50 people really represent a strong statement in support of a cause?

You must remember not to let yourself be used. Do not let the pictures make the viewer think the demonstration was more crowded or more forceful than it actually was. Do not forget that the television cameras often condense the view of the scene. Ten people demonstrating in front of a politician's office may seem much larger when viewed on the TV screen.

Even more caution should be exercised during disturbances. Be careful about using the word *riot*. The racial disturbances of the 1960s may have truly earned the description as riots, but often disorders involve a limited number of people in a limited area and should be described in milder terms.

When you begin covering disturbances and demonstrations, you will notice that when the camera is running or its lights are turned on, the action picks up. The demonstrators shout more loudly, move about faster, and shake their placards and fists. During a disturbance the camera also can spark an increase in the amount of violence taking place.

Most news directors agree that reporters and crews should maintain a low profile at a disturbance. If you believe your presence at the scene is inflaming the situation, you should leave or at least move your camera where it will not be seen by the rioters. Be particularly careful at night. Turning on your camera lights may not only bring about increased violence but also could place you and your crew in jeopardy. Most stations have specific guidelines for covering riots and demonstrations. Follow them.

Covering a Disaster

The radio news portion of this book showed step-by-step how a news team might cover a plane crash. Let's now examine how a television news team might cover the same story.

Once again, assume that you are working for a major TV station in Chicago and the radio station discussed previously is a sister to your TV station.

Your main problem is the same as that of the radio station—getting on the air quickly with the story. But you also will be busy getting pictures on the air, especially live remotes from the airport and the hospital to which survivors were taken. You also will be concerned with commercials. All airline commercials automatically will be dropped.

When the plane crashes, it is 3 A.M. and you are alone in the newsroom. You are the overnight assignment editor. Suddenly, the bulletin buzzer on one of the wire machines goes off. You run into the wire room and see an AP story that reads

> A DC–10 has crashed and is burning on the runway at O'Hare International Airport.

UPI is starting to move the same story. Back at the assignment desk, you turn up the radio that has been monitoring the output of your sister radio station, WXXX. You know that Ben Francis at the station's studios down the hall will get on the air simply by interrupting the disc jockey's overnight music. You are just in time to hear his special report, but it only repeats the same information that you just read on the wires.

You would like to put a bulletin on the air. But whereas Ben could quickly interrupt his programming, it will take you several moments longer. First you have to write the bulletin. You do so in a moment or two and it says

> This is a special report from the Channel 3 newsroom. A jetliner has crashed at O'Hare International Airport. AP and UPI report the plane is burning on the runway. There are no reports yet on injuries. We will have details as soon as possible and a complete report on the plane crash at O'Hare on the 6 A.M. News report. This has been a special report from the Channel 3 newsroom.

Next, you call the engineer at the TV station's air control—the control room that sends your station's signal out to the transmitter. The engineer will push the buttons that will make it possible for the staff announcer to read your special report. But first the engineer must know how many seconds it will take to read the report so he can make sure that no commercials are about to come up. When you arrive at air control, the engineer is ready for you, and the staff announcer reads your story. The TV audience did not see the announcer on the air. All they saw during the program interruption was a slide indicating that a special report was being aired by Channel 3 News.

Now you just begin planning how to cover this major story. But you will not do so on your own. First you will call the news director, Bill Flynn, at home to let him know what happened. You tell him you quickly aired a special report and add that WXXX radio is now reporting that there are survivors and that the plane is still burning on the runway. The radio is also saying that it was a Trans Intercontinental Airways flight number 528 from San Francisco.

You and Flynn decide not to worry about putting another special report on the air until at least 6 A.M. Your TV audience is small at this hour and it would be better to go on the air later with some tape from the scene when your station normally gives a sign-on newscast. The Late, Late Movie will end about 5 A.M. and the station will not resume broadcasting again until 6 A.M. Jack Sheldon, the morning newswriter, will arrive at work at about 4 A.M. He normally would be joined at 6 by Al Jones, the morning tape editor, but you will call him in early. Sheldon's job is to write the 6 A.M. newscast and the local news cut-ins on the morning network news programs at 7:25 and 8:25 A.M.

You also will bring in a second tape editor and another writer to help Sheldon and Jones put the newscast together. Then you wake up two reporters and two camera crews. At your station each crew consists of two people—one who operates the camera and lights and the other who works the audio equipment. One of these two teams will be sent to the airport, the other to a hospital. The technicians will have to come to the station first to get their cameras, recorders, lights, and the vans that are equipped to feed back a microwave signal. The reporters will go directly to the scenes where the crews will meet them. This means that you now have to phone and wake up eight people. The news director also is getting dressed and heading to the station to help you direct the coverage.

While you are making those calls, one of the other newsroom phones begins ringing. It is Merv Levine, a freelance TV cameraman. He tells you he heard about the crash on the police radio and quickly sped to the airport. He arrived in time to get tape of the burning plane on the runway and the rescue crews working on survivors and pulling out the dead bodies. You tell him to hurry to the station with the tape, but before you hang up you ask him what hospital the ambulances came from. He tells you Lutheran General. Neither the wires nor Ben at the radio station had that information yet. Now you will be able to tell one reporter and crew which hospital to go to. You hope they will be able to talk with some of the survivors.

It is 4 A.M. when you are finished with all your calls and Sheldon is walking in the door. You are both joined moments later by Flynn, the news director. You fill both men in on the latest information about the crash, adding that Sally Sullivan went to the airport and Mike Smith to the hospital.

Sheldon and Flynn begin deciding what to put in the 6 A.M. broadcast. Close to 4:30 A.M. Levine shows up and is followed by Jones, the tape editor. You all go to one of the edit rooms to play the videotape cassettes. The picture is vivid, full of drama, action, and excitement. Levine's tape of the scene after the accident will convey the full horror of the crash. Now the two camera crews start coming in. You help them collect their equipment and get out on the road. There is a good chance that Sheldon and Flynn will be able to combine Levine's tape with live mini-cam reports from the airport and the hospital. And by 7:25 and 8:25 A.M.—the local cut-ins—there should be plenty of tape and live remotes to let your television audience know about the accident that occurred while they slept.

You do not call in other reporters or crews early. An hour newscast is scheduled at 6 P.M. and although most of the stories in the broadcast will revolve around the plane crash, you will need some reporters for other assignments. But the news director decides you should wake up one of the evening anchors so she can arrive in the newsroom at about 9 A.M. to do special reports throughout the day with the latest details on the plane crash.

Your news director asks you to remain on duty to help the daytime assignment editor, Bob Stone, who will pick up where you left off.

Planning for the 6 P.M.

The major problem now facing the TV news team is how to tell the story of the plane crash in detail for the 6 P.M. news. The broadcast will run one hour, allowing plenty of time for several different reports and live remotes. The story will not be new to 6 P.M. viewers, but it will be their first chance to see all the pictures and facts in a cohesive package. Those special reports that were run during the day were brief, usually one to two minutes each. And they all promised plenty of details on the 6 P.M. broadcast.

The first question to ask is what the situation will be at 6 P.M. By that time, you are likely to have a fairly complete accounting of the number of dead, injured, and survivors. The accident scene at the airport will probably be cleaned up, although the plane may still be on the runway awaiting heavy equipment to remove the wreckage. The places where things will be happening visually will probably be the hospitals where the injured were taken and the morgue that has been set up for the bodies. Relatives and friends will be arriving during the day at both sites and some probably will be willing to talk to reporters. You also find out later in the day that a popular country music group, The Nashville Five, was among the dead. And the producer of the 6 P.M. broadcast suggests a report on previous major airplane crashes. He wonders if there is enough file footage to do a brief history of them.

As will be discussed in detail later, there usually is a meeting in the morning to discuss what stories to cover and which reporters to assign to them. This meeting usually includes the news director, the assignment editor, and the broadcast producer.

The consensus at this morning's meeting is to do the following.

Begin the broadcast with an umbrella lead that recaps the details of the crash, the number of dead, injured, and survivors, and what is believed to have caused the crash. This probably will be no longer than one minute and will be read by one of the anchor people with silent tape for visuals, probably that dramatic spec tape showing the plane burning on the runway.

From there go to a live remote at the hospital, giving more details on the injured and their chances for survival. Tape showing ambulances bringing the victims in and relatives arriving to see them will precede brief interviews with some of the relatives.

This will be followed by another live remote at the makeshift morgue that was set up at the airport. This report will contain tape shot during the day, showing the covered bodies, relatives arriving to help in the identification process, and perhaps interviews with officials on the identification problems.

At this point it is possible that the producer will want to go to a commercial because several more stories on the plane crash remain and some relief from the emotions of the story is needed.

The next item probably will be a live report from the airport showing the cleanup equipment in place to begin work tomorrow and recapping the events of the morning with the tape of the burning plane and the rescue workers at the scene.

This can be followed by a quick report, perhaps narrated by one of the anchor people, recapping other major air crashes and what caused them. Full coverage of the plane crash would end with a story on the career of the Nashville Five, whose deaths in the crash were reported in the first section of the broadcast.

These reports probably will take about twenty minutes of the broadcast. For viewers who tune in late, a recap of the crash will come late in the broadcast with another live remote from the hospital.

A major problem for the producer of the broadcast is to make sure that the same shots are not repeated in each story. One way to do this is to have one writer or associate producer act as a clearinghouse for all the material, learning what each reporter shot and what he plans to use in his story so as to keep reporters from stepping on each other's toes.

It's a Circus

Television and the circus have a lot in common. The combination of frenzy and organization that go into a three-ring circus is similar to putting on the 6 o'clock news. But there is more than analogy to be gained from a look at the circus.

The circus probably is the best example of a staged event that you will be expected to cover during your broadcast journalism career. It is unlikely that you will escape this story because the circus finds its way into almost every corner of America. And no news director or assignment editor can pass one by. After all, a circus has everything—animals, pretty women dancing on horses and dangling precariously from trapezes, lion tamers risking their lives, and clowns for comic relief. Can you think of any better cover footage?

This is a good two- or two-and-a-half-minute news feature for the evening news, and you can bet it will be on the late news as well. But a warning about shooting your video at a circus . . . and just about any other brightly lighted scene: Do not point your camera directly at the lights. The temptation is great, as the acrobats tumble high into the air and the trapeze artists reach out for their partner's hands. But those bright lights could damage the sensitive tubes in your cameras ("burn-ins"). Remember, too, that burn-ins can be caused even when the cameras are off. Cap your cameras when you are not using them.

Here's an example of a circus story that aired in Richmond, Virginia.

Video	*Audio*
V/O (natural sound under)	For more than 100 years, Ringling Brothers, Barnum and Bailey has
Cover footage of circus wagons, clowns, and animals	brought a festival of comedy, color, and spectacle to countless millions of Americans in every corner of the nation. Many circuses have been forced out of business during the past 30 years, but this one has survived
Caravan moving down the street, more animals and performers	and prospered. It arrived in Richmond with the traditional parade from the railroad station to
Shots of crowd, CU of kids	the coliseum, and hundreds of happy children, and adults too, enjoyed the free show.
Shots of workers setting up the rings	But it's not all fun. A lot of work also goes into putting on a circus. The elaborate rigging takes nearly nine hours to set up. And unlike other stage productions, the crew has to take extra precautions while constructing the sets. Bogdan
Establishing two shot	Jakubowski, who heads the rigging team, says he runs into all sorts of problems.

SOT (Head shot) RUNS: :10	TRACK UP OUT: ". . . . at this time."
Super: Bogdan Jakubowski	TIME :10

Video	*Audio*
V/O Transition Cover of the various entertainers Clown cover	After the maze of wires, trapezes, and rings have been assembled, the arena is turned over to the performers. Night after night, every acrobat, animal trainer, trapeze artist, and clown must prepare for another evening of live entertainment. And even the clowns get nervous sometimes.
SOT (CU of clown) RUNS: :26 Super: Chuck Sidlow	TRACK UP OUT: ". . . once in awhile." TIME :26
V/O Transition Cover of kids and adults in audience	Sidlow says it gives him great pleasure to see the young kids enjoying themselves, but the pleasure is doubled, he says, when he gets a laugh from the "old" kids in the audience.

SOT (Clown's head)
RUNS: :22
Cover with laughing
  crowd shots about
  :08 into bite
	TRACK UP
	OUT: ". . . great time"
	TIME :22

V/O Transition Cover of high wire performer (Tosca)	Another highlight of the circus . . . the high wire performers, and Tosca Schroer triggers a variety of emotions ranging from admiration to fright. She says there's some danger, but she wouldn't trade her circus life for anything.

SOT (Tosca's voice over cover of her on the trapeze) RUNS: :18 Super (Tosca Schroer)	TRACK UP OUT: ". . . really terrific" TIME :18
V/O Cover close Quick shots of performers and crowd	It's called the greatest show on earth . . . and from the applause and laughs from this packed house it would be difficult to argue the point. This is Mark Powers reporting from the Coliseum in Richmond.

The Specialty Reporters

The beats and assignments examined so far—local government, politics, crime, and courts—usually do not require any previous specialized knowledge. It is as a general assignment reporter that you most often will be sent out to cover these beats and stories. Your expertise and development of sources on the beat will come from your experience in covering these types of stories.

But there are some beats that usually require a specialized knowledge before you can cover them well. These include sports, weather, health and science, movie and theater reviews, and consumer news. Reporters assigned to these beats usually know their subject well because they studied them in college, have done some work in the field, or have spent a great deal of their spare time learning about the subject. In short, they have some background in the field.

These beat reporters often become subanchors of the local news team. They usually appear live on the set with their stories. And their personalities play an important role in building a following. Some, like John Stossel, an award-winning consumer reporter, have gone from local news in New York City to national TV (ABC). Others, like Warner Wolf who does sports on WCBS-TV in New York, have inspired imitations around the country.

Sportscasting

Wolf is known for his breezy, entertainment style of delivering the sports news and the use of such phrases as "Let's go to the videotape," "Gimme a break," and "swish" (everytime a basketball player scores a basket). His performance has made him the most followed sportscaster in New York.

Along with the anchor or anchor team of the newscast, the sportscaster often is given top billing in the promotion and advertising campaigns for the news broadcasts. The top stars among these specialty reporters often can command a salary equal to that of an anchorperson. Often, TV stations will run separate promotions and ads for these beat stars to help them build a following and increase the size of the news audience.

How do you get started as a sportscaster? Jack Whitaker, who spent more than 20 years with the CBS organization before joining ABC in 1982, started out as a newswriter and newscaster in Philadelphia. When the sportscaster at WCAU-TV quit, Whitaker was offered the job and took it. "I had played some baseball and basketball around the neighborhood but had no more than a normal interest in sports," he recalled. "I did not realize how little I knew about sports," he added, "until I started working as a sportscaster."

When ABC President Roone Arledge hired Whitaker, he described him as one of a small group of sportscasters who "transcend the play-by-play types." Whitaker said he tries to accomplish this by "seeing the game in different terms than just the box scores, downs, and yardage. When doing play-by-play," he said, "you concentrate on the event . . . and try to avoid the clichés."

Whitaker noted that *New York Times* critic Jack Gould once wrote that most sportscasters are just glorified caption writers. "I got pretty mad about that at first," Whitaker said, "but then I realized that caption writing presents a real challenge. It's difficult to do. You can't caption pictures with obvious comments like 'he swung at the pitch and missed.' You have to be laconic, terse, and at the same time get your message across," Whitaker said.

How do you develop a good style? "I try to get the feel of it, the smell of it, the sound of it. I try to tell people what they might not see from just watching the pictures."

His advice for young people: Take a lot of liberal arts courses, go to as many games as you can, and read the sports magazines and columns. He recalled that columnist Red Smith probably had the greatest influence on his own writing. "You have to steal first," Whitaker said, "but after emulating someone, you must develop your own style."

Weather Reports

The combination of meteorologist and communicator is not easy to find, according to Gordon Barnes, who reports the weather each morning for the Cable News Network and WDVM–TV in Washington, D.C. Barnes said, "There are a lot of good meteorologists around the country who are good at forecasting the weather. They understand all the technical terms but they cannot communicate."

Barnes said there is a real shortage of good communicators who have a good background in meteorology or science-related subjects. "You have to know the weather business, the terminology, and at the same time

Meteorologist Gordon Barnes. (Photo by Robert D. Kaplan, CNN)

know how to convert all that into something that the audience will understand.''

Barnes also said that only about ''20 percent of the stations in the nation have legitimate weather forecasters.'' By legitimate, Barnes said, he meant those who had studied meteorology and other science-related subjects. ''Unfortunately,'' Barnes said, ''most station managers are still trying to find some kind of gimmick in the person's personality or presentation, or rely on computer-type gimmicks to attract an audience.'' We'll discuss some of those gimmicks later in the book.

Barnes' advice for broadcast students who want to specialize in weather reporting is to study as much math and geography as possible. Physics and chemistry also are important, Barnes said, and if you can take courses in meteorology or climatology that is even better. Barnes said that if you can earn a degree in meteorology in addition to your broadcast journalism degree, you will have an excellent opportunity for a well-paying job in a large market.

Consumer News

Another important specialty reporter is the consumer news correspondent. In an era of inflation and economic woes, accompanied by consumer ripoffs and lax regulation, people are looking for help in dealing with the marketplace.

John Stossel, mentioned earlier, believes the area of consumer news is underreported. ''What runs this country is not Congress, but money,'' says Stossel. He said a good consumer reporter covers the whole spectrum of news that affects people's lives from changes in the prime lending rate to tips on what vegetables are good buys at the supermarket to how those micro chips are about to change the way we live.

Stossel also believes that a good consumer report has the elements of a good investigative report, because "we often tell people what sellers don't want them to know." He cited as examples reports he did while at WCBS-TV in New York on milk price fixing and how expensive and cheap cosmetics come from the same batches in a common factory. The only difference between the cosmetics were the ad campaigns and packaging.

Stossel added that an important technique in all consumer reporting is to get background information and a list of experts who can tell you all about the subject. He suggested avoiding publicity-seeking doctors and public relations firms because "the information they give you often is wrong." He has found that the best experts on a subject can be found through articles in obscure journals because they have no interest in getting on TV. The trick is to convince them to talk to you in front of a camera.

Stossel believes there is a need for many more consumer reporters around the nation. And he urges broadcast journalism students not to be afraid that they will become locked into a narrow field. He said his role has usually been interpreted broadly wherever he has worked. "The consumer reporter can usually cover any type of story except crime and politics," Stossel said.

Whichever specialty may interest you, it can lead you to a career in broadcast journalism that sets you apart from the rest of your colleagues and enables you to move up to larger markets faster.

Misuse of the term "Reporting"

In the radio section of the book, we wrote about the dishonest practice of using news staff to record voice reports in a studio when they actually have not covered the stories. Unfortunately, the practice also exists in television.

We disapprove of CNN's use of writers, producers and others on the staff who add their voices in a studio to video collected from other parts of the nation and world without informing the viewer that the narration was not done at the scene.

If it is impossible to use the voice of a reporter covering the story in the field then ethics dictate that the public be made aware of this by identifying where the voice was added to the pictures.

If video is being shown of fighting in Lebanon it is dishonest to have a producer in Atlanta add his voice to the pictures without a close saying, "This is John Doe in Atlanta." Otherwise, the viewer will assume, logically, that John Doe is reporting from Lebanon.

Adding to the problem is CNN's use of supers that identify the narrators as those "reporting" the stories. We believe strongly that this is a misuse of the term "reporting."

Electronic News Gathering (ENG)

The film camera has become a rarity in television news. It has been replaced by the minicam, a lightweight, electronic camera. The use of this new electronic equipment is referred to in TV news as electronic news gathering, or ENG.

The importance of this new technology as a journalistic tool was dramatically illustrated during the assassination attempt on President Ronald Reagan. Within eight minutes of the event, ABC News was replaying the tape to the entire nation. CBS and NBC did the same within 20 minutes. Before the president had entered surgery, all three networks had interrupted their regular programming and established ENG cameras in strategic locations at the hospital, White House, and other spots.

Microwave Magic

It was not only the ENG cameras but also the microwave units that were quickly sent to key locations that made it possible for the networks to

KSL–TV photographer Karl Petersen prepares for "live" microwave relay to the station for the evening newscast. (KSL–TV photo)

provide such swift coverage of the events following the Reagan assassination attempt. Microwave made it possible for correspondents to report live from the hospital and other key locations.

Without microwave, reporters would have had to videotape their reports and much time would have been lost getting the cassettes back to the network bureaus for broadcast to the nation.

All that is usually needed to set up this sort of microwave link is a news van with a microwave dish and a receiving dish located either at the TV station or at some relay point, usually at the top of the tallest building in the city. To complete the link, there has to be what is referred to as "line of sight" between the transmitter dish on the van and the receiving dish. The signal from the receiving dish is then transmitted to the studios for broadcast to home receivers. The process is, for all practical purposes, instantaneous. Because of the limited power of the microwave transmitter, the minicam unit must remain close to the receiving dish. And it must be in a spot where nothing blocks the line of sight.

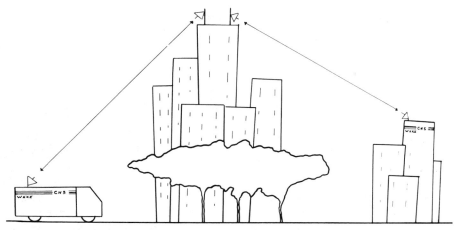

Microwave relay. (Drawing by Irene White)

Live Minicam Reporting

Minicams have made it much easier to report live events as they are happening. In the past, setting up a live remote required at least several hours. The units were usually housed in cumbersome tractor-trailers. Because of the new ENG mobility, today's television news managers look for breaking stories that are happening while the broadcast is on the air.

The minicam has truly brought the image of up-to-the-minute news to the home screen. But the new technology also has brought problems for reporters. Often they are asked to do live remotes for the sake of having live remotes. Even after an event is over, the news director or producer wants you to tell the story from the scene, and you may have to strain to make it work.

The new ENG technology sometimes demands that you be able to handle the pressure of live broadcasting under the most adverse circumstances. The weather may be foul. There may be a crowd behind you gawking at the camera or making a lot of noise. The small earpiece (telex) that feeds you the program audio and cues may not be working. The TV monitor that shows you what the viewers at home are seeing may fail. Still, when you are told that you are on the air, you must try to maintain your composure as you give your report. Think through what you are going to say before you appear live in this type of minicam situation. Expect something will go wrong. It often does.

Among the many advantages of ENG is that it enables reporters to stay longer on a story in the field. This should help them to obtain better video shots and interviews. Once the videotape cassette is back in the newsroom, there is no need for the long processing time that film required. Even more important, the reporter often can microwave the tape, narrative track, and cutting instructions back to the newsroom. If the story breaks during a newscast, the reporter could be left in the field with the minicam live remote to provide updates throughout the news broadcast.

Justifying the Cost

ENG equipment is more expensive than film equipment. Because of the rapidly developing technology, it becomes expensive to update with newer and more innovative models every year. But ENG can help a station be more competitive, attract more viewers, and in the long run produce more advertising revenue.

Although the initial cost of ENG equipment is high, there are eventual savings from the new technology. Many stations are able to reduce payrolls, eliminate film lab technicians, and often cut the size of camera crews.

Videotape is much less expensive than film and, unlike film, can be reused. Another advantage of videotape is that it creates more of a live look than film. The sharpness and crispness of the tape picture, as opposed to the graininess of film, gives the viewer the impression of a more natural picture. The video camera also produces a more acceptable picture in low light situations than is possible when shooting film.

ENG and Accuracy

Some broadcast journalists are concerned that the ENG technology has led to increasing editorial mistakes during live reporting such as was the case during the coverage of the assassination attempt on President Reagan. First reports of that shooting said the president had not been hurt and that presidential aide James Brady had been killed.

Electronic journalism *per se* does not cause inaccuracies any more than typewriters cause the inaccuracies that occur in newspapers. Accuracy depends on how well journalists do their job and how they use the available tools. But ENG does place a heightened responsibility on journalists to check and double check facts before rushing on the air with them.

It is critically important for the anchor in the studio and reporters in the field to emphasize the source for every fact, especially in the early stage of live reporting. Newspaper editors and reporters hear the same "facts," some of which later may turn out to be wrong. But they will have time to sort out conflicting versions of a story and probably eliminate inconsistencies before deadline time.

Television does not have that luxury. It must immediately perform its public service and can do so if broadcast reporters, editors, and producers understand the potential pitfalls. The television audience expects you to be on the air in a crisis. It expects infallibility because you are at the scene or have a direct link to the scene from the anchor desk.

If you personally witness something you know to be fact, report it as such. Otherwise, attribute repeatedly: "The Associated Press says;" "A

Photos taken from an ABC News television screen during the replay of videotape showing the shooting of President Reagan. Photo (A) shows the president moments before the shooting, (B) as the shots are being fired, and (C) as President Reagan is being pushed into the limousine. (ABC News photos)

(A)

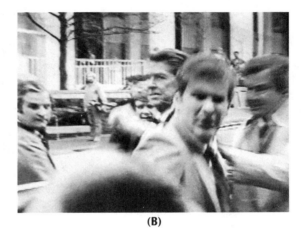

(B)

(C)

Police Department official says." Moreover, point out conflicts and inconsistencies where they exist: "Our reporter says one of the fourth-graders on the bus has been critically injured. We want to point out that United Press International says six children are critically injured." Emphasize that facts are shifting, that you are learning along with the audience, and underscore the things that you do not know.

The one area of reporting that we have not covered is Investigative Reporting. We have left that discussion for later in the book (Chapter 23) so as not to interrupt the natural progression from general assignment and beat reporting to constructing and scripting news stories.

18

Constructing the TV News Story

The television reporter's job does not end when he or she finishes covering a story in the field. The video and audio elements must be put together to make up a "package," a picture and word story. From the moment reporters receive their assignments, they must start thinking about what their completed stories may look like. They should not, however, prejudge or predetermine a story.

A reporter must deal with two different tasks—technical and editorial. The editorial job is to put the elements together so as to tell the story in a concise, clear, and compelling manner. The technical task is to obtain those elements in the first place. Let's look at the technical aspects first.

Cover Footage

You must get good video shots that will clearly illustrate the information being conveyed in your script. This is called cover footage. Without it, there is no picture story.

When you leave the newsroom with the photographer, begin talking about the possible video shots at the scene and your concept of the story. Think about what may be the best possible way to get the necessary shots quickly and efficiently. As you gain experience, you will know in advance most of the shots that will be needed.

First think about getting shots that will introduce the viewer to the general theme of the story. These are known as establishing shots. For example, the firemen in your town may be fighting a three-alarm blaze in bitter, below-freezing weather. When you arrive at the scene, you find flames shooting out of the building, several fire trucks and firemen battling the blaze. Get all these shots. They establish that there is a fire.

Now that you have those establishing shots, think about finding a human focus to make that fire story more dramatic. If it is bitter cold, the building will be covered with ice from the fire hose water. That picture will make this fire look different from other fires. But more important, the firemen will be covered with ice. Some may be huddling around a trash can fire, trying to keep warm. These are shots that will illustrate the human element of the story, firemen doing their job despite difficult conditions.

When shooting cover footage, remember that usually it is too late to get shots that you have missed once you leave the scene. But overshooting can produce a serious problem at the other end of the line. The more material there is to screen, the less time there will be to write the script and edit the story. Sometimes overshooting makes it impossible to use the best pictorial footage or interviews because there is not enough time to locate what you are looking for.

How much cover footage should be shot on a breaking story? As a rule of thumb, try to get the necessary cover shots on one videocassette, usually 20 minutes long.

Interviews and Jump Cuts

The cover footage will give the story its visual impact. Interviews, known as "talking heads," will make it come alive with people. You need an establishing shot for interviews—a wide shot showing you and the interviewee talking. Most often in these shots the camera is behind you. Your photographer will get a head-on shot of the interviewee and part of your shoulder and head (over-the-shoulder shot).

Your photographer should get other shots that will help later in editing the interview. They are needed to avoid what is known as a jump cut, an abrupt change in the position of the interviewee's head when separate segments of an interview are combined.

A cutaway shot is a way of providing a smooth visual flow if you wish to use more than one part of an interview. One such shot is extremely wide, showing the interviewee and the interviewer. Unlike the over-the-shoulder shot, it must be so wide that the lips of the interviewee are not easily distinguished. This shot can be interposed momentarily between sound bites to avoid a jump cut. It also solves another problem. Because

Reporter Chuck Delost, KOVR–TV, Sacramento. (KOVR–TV)

the interviewee's lips cannot be seen clearly in the extremely wide cutaway shot, they will not appear to move out of synchronization when edited.

This wide shot can be done before or after the interview. The photographer should shoot at least 30 seconds of it, and for maximum flexibility in editing, the interviewer and interviewee should speak alternately during this period.

Reversals

Another edit shot involves reversing the camera position so it is behind the interviewee and the reporter faces the camera. This is called a listening or reversal shot. The audience sees from the motion of the head that the interviewee is speaking, but because it can not see the interviewee's lips, you avoid the problems of lip synchronization and the jump cut.

In reversing the camera for the listening shot, care must be taken to place the camera in the correct position. If the camera is set up incorrectly, the interviewee will appear to be gazing in the wrong direction. Even seasoned photographers sometimes get confused, and as an aid some refer to the "cheek" rule or the "center line" rule. During the interview the camera will be to the right or left of the reporter. If the camera is to the right of the reporter, it will favor the reporter's right cheek. In the reversal shot be sure that the camera again shows the reporter's right

(A)   **(B)**

Demonstration of reversal techniques used during the shooting of an interview. (A) Cameraman shooting interviewee (facing camera) over shoulder of reporter. (B) Reverse shot of reporter. (WBTV photos)

cheek. Of course, if the camera had been set up on the left side of the reporter during the interview, you would show the reporter's left cheek in the reversal shot. Another suggestion is to imagine a center line connecting the reporter and interviewee. Don't cross the center line in shooting the reversal.

Never use a reverse shot of yourself when you are doing narration or during your close. Few things are more disturbing than seeing a reporter face the camera as he is doing a voice-over close. If you run out of cover footage for an ending, you should at least do your voice-over close over a wide shot of you and the interviewee or an over-the-shoulder shot with the camera pointed at the other person.

The Reverse Question

Still another editing technique, called the reverse question, requires some cooperation from the person being interviewed if it is to be completely successful. After the interview, the reporter repeats some of the questions asked during the interview, but this time the camera is facing the reporter. As with the listening or reversal shot, reverse questions are best when taken over the shoulder of the interviewee. Part of that shoulder and a profile of the interviewee's face should be in the picture. Avoid the reverse question that shows only a waist or head shot of the reporter. It is the kind of reverse question that could be done in the studio and, unfortunately, sometimes it is done just that way.

It is most important to ask reverse questions exactly the way you did during the interview. If you are running an audio tape recorder during the interview (and you should be), you may play the tape back to make sure you are phrasing the questions the same way. But that is time consuming. If you stick closely to the prepared questions in your notebook and try to remember the follow-up questions, you should have no difficulty.

Another inconvenience of the reverse question, if done over-the-shoulder, is that interviewees must remain while you continue to tape. That is often a problem. When the interviewees do agree to cooperate, it usually means taking time to explain what you are doing. Although you tell interviewees that they need not answer the questions this time, often they forget and jump in with responses anyway.

The reverse question is a popular technique, especially with local news directors, as a method of avoiding a jump cut and getting more visibility for reporters. But it raises some ethical questions. In a sense, it is "fooling" the viewers. When they see a reporter's question in the middle of a story, they may believe that two cameras were used or that the camera was pivoted each time to get both the questions and answers. Most news directors and producers see no harm in reverse questions provided that the technique does not distort the interview.

The executive producer of Walter Cronkite's Evening News for many years, Sanford Socolow, surprised many when he started using jump cuts. "Reversals and cutaways are more distracting," he argued, "and take your mind off what is being said much more than jump cuts."

Although the question of ethics was secondary in his decision to use jump cuts, Socolow said it is "more honest" because the viewer knows that you are chopping something out. "I didn't ban cutaways and reversals," Socolow stressed, "I simply told people to do what is less intrusive and jump cuts are less intrusive."

But news executives at NBC and ABC disagree. Paul Greenberg, the executive producer of NBC's "Nightly News," says he never uses a jump cut unless it is almost impossible to notice. The classic jump cut in which the head and hands move in and out of the picture are "disconcerting" to the viewer, in Greenberg's opinion.

Jeff Gralnick, the executive producer of ABC's "World News Tonight," said that when someone's head "flies from one side of the screen to the other, people stop listening and say 'there's something wrong with my television set.' " Gralnick said he is a firm believer in properly executed reverse angle questions and cutaways.

As for the ethics of reverse questions, Gralnick said he does not see anything dishonest in them. "I believe in the sophistication of the viewer," he said, "and think more often than not they understand that unless the program is live, it has been edited."

Howard Stringer, who succeeded Socolow as executive producer of the CBS Evening News with Dan Rather, is opposed to jump cuts. "I have never used jump cuts in documentaries," Stringer said, "and I will not use them in hard news pieces."

Stringer said he considers the jump cut jarring. He said he believes the audience knows an edit has been made, whether it is done with a jump cut or a reverse shot. Stringer said although he would not rule out using a reverse listening shot of the correspondent alone, he prefers a reverse shot over-the-shoulder of the interviewee because "a two shot is more interesting" and shows the spatial or pictorial relationship of the correspondent and the interviewee.

There is a more sophisticated method of covering up jump cuts than using cutaways or reversals. It was referred to in the beginning of this chapter as cover footage. It is used as a visual companion to the reporter's audio track and sound bites. Cover footage is best when it is related to the reporter's narration and to what the person is talking about in the sound cut. The use of cover footage often can enliven a TV news story.

Most news directors insist that cover footage be used to replace the talking head as soon as possible. The theory is that viewers prefer to see pictures that illustrate what the head is talking about rather than the person being interviewed. The exception is when the person is particularly compelling or saying something dramatic or controversial. Obvious examples are someone who narrowly escaped a disaster or witnessed one, a circus clown, a famous actress, or a councilman accusing a mayor of embezzlement. If the talking head is your typical fire chief speaking about alarms and equipment, go to the cover footage of the flames as soon as you can, usually within five to ten seconds.

Too often meaningless footage is used to cover talking heads. A common misuse of cover footage is the crowd shot—people just walking down the street.

One view about selecting cover footage is that audio and video should complement each other but not be redundant. The other position is that cover footage must literally illustrate the words in the script.

Editorial Structure

In preparing a TV story you must decide what is important and how to convey it most clearly, concisely, comprehensively, and compellingly. What is the most effective style? Is it a sober subject requiring a straight approach? Is it a humorous story requiring a touch of whimsy? Why is this story being told? The point of the story should determine how you approach it. Humor sometimes can be in bad taste. Straight writing often can be boring. Let the story you are covering suggest the necessary approach.

A major element in many TV news stories that really draws the viewer's attention is emotion. In the aftermath of a natural disaster, TV news can depict the faces and the voices of those struck by the tragedy. During a teacher's strike, TV news can show the anger of those on the picket line and the parents of children who are losing part of their education.

Remember that sometimes understatement or irony can be as powerful on the home screen as people crying or shaking their fists at each other or squealing with delight.

Broadcast news is frequently criticized as being interested only in emotion and controversy. Sometimes reporters gratuitously stress emotion or controversy through their own bad judgment or the demands of editors or producers. But broadcast reporters also put emotion to good use to make a story vivid. Properly employed, emotion in a TV news broadcast story needs no apology.

Other major ingredients in the TV news story are clarity and conciseness. Accept early that you will not be able to tell the viewer all there is to know about any particular story. Distill that story down to one or two basic ideas. Always look for a central focus and stay with it. Many stories stumble because they really are a story and a half or even two. Hone your information and your ideas.

Once you have determined the approach you wish to take in your story, you must consider the best method of telling the story. The three methods are the stand-up, the voice-over, and the package.

In the stand-up the reporter stands in front of the camera telling the story. All the viewer sees is the reporter and what is in back of him.

The stand-up dates from the early days of TV news. By today's standard, it is a tedious way to deliver news, without the production techniques and visuals so highly regarded by today's generation of TV journalists. But it is the fastest way to get a story on the air when close to deadline. The stand-up often is the most appropriate form of live reporting, such as from a candidate's campaign headquarters on election night, from a railroad station during a commuter rush hour tie-up, or during the final hours of a key labor negotiation.

The stand-up should be simple in language. A lack of clarity will confuse the viewer because there is nothing to illustrate what is being said. Casual, ad-libbed stand-ups often look sloppy and make the reporter less believable.

The best stand-ups are prepared carefully and are scripted. Do not be afraid to use that hand-held script, but avoid looking down at it constantly. An occasional reference to it confirms that the broadcaster is trying to get the facts straight.

More than with any other form of broadcast news the stand-up requires the tightest of news writing. The average stand-up report runs no more than a minute. Most broadcasters will read about 150 words in this time, really nothing more than a few paragraphs of information.

Because of the new technology, stand-ups can be timely. Mimicams make live reporting from the field easy for the producers, but tougher on the reporters. Some TV news directors insist on at least one live report in each major newscast. This is to show the viewer that the news team is aggressively covering events as they happen.

Stand-up Opens, Closes, and Bridges

As a reporter, you also will be expected at times to appear on camera in your field reports. These appearances are referred to as stand-up opens, stand-up closes, and stand-up bridges.

The stand-up open shows the reporter on camera at the beginning of the story. It is a useful technique when it is important to establish the reporter's presence at the scene of a story. It also is a common way of starting a live ENG report of a breaking story. A tape package on the 6 P.M. news from the scene of a fire might open with a wide shot of the reporter standing in front of the burning building. His opening might go something like this:

Video	*Audio*
O/C Wide shot of reporter Flaming building in background	The fire in the Weareasy Shoe factory has been burning like this for more than three hours . . . and fire officials say they do not know when they'll be able to bring it under control.
V/O Cut to tight shots of burning building	Right now the fire is concentrated on the third floor where it apparently started around 3 o'clock this afternoon. So far no one seems to know how the fire broke out. Company officials are pleased though that all of the 35 workers who were inside the building escaped.

At this point in the story, the reporter's voice would be heard over more shots of the fire, followed probably by an interview with the fire chief. A stand-up open lets the viewers know that the fire is still in progress and that a reporter is there.

The story might end with more on-camera narration by the reporter, a stand-up close, which would either review important information given during the report or add some new information.

Video	Audio
O/C Wide shot of reporter	This is the second fire in the Weareasy Shoe factory this year.
Waist shot of reporter	Last summer the building suffered almost 100 thousand dollars damage when air conditioning equipment short-circuited. This is David Hutchings, WXXX News.

Stand-up closes are more common than stand-up opens, although most field reports seen on television news open and close with narration by reporters over cover footage.

The third use of a stand-up in a field report is the stand-up bridge. This is narration delivered on camera by the reporter in the middle of a story to help the viewer understand better what is going on. It is often used in crime stories. Here is an example:

Video	Audio
V/O Shots of canal, police "crime area" sign	This is where the body of Sharon Price was found early this morning by a man walking his dog. The 19-year-old woman had been missing from her home for more than two days, and a search for her in Hanover and neighboring Henrico County by scores of police officers and volunteers had failed to locate her. Sheriff Paul Ludwig says it's too soon to say how Sharon Price died.
Shots of police officers and vehicles	
Establishing shot of Ludwig	
SOT :22 seconds Font: Sheriff Paul Ludwig	TRACK UP OUT: ". . . . matter of days." TIME: 22 seconds.
Cover shots of deputies going through brush	

Video	*Audio*
O/C Bridge	Although the body was found about a quarter of a mile downstream, police officials say it was here—by these rocks—that the woman was killed and her body shoved into the water. They would not discuss in detail how they know this, but apparently parts of the young woman's clothing were found here near these bushes.
V/O Cover shots of roped-off area; Police officer standing guard; Flashing lights on car	An autopsy is being performed on Price this morning in an effort to determine the cause of death and whether she had been sexually molested. As far as we can determine, police have no suspects and—it would appear—very few clues at the moment. This is Paul Dodge, WXXX News.

In this example, the only time the reporter was seen on camera was in the middle of the report when he was showing where the woman apparently had been killed. It would be quite natural for him to point as he glanced in the direction of the water and rocks, and perhaps even move toward the bushes as he was describing them in narration. After doing this, the reporter returned to cover footage while closing the story with off-camera narration. The on-camera bridge was used to clarify and to dramatize the story. It served a purpose and demonstrates how a reporter can make effective use of a stand-up bridge.

Do not overuse the stand-up technique. As mentioned earlier, young reporters sometimes abuse the technique in an effort to get more visibility. Often the news director encourages reporters to become more involved in their stories.

The Voice-over

The voice-over is a reporter's narration over cover footage of the story. There are no stand-ups and no sound cuts from interviews. It is rarely used by itself because it is somewhat dull. Just as the stand-up by itself offers no variety, the same is true for the voice-over that is used alone.

On today's television news broadcasts, if a producer has a choice between a reporter's voice-over story with no other elements and a quick 20- to 30-second voice-over by the anchorperson, he often will choose the latter.

The Package

The voice-over technique when used with good sound bites and perhaps a stand-up of some sort is the most common method of telling a story for television news. In TV jargon, it is known as a "package".

The term *package* is appropriate to describe the presentation of a complex news story. Like most packages, the TV news package contains something inside, has to be wrapped properly, and neatly tied and addressed. When TV producers or assignment editors tell you they want a "package," they're telling you, in effect, that they expect you to prepare a story that is more elaborate than the stand-up or voice-over report. Your package can be constructed in simple fashion. But its sophisticated possibilities are as unlimited as your imagination and as the boundaries of clarity and understanding will allow.

The simplest form of package consists of reporter narration at the opening and close over cover footage (voice-over) and part of an interview (sound cut) in the middle:

Video	*Audio*
Anchor lead-in	A scandal is rocking the quiet suburban community of Suffern. Police say a church official has run off with church funds. Roberta Roe reports.
V/O Police alert bulletin	The Rockland County police say Bill Smith vanished last month. The 59-year-old retired accountant was treasurer of the All Saints Episcopal Church here. But foul play is not suspected.
Still picture of Bill Smith	Officials of the church and the District Attorney say Smith
Shot of church Shot of church office	systematically transferred the church monies to his personal accounts for nearly a year and a half. Perhaps as much as 300 thousand dollars is missing. The

Video	*Audio*
Set-up shot of pastor	pastor, the Reverend John Dunn, said he cannot believe what has happened.
SOT :22 Font: Rev. John Dunn, All Saints Episcopal Church	TRACK UP OUT: ". . . would do something like this." TIME :22
V/O Shot of church Shot of Smith's house	Still, the police say the quiet, respected church official did run off with the funds, leaving behind a beautiful suburban home, a working wife, and grown children. The police have issued a nationwide alarm for his arrest. This is Roberta Roe in Suffern.

The story can be enhanced by adding another interview that presents additional information, for example, obtained from the district attorney.

V/O Police alert bulletin Still picture of Bill Smith Set-up shot of DA	The Rockland County police say Bill Smith vanished last month. The 59-year-old retired accountant was treasurer of the Episcopal Church here. But District Attorney Ken Gibbons says Smith was not the victim of foul play. Instead, he is wanted for a crime.
SOT :19 Font: Ken Gibbons, D.A.	TRACK UP OUT: ". . . We believe he took as much as 300 thousand dollars." TIME :19

V/O Shot of church offices and books	Gibbons and church officials say Smith systematically transferred church monies to his personal accounts for nearly a year and a
Set up shot of pastor	half. The pastor, John Dunn, cannot believe what has happened.

SOT :22 Font: Rev. John Dunn, Pastor Shot of church	TRACK UP OUT: ". . . would do something like this." TIME :22

V/O Shot of Smith's house	Still police say the quiet, respected church official did run off with the funds, leaving behind a beautiful suburban home, a working wife, and grown children. The police have issued a nationwide alarm. This is Roberta Roe in Suffern.

This package, which now contains two "talking heads," could be made more sophisticated by adding a stand-up bridge in the middle or perhaps a stand-up close, or both. The use of sound bites back-to-back to produce a montage or debate effect is another technique that adds interest. When used properly, along with the imaginative selection of cover footage, the package should please viewers.

Cold Open

The "cold open" is a sound cut, usually less than 10 seconds long, that starts the package on a dramatic note. The drama comes from the words or the emotion of the sound cut. It is usually followed by the voice-over narration of the reporter. On stations that follow an "eyewitness" or "action" news concept, most packages start with a cold open because the reporter is often live on the set or doing a live remote from the scene. Variations in the use of the different elements is endless. Overuse of the cold open, however, destroys its effectiveness.

Length of Package

Local TV news directors usually like reporters to deliver packages that are about a minute and a half to two minutes in length. But at many stations where the news has expanded to an hour or longer, reporters are encouraged to make their stories somewhat longer, two or two and a half minutes and sometimes three minutes. This is particularly true if a reporter is working on a special series or investigative story.

Volume of news determines how long your story should be. Your producer might be light on news and ask you to "stretch" your story an extra 30 seconds. If there are more stories than expected, you may be told to keep your story as short as possible or to chop 15 seconds out of your script. You may think you have a good two-minute story only to discover that you really do not have sufficient cover footage to let the story run that long. There will be times when, because of the importance of your story, you may allow your package to run longer than you would like without good cover footage, but keep those instances at a minimum.

Instructions from the Field

Sometimes you must write and record your script in the field, either because the story is still developing or you are being sent on to another story. You must send back the fullest possible instructions on the story so the producer or videotape editor can select appropriate sound bites and cover footage. The editing will go much faster if you indicate the in-cues and out-cues of the sound cuts and where they are located on the videocassette. One way to do this is by logging footage numbers off the videotape recorder. Some of the newer equipment puts a time code on the cassette. Then you need only glance at your watch as the story is being shot to log the times that you think will be important.

When you record your narration on the cassette, it is a good idea to count down, that is, say, "three, two, one" before you begin each segment of the narration. This makes it easier for the ENG editor to cue up to the start of the narration and it allows the automatic audio gain control circuits on the videocassette recorder to stabilize. This will eliminate any possible distortions in your audio track.

19

Scripting Television News

Physical Preparation

The physical preparation for the TV newscast is much more demanding than for the radio newscast. In radio the newscaster must be able to read the script easily while talking into the microphone and know when to play the audiotape inserts. A television script is much more complicated. The anchor must be able to read it while looking into a TV camera. The newscopy must be typewritten in a narrow column on a special type-writer with large letters, and the writer must be familiar with technical terms and know how to express them properly on the script.

Split Page

In radio, you can type your script across the entire page. But to make room for instructions for the director, TV news invented the split page. This is a page divided in half, vertically down the middle. The left side of the page contains the slug of the story, the date, the writer's initials, the name of the broadcast, and all the video and audio instructions. The writer must indicate whether the script is leading into a tape package, a live remote, a reporter on the set, a silent-to-sound piece of tape, or a voice-over. The times of the tape and its outcue also must be given. The right side of the page contains the script, the outcues of the tape inserts, and their complete running times. If there is more than one anchorperson, the name of the person who is reading the script will be indicated. When you are dealing with a complicated TV news broadcast, all these instructions can make the difference between a smooth one and a mess.

A sample page for a read story with a slide beside the anchorperson looks like this:

```
BANK ROB 4/11 ajm 6 P.M.                      JONES
O/C  SL                     Three  men  robbed  the  Hometown
                            National  Bank  late  this  afternoon.
                            They  escaped  after  a  gun  fight  with
                            police.  It's  believed  the  bandits
                            took  more  than  25  thousand  dollars.
```

Many stations have copy books, a preassembled set of paper and carbon to produce several copies of the script at once. They may be printed with a line down the middle, dividing the page in half. If not, many stations instruct their writers on how they want the margins and tabulators set. Usually, one line of script should take an average of one second to read on air. For this, set your margins at 60 characters or spaces, and a tabulator at 30 spaces from the left margin. This will divide the page in half. Set another tabulator at 35 spaces from the left margin. This will provide an indentation for the paragraphs of the script. That space also can be used to write the outcues and running times of the tapes so they stand out for the director and anchorperson. Whatever system the station you work for uses, follow it. To do otherwise would be to create confusion.

Some Basic Rules

All TV news scripts are typed *double space*. This rule must be followed at all times. This leaves space for the editor to write and also makes the words stand out clearly for the anchorperson. Triple space with bulletin-size type would place the lines too far apart and use up too much paper, creating a cumbersome script.

The left side of the split page contains all the production information. It would be cumbersome here also to write out each bit of technical information completely. The director is watching a dozen different things in the control room besides the script. He must be able to glance at the script quickly and follow the instructions without difficulty. For these reasons, the following standard abbreviations are used:

1. SIL for <u>silent</u> <u>tape</u>.
2. SOT for <u>sound</u> <u>on</u> <u>tape</u>.
3. VTR for <u>videotape</u> <u>replay</u>. This applies only to 1- or 2-inch tape.
4. ENG for <u>three-quarter-inch</u> <u>videotape</u> <u>cassettes</u> only.
5. SL for <u>slide</u>. It can be followed by the words <u>full</u> for full frame or <u>box</u> to indicate it goes into the box beside the anchorperson. If there is no such indication, the slide will be placed in the box.
6. ESS for <u>Electronic</u> <u>Still</u> <u>Storage</u>. This is a system that electronically stores graphics and video images on discs in a computer for random recall. The ADDA computer is used by many news organizations for the same purpose. Again, if the word <u>full</u> does not accompany ESS or ADDA the image will be put in a box.
7. FF for <u>freeze</u> <u>frame</u>. It also can be followed by the words <u>full</u> <u>frame</u> or <u>box</u>. When used alone, it will be placed in the box next to the anchorperson.
8. Font or Fonts or Supers. These are titles or captions that are superimposed over graphics or videotape to help identify such things as names, titles, and locations and to help clarify statistics.
9. V/O for <u>voice-over</u>. This indicates that the anchorperson will voice-over graphics, silent tape, or tape with natural sound track under.
10. O/C for <u>on</u> <u>camera</u>.

Technical Instructions

All technical instructions are written on the left side of the split page. Leave ample spacing around those instructions for clarity. Include in the technical information the running times for tape. Indicate only the elapsed times, and write the technical information directly opposite from where the tape should begin. For example, in the following illustration are the letters SL. That means the anchorperson, Jones is going to read two seconds of copy with a slide shown next to him on the scrren. Then silent videotape will begin to roll on an ENG machine. The videotape will run 11 seconds and that is indicated in parentheses (0–11). The videotape will replace the anchorperson on the screen as he starts to read the words "they escaped after . . ." The newscaster's voice will continue to be heard as a voiceover (V/O) silent videotape. Because the tape runs 11 seconds and has no sound, that means the newscaster must have enough copy to carry him through this voice-over video.

JONES

O/C SL	Three men robbed the Hometown National Bank late this afternoon.
V/O SIL ENG(0–11)	They escaped after a gunfight with police. It's believed the bandits took more than 25 thousand dollars.
	It was shortly after noon when the gunmen entered the bank and forced about 15 customers to lie on the floor. Witnesses said one of the men held a shotgun on the customers while the other two scooped up the cash. No one was injured.

The voice-over story read by the newscaster is the simplest use of videotape. In the next example, the script becomes more complex. It is called a *silent-to-sound*.

BANK ROB 4/11 ajm 6 P.M.

JONES

O/C Jones SL	Three men robbed the Hometown National Bank late this afternoon. They escaped after a gunfight with police. It's believed the bandits took more than 25 thousand dollars.
V/O SIL ENG (0–10)	The robbery began shortly after noon when the gunmen entered the bank and forced about 15 customers to lie on the floor. Witnesses said one of the men held a shotgun on the customers while the other two scooped up the cash. Bank cashier Sara Smith described what the bandits did next:

```
SOT ENG (10-40)
                        TRACK  UP
                        OUT: ".  .  . was scared stiff."
                        TIME  :30


O/C SL                  Bank officials have offered a
                        five thousand dollar reward for the
                        capture of the three bandits.
```

You will notice in this example that the newscaster, Jones, was again on camera and a slide was up while he was reading an opening to the video portion of the story. The tape ran silent for ten seconds, and then the sound was brought up for another 30 seconds, so the total length of the tape was 40 seconds. The SOT ENG is typed directly opposite the point in the script where the sound is to be brought up. To help the anchor and the director, many writers type lines above and below the TRACK UP and out cue, as you see in the example.

After the sound bite, the anchor returned on camera, with a slide, for a final word—a tag—on the story.

The following example shows a script for a lead-in to a tape package by a reporter.

```
BANK ROB 4/11 ajm 6 P.M.
                             JONES
O/C SL                  Three men held up the Hometown
                        National Bank late this afternoon,
                        escaping with about 25 thousand
                        dollars. The robbers shot it out
                        with police before escaping.
                        Roberta Roe has this report:
ENG  Runs 1:48

                        TRACK  UP
                        OUT: ".  .  . Roberta Roe
                          reporting."
                        TIME  1:48
```

In this example, you will note that the time of the tape is written in the left column. Most anchors like to have the time of the tape in the right column as well, so they know exactly when they will return on camera. Remember, the anchor cannot see the information in the left column on the prompter.

The bank robbery example is a self-contained report that was packaged before the broadcast. Once the tape begins, the director and the anchor have little to do for the next one minute, 48 seconds except prepare for what is to happen next in the script. In this situation, the tape continues to the end without interruption unless there is a technical problem. If a problem does occur, the anchor should have a copy of the reporter's script, or at least be familiar with the contents of the piece, so he does not appear foolish. Most often, the anchor will say, for instance, "We'll try to get back to that story later in the broadcast" if that possibility exists. Obviously, if the newscast is reaching a conclusion, the best the anchor can do is apologize for the problem and give a sentence or two about the contents. This is particularly important if the tape includes some important news development. A simple apology would suffice if the malfunctioning tape was a feature story.

Dealing with Names

In radio, a broadcaster often will mention a person's name or title at the end as well as at the beginning of a sound bite. You do so because the identification is the only one that listeners have, and they might miss it the first time. The same principle can be applied in TV news broadcasts, but it is not as necessary. The name often is used during the introduction to the sound cut. But when the person is seen talking on the videotape, the name usually will be fonted or superimposed as a visual form of identification. This makes a second audio identification unnecessary. However, it is best not to rely only on the visual identification. Machines have a tendency to fail or to do the wrong thing. If the supers do not come up when they are supposed to, the viewers may never know who was talking unless they happen to recognize the person or the anchorperson makes an ad lib identification after the tape has played.

Some reporters like to package their stories without using establishing two-shots before sound bites. These shots can be used effectively to identify the newsmakers. But they slow the pace of the report somewhat. Some reporters prefer to go right to the talking head and rely on the super to identify it. It is a good technique *only* if the reporter makes the identification during the narration following the sound bite.

Let's review the preceeding example of the bank robbery report and examine how reporter Roberta Roe could have led into the first sound bite.

Video	*Audio*
V/O Shots of the bank Police officers and patrol cars	The bank was crowded with customers when the gun battle broke out. At

Two-shot	least 20 shots were exchanged and Police Captain Frank Jones said it was very fortunate that no one was injured.

SOT Runs: :18
 	
SUPER: Capt. Frank
  Jones, Hometown
  Police
	TRACK UP
	OUT: ". . . . as they fled down
	  the road."
	TIME :18

Roe used an establishing shot to identify the police captain. She also would call for a super midway through the sound bite to support the verbal identification. But she also could have lead into the sound bite this way:

Video	*Audio*

V/O Shots of the bank
Police officers and
  patrol cars
 	
Bullet holes in bank
  window
	The bank was crowded with customers when the gun battle broke out. At least 20 shots were exchanged and police say it was very fortunate that no one was injured.

SOT Runs: :18
 	
Super: Capt. Frank
  Jones, Hometown
  Police
	TRACK UP
	OUT: ". . . as they fled down the
	  road
	TIME :18

Shots of Lt. Jones
  conferring with other
  officers
	Captain Jones said there's a chance that at least one of the bandits was shot.

In this example, there was no verbal identification of the police captain at the beginning. The reporter is relying on the super to make the first identification. But coming out of the sound bite she mentions the officer's name. It supports the identification and could be critical if the super did not come up.

Statistics

In the section on radio writing, you were warned away from the heavy use of statistics. The radio listener has nothing to visualize. The overuse of statistics becomes too much for the radio listener to grasp. It can be clearer in television. Although extensive use of statistics should be avoided, the special video effect machines will allow the writer to illustrate facts and figures. You should still keep the printed information displayed on the screen as simple and easy to read as possible. Often fonted information can be used to replace a stretch of footage that is visually unexciting.

Upcutting

Upcutting occurs when the first one or two words of a tape insert are missed by the viewer as the anchorperson leads into that tape. It is a problem in both radio and TV, but more so in TV during silent-to-sound pieces. The cause is that too much copy was written for the voice-over portion of the story. And it cannot be remedied by the director because the silent and sound portions follow each other on the same cassette.

A typical example might be where there is ten seconds of tape to voice-over followed by the track up. If the writer provides exactly ten seconds of copy, the track up will have to come instanteously after the anchorperson's last words. There is almost no break between the anchor's voice and the track up. And if the anchor slows down in the reading, the viewer will never hear those first few words.

The solution is to write a bit less copy than needed to cover the voice-over portion. This allows for a slight slowdown in the brief reading by the anchorperson and still leaves a half-second for a break between the two different audios.

Writing Style

Everything said earlier in this book about writing style for radio also applies to television news. But the big difference is television's added visual dimension. The viewer usually sees what you are writing about. Even read stories in TV usually have a slide or graphics that at least shows the newsmaker or illustrates something in the copy.

You must always keep this visual aspect in mind. If your read story is about the mayor, you must mention the mayor's name in the first or second sentence so that it matches the slide the viewer is seeing.

The same is true for the silent tape that the anchorperson is voicing over. The words must complement or explain further what the viewer is seeing on the tape. To do otherwise presents an audio and video conflict, creating confusion for the viewer. Some tape scenes are so general that any pertinent information can be written over it. An example is a fire story in which the tape shows only wide shots of the blaze and fire trucks. But once the tape becomes specific, such as showing a tight shot of flames leaping out of a fourth-story window or a fireman's face caked with ice, then your script should match the tape shots.

Less Is More

You must find the time to reread and edit your script objectively. Almost always you will spot entire sentences and sometimes paragraphs that are not absolutely essential. Sometimes they make better lead-in material for the anchor. Frequently, nonessential sentences contain interesting secondary information but slow the pace of the story. Sometimes a tip-off will be that you are hard-pressed to figure out how to "cover" these sentences; you already have used your best shots relating to that aspect of the story. The problem is not that you lack cover material but that you are dwelling too long on a secondary thought.

We do not believe that some ideas are too complicated for television. And you should not drop crucial information if it is difficult to illustrate. When you find it hard to cover your copy, your script may be too long. And it is too long usually because your writing is verbose. Television stories need not be simplistic. But they must be clear and direct.

Kuralt Script

Some of the most colorful writing for television has been composed by CBS News Correspondent Charles Kuralt. The word *compose* is appropriate because Kuralt's scripts—particularly his "On the Road" series—often have a melodious quality. He knows how to make the best use of natural sound and pictures. He creatively blends those elements with words. As important as the pictures are to Kuralt's stories, it is his skillful use of words that distinguish his packages from most. Following is an example of one of Kuralt's favorite scripts.

Video	*Audio*
O/C Cronkite	President Kennedy once hosted a dinner for fifty Nobel Prize winners and he said: "This is the most extraordinary collection of talent, of human knowledge, that has ever been gathered at the White House, with the possible exception

CBS News correspondent Charles Kuralt "On the Road" in Gettysburg, Pa. (CBS News photo)

Video	*Audio*
	of when Thomas Jefferson dined alone." It's that towering figure in American history who is profiled tonight by Charles Kuralt, On the Road to '76, in Virginia.
Take SOT	This is what he directed to be
Charles Kuralt	written on his tombstone, this and,
Stand-up at tombstone	as he said, not a word more: "Here
Close-up of tombstone	was buried Thomas Jefferson, author of the Declaration of American Independence, of the Statute of Virginia for Religious Freedom, and father of the University of
Close-up	Virginia" — nothing about his
O/C Kuralt	having been President of the United States. He thought of that as just an honor he had once, to be for a time an employee of the people. He

	wasn't interested in honors. He was interested in liberty.
Medium wide	Don't look for him down here in
Kuralt walking through graveyard	the mists of the family graveyard. Up on top of this hill, in the
Close-up of house	sunshine, he's still living. He was
Pull back	the architect of Monticello, but
Wide shot house	architecture was his pastime;
Reflection of house in pool of water	liberty was his passion. Walk around here, where he lived and
Pull back to wide shot of house	thought, and you can hear him on the subject of liberty. "The God who gave us life gave us liberty at
Close-up trees	the same time." "I have sworn upon
Pull back to wide shot from balcony	the altar of God eternal hostility against every form of tyranny over the mind of man."
Close-up on flowers in window	You almost expect to find him up here, cultivating his begonias. He
Zooms out	could raise flowers. He could, a biographer wrote accurately,
Wide shot of house	calculate an eclipse, survey an estate, tie an artery, plan an edifice, try a cause, break a
Dining room	horse, dance a minuet, play a
Willow tree	violin. Never mind. He gave up all those pursuits to pursue liberty.
Pan to garden Medium shot	He wrote: "I have such reliance on the good sense of the body of
Writing desk	the people that I am not afraid of
Close-up of desk from above	their letting things go wrong to any length in any cause." He
Close-up of quill pen	believed in us. Maybe that's why we
Zoom out, pan down to inkwell	feel that he is still with us somehow.
Close-up of books	Would he be on the side of black
Trucking backwards	people and poor people trying to gain their civil rights today?

Video	*Audio*
	Beyond a doubt. Would he support women trying to achieve the same rights as men? We can be sure of it. Liberty was his work.
High angle, medium shot of bookcase, pan down	
Zoom in to plan in frame on wall	On the wall of his study hangs his plan for the University of Virginia, to be built down the hill from Monticello. "If a nation expects to be ignorant and free," he wrote, "it expects what never was and never will be." He founded the university as an act of liberty.
Dissolve to exterior shot of university and pan of grounds	
High angle of building	
Bust of Jefferson through window zoom in	Thomas Jefferson wrote the Declaration of Independence as a red-haired young man of thirty-three. Over the years, he changed his mind about many things, but not about liberty. As a white-haired old man of eighty-three, he cared about nothing else so much.
Dissolves to painting of Jefferson as an old man, then zooms out	
Dissolves to another painting of Jefferson over mantel, then zooms out to Kuralt	The fiftieth anniversary of the 4th of July was coming and was much on Jefferson's mind. The mayor of Washington sent him an invitation to attend. On June 24th, 1826, Jefferson sat down here and took his pen in hand to write that he was too old and weak to accept. There was nothing old and weak about that letter. It was a democratic outburst as clear as a liberty bell. ""The mass of mankind," he wrote, "has not been born with saddles on their backs nor the favored few booted and spurred to ride them legitimately,
Stand-up	
Kuralt walks to writing desk Kuralt takes pen in hand	
Very slow zoom in to Kuralt	

by the grace of God." It was a
youthful letter, full of power. It
might have been the first thing he
ever wrote. As it turned out, it
was the last.

Dissolves to American
flag

Cut to shot of
Jefferson's bedroom

He wanted to live until the 4th
of July, and he did. Fifty years to
the day after the Declaration of
Independence, having said all he
had to say to us, which was enough,
Thomas Jefferson died on this bed,
a free man.

Dissolve to bust of
John Adams at
bedroom window

Zooms out to Kuralt
standing by
Jefferson's bed with
Adams' bust in
background

Zooms back to wide
shot

On that same day, a few hours
later, away to the north in
Massachusetts, John Adams, also old
and weak, also satisfied to have
lived until the 4th, also died. His
last words were: "Thomas Jefferson
still lives." You were right about
that, Mr. Adams. Charles Kuralt,
CBS News, On The Road to '76, in
Virginia.

Using the New Hardware

The ENG Camera

The day was filled with frustration for a news director colleague. There was a burn-in on one of the ENG cameras that could not be removed. One of the editing consoles was stretching tape. The engineering department said a minicam would have to go back to the factory because the problem could not be solved in-house.

"Sometimes," the news director said, "I wish we could go back to the CP–16's." He was talking about a 16-millimeter sound film camera that was a particular favorite of news directors and reporters who had to shoot their own stories. They were light—less than 20 pounds when loaded with a 400-foot magazine—and they were dependable most of the time. But our friend's nostalgia vanished almost as quickly as it came because he knew that despite its complexities the ENG camera was undoubtedly the most important piece of equipment in his arsenal of sophisticated hardware. Following are some things you must know about the ENG camera.

White Balancing

Before you can start shooting your story, you must "white balance" your camera to ensure that the camera produces video information faithful to

216

ENG cameraman Hank Brown
and technician Harry Weldon.
(ABC News photo)

the original colors. To do this, aim the camera at a white object and press
the white balance button or switch. Each time your light situation
changes, you must white balance the camera.

Electronic circuits inside the camera make the necessary adjustments
to achieve other colors after being given the white reference. If you fail
to rebalance the camera, as the day progresses the colors will be less true.
The reason is that ordinary daylight is bluer or cooler during midday
than it is early in the morning or late in the afternoon. As the sun rises
and again as it sets, light tends to be redder or warmer.

Db Boost

You can improve the ability of an electronic camera to shoot pictures in
low light situations. This is accomplished by operating a switch that increases the video gain of the camera. Often by using the Db boost switch
you can get at least an acceptable picture, rather than none at all.

V.C.U. broadcast news students get a white balance before reporter does her "stand-upper."

But increasing the gain of the camera, or the amount of video signal produced in dim light, also increases the electronic distortion of the signal. The resulting video picture will have a graininess that resembles film that is processed longer than normal because it was shot in a low light situation. The electronic picture, however, will be better than the picture you could normally expect with film.

Depth of Field

The television camera lens (just like a film camera lens or a 35-millimeter camera) has an iris or diaphragm that controls the amount of light which can get through. The smaller the iris, the less light can pass through and the greater the range in which objects will be in focus. Making the iris smaller, "stopping down," improves the depth of field.

When you are shooting a news story, you should adjust your lens so you have sufficient depth of field to keep everything at the scene in focus. For example, when you are shooting a fire story you will want to make sure that you can get good pictures of the flames shooting out of a window as well as the firemen and ambulances that are between your camera and the building. To keep everything in focus without adjusting the lens each time, zoom into the farthest point from your camera, in this case, the flames in the window. Get a sharp focus on those flames and when you zoom out again everything between those flames and the camera also will be in focus.

Videocassette Recorder

You are probably familiar with home models of videocassette recorders. Professional recorders are similar in many respects, but they also contain significant differences. The chief difference is in the width of the tape on the cassette. Home videocassette recorders use one-quarter-inch or one-half-inch wide tape. Most professional videocassette recorders use tape that is three quarters of an inch wide. The professional models are capable of recording a scene with much greater faithfulness and clarity.

Be especially careful when working on very hot or very cold days. If you take a videocassette recorder from an air-conditioned environment to the hot, steamy outdoors, it will often fail to operate for several minutes or longer. That is because moisture has formed on the video record head, causing what is called a tape clog.

A cold weather problem affecting both camera and videocassette recorder gear is short battery life. Bring more batteries than you think you will need. In cold weather battery charge is dissipated quickly. A battery

WWBT–TV photographer Mike O'Hara. (WWBT photo)

that powers a recorder through six videocassettes in warm weather may get you through only one or two cassettes when it is really frigid outside. Protect the batteries from the cold.

Remember that it takes time for many videocassette recorders to lock up electronically and to stabilize. Some have the ability to start up almost instantly, but most need a few seconds. The average scene in a typical news story runs about four seconds. Add a few seconds at either side of the intended shot, and you can see that individual scenes should be held for no less than 10 seconds.

Remember that all your ENG equipment must be treated with care. Film cameras are sturdier than the ENG models. And the videotape recorders will not take too much abuse. Do not, for example, try to depress any of the buttons until the cassette is properly in place and the protective glass cover is completely closed. To do so is to invite an expensive repair bill. Also, do not force the record button or any of the buttons. If they refuse to go down, something is wrong. Forcing them down will only make matters worse.

Often the record mechanism will not work because the red button has been removed from the cassette. Removal of the button makes it impossible for someone to accidentally record on the tape. The button always should be removed when you wish to preserve material on the cassette. If you are in the field and discover that the red button is missing, you can record on the tape by covering the buttonhole with masking tape.

Video Camera Techniques

In your first job as a TV news reporter you may have to know how to use a video camera and how to edit your own videotape.

Jane Lurie, a camerawoman for WCBS–TV in New York City, said that the most important point to remember when you begin using a video camera is to "get to know it so well that it becomes second nature to you. In time," she said, "you won't be thinking about the steps you must take before you begin shooting . . . . you will do it automatically."

Getting comfortable with the camera is essential. If you're a reporter shooting your own story, you will have to tell that story pictorially as well as verbally. "You must tell your viewers what it was like to be there," said Lurie, "and you must do it quickly. That means you must shoot carefully . . . editing in the camera as much as possible so that you do not overshoot."

Ideally, Lurie said, you should only shoot "what you know will actually get on the air."

Good composition also is important. Lurie said that to get good pictures "you must be aware of what's going on around you. You must remember that you are not just shooting people . . . but what is behind and in front of them." "If you are at a fire," she said, "you want to get shots that show people doing things, with the burning building in the

WCBS–TV camerawoman Jane Lurie. (Photo by Lionel Phillips)

background. Get shots of the shooting flames . . . the struggle of the firemen, the family crying . . .''

But Lurie warned about too much zooming and panning. "There always should be a purpose for camera movements," she said. "Otherwise, it is better to cut from one shot to another." She said an excellent exercise is "to shoot for an entire week without zooming or panning once. It forces you to make interesting shots. You'll learn how to show the action through the shots and not by moving the camera," she said.

The WCBS–TV camerawoman also said that if you are going to work in TV news "you have to learn to live with the fact that you will have to shoot some things that you really don't feel good about shooting . . . such as people in moments of grief and tragedy." Lurie said that for her the hardest shots she must take are those of bodies and grieving families. "There are still some scenes," she said, "that will haunt me forever."

Lurie also said that if an editor will be putting your story together, it is an excellent idea to watch the process. "You will find out if you got all the shots that you should have, and if you didn't," she said, "that will help you the next time you shoot a story."

Here are some other things to remember when shooting tape. Instead of zooming and panning, move around if you are the camera operator, or, if you are not, suggest shots that change the relationships between objects. If an accountant is working at his desk, do not zoom in for a closeup of his face. Move around to the front or corner of his desk, crouch down, and compose the scene so that a large calculator on his desk dominates the scene with the accountant revealed behind it. If the story is about children and you want to stress their vulnerability, stand tall and shoot down on the child. Or better still, get on a table or chair and shoot down from a greater height. Or if you want to show the child's point of view, exaggerate the effect. A low-angle shot will make the world appear large and imposing.

Arrange objects in the frame in an interesting way. Strictly balanced frames tend to be boring. Setting the subject to the right or left of center frame and above or below the center line is more interesting than placing the subject dead center.

Compositions that follow the diagonal of the television frame are more dynamic and interesting than those that are arranged horizontally and vertically.

Editing Techniques

An ENG editor for WCBS–TV in New York City, Joe Blanco, said one of the major problems for videotape editors is overshooting. "It's more of a problem," he said, "as you get closer to deadline."

Blanco says the reporter and cameraperson should know what shots they want and need and keep the shooting under control. He acknowledged that sometimes you cannot tell what is going to happen. But when you do, Blanco said, "you can almost edit as you go along in the camera."

When you have to deal with too much tape close to air time, Blanco said something has to suffer. The priority, of course, is getting the story on the air. When there is not enough time to screen all the material and edit it as well, "you have to sacrifice something esthetically," he said. Blanco said he sometimes is forced to use long scenes instead of several different shots, and this "distracts from the effectiveness of the piece."

Blanco said the first thing he does when he is given a story to edit is to screen everything on the cassettes. He takes notes as to where each scene is located. He said he never gets shot sheets from the reporters.

After he compiles his own shot sheet, Blanco said he then needs a script. It is up to the reporter or an associate producer to indicate which sound bites are to be used, Blanco added. "The ENG editor is not concerned with what is in the sound bites—only in the visual aspect of the story," he said.

As for the visuals, Blanco said he usually has his own idea about how the piece should be put together once he has seen the script. But if reporters want to stress a certain point visually, "they'll mention certain shots they want, and I will work with them," Blanco said.

The WCBS–TV editor advised young reporters to tell their stories as straightforward as possible. "Stick to the basic theme," he said, "don't get off on tangents."

Asked about creativity, Blanco said that unfortunately he does not have too much time to be creative. "You do the best you can with the time you have," he noted, adding that ENG does not provide as much cre-

WCBS–TV ENG editor Joe Blanco. (Photo by Lionel Phillips)

ative flexibility as film. "Everything is 'cuts' with tape. The dissolves and other special effects used in film are rarely used in an ENG piece," Blanco said. "The director's input was more important in the old days," he added, "because he called for those effects when the show was on the air."

But a good editor can still produce an effective story with ENG, Blanco stressed. He gave as an example a story dealing with the troubles in the trucking industry. The piece dealt with the drivers' problems, the use of drugs to stay awake, and the failure of some trucking firms to maintain safe equipment.

Blanco had a problem too: How to naturally take the viewer from the "popping pills" to unsafe vehicles in the same story. "You have to find a way to go from A to B," was the way he simplified it. After doing the first part of the story about the use of drugs, the reporter did a voice-over transition in which he said, "the danger that goes with driving a truck is not always the driver's fault . . . it's sometimes the trucks themselves."

Blanco showed shots of the pills for the first part of the narration and then abruptly cut to a tight shot of a truck wheel coming to a screeching halt. "I had full sound up when the viewer saw that wheel," Blanco recalls. "The sound provided an instant transition. It was a 'shock cut' that broke one thought and moved on to another instantly." He added, "even before the reporter's bridge was completed, we had a strong picture and sound transition to support it."

News staff members working at computers in electronic newsroom at WBTV, Charlotte, N.C. (Photo courtesy of WBTV)

The Electronic Newsroom

Computers have revolutionized the military, the world's banking and business operations, replaced the pinball machine, and are being used by tens of thousands of Americans in their homes to keep track of their bills, to store recipes, and even to help write books. Computers also have had dramatic effects on the newspaper business. But to date, the computer has played a relatively small role in radio and TV newsrooms. Computer experts predict that within a few years most large radio and TV newsrooms will have the new hardware and that eventually the transition from paper to computers and video display terminals will filter down.

The chief reason for the success of computers in print journalism is that it has saved money. With the elimination of compositors, payrolls were trimmed substantially. Computers replaced many typewriters in the newsroom, and the systems also were used for a variety of nonjournalistic business operations.

The major reason that computers have not made a significant impact in the broadcast newsroom is that it is difficult to show how they will save money. The few broadcast managers who have accepted the elec-

Producer Jim Shepherd working on a rundown for a CNN newscast. (Photo courtesy of CNN)

tronic newsroom concept have done so because they think it gives them greater efficiency and, perhaps in the long run, a better product. Those benefits have not convinced many broadcast news managers to invest in hundreds of thousands of dollars in new technology when most are still trying to pay for the move from film to expensive ENG cameras and microwave facilities.

Some Innovators

Among the few operating electronic newsrooms are WBTV in Charlotte, North Carolina, and Ted Turner's Cable News Network (CNN) in Atlanta. Computer systems have been installed in radio newsrooms at KCBS in San Francisco, KIRO in Seattle, and WRC in Washington, D.C.

WBTV in Charlotte was the first station on a regular basis to replace its paper-fed prompter with an electronic system that moves copy from the computer bank to the prompters. CNN has been doing much the same thing, but on a limited basis because of the magnitude of its operation.

Both CNN and WBTV are using computer equipment at the assignment, producers', and writers' desks. The wire services are also fed into the computers, enabling the editorial staffs to monitor the wires at their desks. The computers also are being used to turn out "lineups."* The

*The "lineup" or "rundown" lists all the stories to be used in a newscast. For details, see Chapter 22.

systems automatically compute the time of each story and package in the newscast and make adjustments as stories are added or dropped. This allows the producer to pinpoint the exact length of a newscast, if necessary, to determine how much must be added or removed from the broadcast to make it the right length.

Such computer capability is particularly useful when the newscast is endless. CNN installed its computer system to simplify the processing of its 24-hour nonstop news operation. In the opinion of CNN executives, if the computers did nothing more for the operation than to eliminate the endless miles of wire copy that otherwise would be needed they would be "worth their weight in gold."

But relying on the computers to take care of some of the other needs is what worries CNN executives and news managers elsewhere. CNN Vice-President Ted Kavanau has never been convinced that the computer system is reliable enough to store (bank) scripts and to send them electronically to the prompters. More than one newspaper reporter has banked a story in a computer only to see it vanish from the system shortly before deadline. Kavanau said he has nightmares about an entire hour newscast being wiped out by a computer malfunction.

Those nightmares became reality for two TV news directors who installed electronic newsrooms. Spence Kinard of KSL–TV in Salt Lake City and Michael Bille of WQAD–TV in Moline, Illinois, ran into "insurmountable problems" with the computer hardware. Kinard lost a news-

Rob Barnes, CNN Data Resource Director, using a Basys terminal. (Photo courtesy of Al Stephenson)

cast one evening because of a malfunction and scrambled to put together a new script, which delayed the broadcast a half-hour. Bille said he almost did not get on the air a number of times because of computer breakdowns. Bille said the computer system did not do anything to improve his product and was destroying the morale of his staff. The major problem with the system was its inability to retrieve script material quickly once it had been written and banked.

"If technology can help you improve your product, as in the case of ENG cameras, then it makes sense," said Bille. "But our computer system didn't help our story ideas or shorten reporter work loads or make them more efficient."

Bill Ballard, news consultant for Jefferson Data Systems, argues that his company's computer system *does* make the WBTV newsroom more efficient and that means a "better product."

Some increased efficiency comes from the improved use of the wires. Both the Jefferson Data and the Basys system installed at CNN have a split screen capability that permits a newsperson to look at a wire service story on one side and rewrite the story on the other side.

Steve Greenwald, WBTV news director, said some of his news staff was nervous at first about using the terminals to write stories. "But now that they are used to them they complain when the system is down and they have to go back to the typewriters," he said.

The Do-It-Yourself System

Howard Kelley, general manager of WTLV–TV in Jacksonville, Florida, says computers bring greater efficiency to the newsroom and, in the long run, provide a better product. He said most stations have not wanted to make a large capital outlay for computer systems because "they cannot promote them as they can a helicopter or a microwave system." Kelley's own move into an electronic newsroom was cautious and modest. He put it together himself with equipment purchased for about $1,800, and he said it has been "worth every penny."

The major difference in Kelley's system and those developed at CNN and WBTV–TV is that Kelley does not have word processing. Stories cannot be written on the computer terminal or banked for use in a newscast or for future reference. His do-it-yourself system also does not provide wire service screening. But the system performs eight other functions, as follows:

1. Provides archive of stories.
2. Keeps track of stock footage.
3. Organizes assignments and futures file.
4. Stores and locates slides and photographs.
5. Turns out producer rundowns.
6. Helps the weather department keep records of yearly lows, highs, rain accumulation, and so forth.

7. Serves as electronic file of sources and contacts.
8. Handles some housekeeping duties, such as maintaining an up-to-date list of the station employees' telephone numbers.

Electronic Radio Newsroom

As in television, computers have been triggering commercials, starting and stopping pre-recorded programs, and handling a variety of other functions at radio stations for some time. But, as in television, their move into the radio newsroom has been slow.

The first station to use a computer system was KCBS in San Francisco. As mentioned earlier, Integrated Technology installed that system. But two years later, it had sold only two additional systems to other radio stations. Greg Endsley, Vice President of Integrated Technology, said radio news directors like his product, but station managers ask the same question as their counterparts in television: "How will it save me money?" The answer is also the same: "It doesn't."

Endsley, like Bill Ballard, argues that his computer will provide a more efficient operation and a better product. The Integrated Technology system provides sophisticated word processing and access to a variety of news wires. As editors scan the wires on their VDTs they can transfer the stories that interest them to a "current" or "active" file. Once in that file, the stories can be moved about until the editors have them in the right order for their lineup. A writer assigned to a particular newscast will then call up the stories on the lineup and rewrite them on the VDT's split screen. Once the stories are rewritten they are printed out by a high-speed typewriter for use by the anchors. Display terminals also are in the broadcast studios so that the anchors can read late-breaking stories or bulletins right off the terminals instead of waiting for rewrites or print-outs.

Another interesting function of the Integrated Technology system is its ability to accept information fed from the field via portable terminals. Reporters in bureaus can use the portable terminals to send suggested lead-ins for their voice reports, wraparound material for actualities, and details about stories that were not included in the reports themselves. Once the material is sent it will appear on the editors' terminals, along with the wire copy stories, in the main newsroom.

Although most radio stations are reluctant to spend a lot of money on computers like those found at KCBS, some news directors are convincing management to invest in modest systems. In Richmond, WRVA's News Director, John Harding, convinced his boss that a computer "would be cheaper than hiring a secretary" to do all his filing. Harding uses his equipment mostly to keep track of sources and sound bites but he does have word-processing capability and plans to make use of it in the future.

Managing editor Ed Cavagnaro (right) and other KCBS Radio News personnel. (KCBS News photo)

New Production Gadgets

"The 22 minutes of information-packed, ultra-slick global flashes are delivered from London, Chicago, and Washington with so much pinball wizardry that the remaining six minutes of commercials seem like restful interludes," is how TV critic Desmond Smith describes ABC's "World News Tonight." That wizardry is working so well for ABC, Smith said, that CBS and NBC are playing a "catch-up game, spending millions on new electronic hardware . . . and changing the 'look' of their prime evening news broadcasts. Ironically,'" Smith said, "the more they 'improve' their broadcasts, the more they are beginning to look like 'World News Tonight.' "[1]

The senior producer of that newscast, Rick Kaplan, said, "We can see now that Cronkite's departure represented more than the end of an era. He represented the end of a certain way of broadcasting the news. We're all sharing the new technology now," he added, "so the big difference, I suppose, will be the way we use it."[2]

Critics and ABC's competitors generally agree that ABC President Roone Arledge is responsible for the resurgence of ABC News, which, like NBC, lingered in the shadows of CBS News for so many years. And it was Arledge who brought the new technology to the "World News Tonight" after years of experimenting with the new gadgets as head of ABC Sports.

WRVA News director John Harding feeding information into a Radio Shack computer.

The late ABC News correspondent Frank Reynolds. (ABC photo)

Not everyone agrees that the new technology represents a move in the right direction. NBC's Paul Greenberg said, "I always have to ask whether viewers are watching a picture spin instead of listening."[3] Veteran CBS News correspondent Charles Kuralt said there is an "unseemly emphasis upon image and flash and the tricks of electronics as substitutes for the hard facts."[4] CBS News Executive Vice President Van Gordon Sauter acknowledged that there is "an increased emphasis on the technical aspects of our evening news." He said these aspects are important to the "overall ambience of the broadcast and in no way diminish its journalistic credibility or efficiency."[5]

Dan Rather commented that "ABC has lots of bells and whistles and red slashes but it still doesn't have good strong scripts."[6] Arledge admits that some of ABC's news pieces use excessive graphics but argues that "people don't tune in to see the graphics, they don't tune in for the . . . technical tricks of any kind—particularly now that everybody is doing it." Arledge said the reason more people are watching ABC is because "we're better at covering things than we ever were before."[7] CBS and NBC are taking no chances. They seem convinced that technology has played a role in ABC's move upward in the ratings, and 1982 saw the introduction of new visual techniques at both CBS and NBC.

Richard Mutschler has occupied the director's chair on the CBS Evening News for 14 years. He does not miss the "old days," the complications of A and B rolling film, and the difficulties that animation posed.

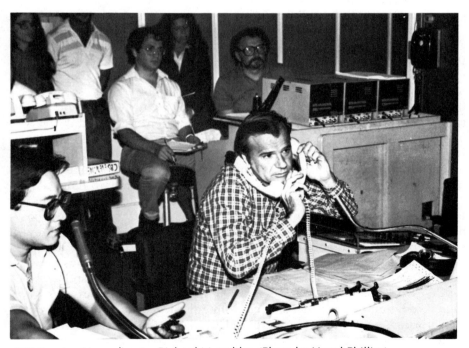

CBS Evening News director Richard Mutschler. (Photo by Lionel Phillips)

CBS News graphic artist working with the AVA machine. (Photo by Lionel Phillips)

"When we had a space flight," Mutschler recalled, "we had to use an animation company. With the new technology," he said, "we can whip out animation in an hour."

The machine that does this for CBS is called AVA, abbreviation for Ampex Video Art. "This machine would have been a great help during the Vietnam war," Mutschler said, "when we attempted to show people what was happening on the battlefield." Mutschler recalled that it once took two or three days to construct a scale model of a battle scene on a table top for the Cronkite newscast. "Then," he said, "we set off some smoke pellets to create an artillery effect. And each time we did, everyone had to leave the studio because of the smoke. Today," he said, "we would tell our graphic artist to reproduce the battle electronically. Using his electronic pen and palette," Mutschler said, "our artist could reproduce the entire battle, complete with smoke puffs, within an hour."

Mutschler did have an opportunity to do all this during the fighting between Britain and Argentina in the Falklands. His artists drew soldiers, helicopters, warships, and missiles, and AVA did the rest. Viewers at home saw Argentine missiles skimming along the water and exploding as they hit the British ships. British helicopters and troops moved across the screen to simulate the British landings on the Falklands.

AVA works on a minicomputer system that translates the artwork into digital codes and then remakes them into graphics for playback. The next step beyond AVA is a machine called the DUBNER. It is basically the same as AVA, but it allows the use of more colors and can produce more animation.

An advantage of AVA or DUBNER machines is that the electronic drawings can be banked for future use. This is done with a machine known as ESS, or Electronic Still Storage. The computer breaks the pictures down into digital code and stores the graphics on discs in the computer's memory bank. The machine can recall any graphic stored on the disc within seconds and by random access. Before this, artwork had to be transferred into photographic slides that were filed for possible future use. But valuable time was lost indexing the transparencies and finding them when needed. The slides were played back on air with a slide machine. This meant they had to be pre-loaded, and random access was virtually impossible.

Mutschler pointed out that when the graphic is recalled during the newscast he can change the animation if he wishes. For example, if during a spaceshot there suddenly was word from NASA that the spacecraft was off course, Mutschler could redirect the position of the spacecraft on the home screens during the broadcast.

Although Mutschler was enthusiastic about the new technology, he also had a warning. "One of the concerns," he said, "is that the eye should not dominate the ear. If you're not careful the visuals can overpower the story . . . you can lose the concept of what the story is about. The artist's re-creation sometimes can get too gimmicky." Mutschler added, "We should not use the new technology to 'vulgarize' the newscasts . . . it's still news, not show business."

Mutschler said the technology changes so fast "it's hard to keep up

CBS News graphic artist. (Photo by Lionel Phillips)

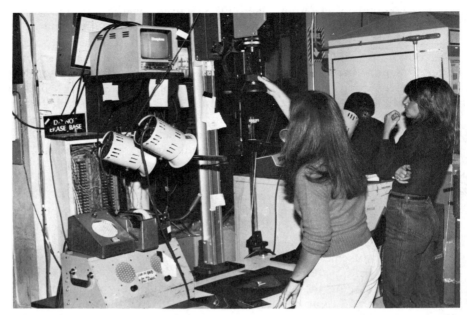

The graphic material being viewed by this camera is being electronically transferred to the ESS computer at CBS News for use later during the newscasts. (Photo by Lionel Phillips)

CNN uses an ADDA system to electronically store its graphic material.

WWBT–TV meterologist Jim Duncan using a Colographics Weather Systems computer. (WWBT–TV photo)

. . . there are changes every month. Sometimes you're sitting in the control room and you get a call from an executive who's watching the graphics in a newscast on another network and he asks 'Why can't we do that?' "

The machine responsible for most of the other electronic tricks that you see on television is known as a digital video special effects machine. It sometimes goes by the trade name of Quantel. This machine can take anything that comes into the control room, such as tape, slides, live remote pictures, the output of a studio camera, and even the output of AVA and ESS, and break it down into digital computer codes. This is the machine that creates the spins, dissolves, wipes, zooms into and out of infinity, and squeezes effects into smaller or larger boxes that are seen every night on the tube. The machine can create as many effects simultaneously as it has channels. Quantels have a maximum of four channels. A new machine called VITAL has five channels. And a machine is promised soon that will make use of a drop shadow graphic effect to produce three-dimensional pictures.

The new computer electronics has also changed the way TV news presents printed information, that is, alpha numerics, on the air. This effect, called mattes or supers in the past, used to be produced by a photographic process. It was time consuming and the TV graphics needed had to be ordered in advance. Now they are produced by computers with memory discs. They are called Chyron or Vidifont machines. An operator sitting at a keyboard similar to a large typerwiter punches out the printed

CNN video journalist operates Vidifont machine.

Supers, or "fonts", produced by a Vidifont machine. (Photo by Robert D. Kaplan, CNN)

information required while viewing the end result on a terminal display attached to the machine. The operator can make instant corrections or changes at any time, even while on the air. Once the desired effect is established, the printed matter is transferred to the memory disc for instant, random access playback. And newer models can produce the alpha numerics in different colors.

Despite the new technology, an old electronic trick is still used to display many of the graphic effects on the air. This is chromakey. It works on the principle that the TV camera sees three basic colors: green, blue, and red. The chromakey effect removes one of the colors by electronic means from the TV camera. This enables the director to insert anything, such as a slide or tape, for example, in place of the missing color. If the area behind the anchorperson is painted blue and a blue chromakey effect is used, a slide or tape can be shown next to the anchor. A vast majority of TV stations still use chromakey. A few are switching to a new gadget that costs more money but allows the different types of video material to be shown inside an electronic box alongside the anchorperson.

21

The Production Team

Executive Producers

If a news operation is large enough, there will be executive producers for the early and late broadcasts. In medium-size newsrooms, there might be only one executive producer, and in small markets, probably none at all. An executive producer usually will be involved in helping the newscast producer draft the lineup, making sure the desk is getting the reporters and crews out to and back from the stories in time, and consulting with the news director on a variety of problems extending to the hiring of talent, choice of sets, and long-range planning of the broadcast format.

Newscast Producer

Reporting to the executive producer is the newscast producer whose most important job is to block out the lineup of the broadcast. The newscast producer decides what stories will appear in what order and the approximate time they will be given in the broadcast. He or she talks over the stories with the reporters after they have finished covering them and often suggests ways to structure the final package. Sometimes the news producer will decide that the story is not worth a package and will reduce it to a voice-over report.

WCBS–TV producers working on the 5 P.M. news. (Photo by Lionel Phillips)

While the broadcast is in the process of being put together, the producer must make sure that all operations are running smoothly—checking out the desk, answering the questions of the editor, associate producers, or writers.

When the broadcast is ready to go on the air, the producer joins the director and his assistants in the control room. If any changes must be made while the broadcast is on the air, the news producer makes the decisions in the control room.

Need for Energy

Cable News Network Vice-President Ted Kavanau says energy is a key to success for a TV producer. "An energetic producer always does a more exciting program," Kavanau told his staff, "and a casual person rarely makes a good producer." He added, "The more you force the material to bend to your will, the more it will spring back to the other side of the tube."

Kavanau sent all CNN producers a list of suggestions that he said would help them to produce a "fast-moving and interesting-looking newscast."

Kavanau said newscasts should have logic. "As your experience grows," he advised, "you will be able to do things differently because you already have an understanding of some basics. Until you do," he added, "make the programs flow. Find the most important reason a story should follow the previous story."

Following are some of Kavanau's other suggestions:

Ted Kavanau, Executive Vice President, CNN Headline News. (CNN photo)

1. Bridge your stories. Use stories that help bring you from one category of story to another. The bridge story has something in common with the story it follows and the story it precedes.

2. Write short leads to tape. Get into tape stories fast. The less time spent on getting into tape the better. Don't punish people with talk when you have tape available.

3. Always write to make the good picture last. Never write short copy if you have a good picture. If you have 47 seconds of good action tape, make sure your writer makes good use of the material.

4. Use packages to give anchors and audience relief. Forcing anchors to read a lot of uninterrupted copy is bad technique. The package gives your anchors time to look over the next problem they face and also gives the audience something substantial. Shows with nothing but voice-over and copy look thin. Space packages properly and don't clump them.

5. End segments with strength. Don't put weak or uninteresting stories at the end of segments. Putting a weak story before a commercial is poor strategy.

6. Start segments with strength. You have just come out of a commercial break, so reward your audience for staying with you. Never come out of a commercial with a weak or uninteresting story.

7. Don't back features up against each other. This is a bad technique and the sign of an insecure producer. One feature is a reward and a break for the audience. A second right behind it weakens the first. It often means that the producer is not using enough news

stories in a manner that creates a total product with graceful flow from copy and picture to tape stories.

8. Use voice-over tapes to pace your segments. Learn to create rhythm between packages. It should look something like this: tape–copy–tape–copy–package–copy–tape–copy–package–copy.

9. Build your segments to create peaks and valleys. One-level segments usually are not very interesting. Build to a package. Build to an emotional story. Then if your segment is not over, start the process again . . . creating a rhythm as you go. Finally, a kind of peak is reached and you go to a commercial to give the audience a moment of respite. The audience should welcome the commercial as an opportunity to recharge its emotional batteries. Then you have removed the onus from commercials as burdens. You have made them welcome and brought the audience back for more when they are finished.

10. Dictate times of copy to writers and the method of writing the story. A strong producer maintains all decision making in relation to how copy stories are presented. If a copy story is illustrated well, that's a sure sign of a creative producer.

11. Cross roll tapes. A good technique is to cross roll tapes to keep the visual action flowing. You can cross roll from tape to tape indefinitely, changing anchor voices under the tape rolls to help define the changing stories.

12. Use news pictures as much as you can. News pictures toughen a show. Putting news pictures together in a sequence is almost as good as a tape and it shows a good deal of imagination and effort on the part of the producer.

13. Use maps for any foreign story and for national stories where there is no news picture or tape available. Call for something on the map to tell where the story is happening.

Editors, Associate Producers, and Writers

Each broadcast will usually have an editor in large market stations. If not, the producer, who also may be the anchor, will assume these duties. The editor will go through the wire service, pulling out copy that will be the basis of the news stories in the broadcast. He and the producer will decide what graphics or slides to order for the broadcast. The editor will also assign the associate producers or newswriters to the stories for which they will be responsible that day. And the editor will edit the script, approving it for broadcast. He or she will inform the producer of late-breaking stories when the broadcast is on the air. If there is no executive producer, the editor will worry about those late tape pieces still being edited.

The writers supply the lead-ins to the tape packages or to a reporter live on the set or at a live remote from the scene. They also write the

CNN News editor Randy Harber scans the news wires on his video display terminal (VDT). (Photo by Robert D. Kaplan, CNN)

CNN writer/producer desk in Atlanta.

silent to sound stories, the voice-over silents, and the read stories. Some of these writing chores also may be handled by the producer and the anchor people. But usually several people are needed to write the script for an hour or half-hour broadcast. The writers also may be assigned to work with the reporter in structuring the tape package for broadcast. At some stations, the writers who do this are given the title of associate producer. But many times there is no extra money in that week's paycheck.

The Field Producer

At the network level, people called producers, associate producers, or field producers do not do the same type of work as those in the same position on a local level. Network producers often are on the road helping the reporter cover the story. He handles relations with the local affiliate that is providing facilities; keeps in contact with the network broadcast producers; works closely with the reporter and cameraperson in shooting the story; sets up interviews; and helps the reporter structure the final package.

Sometimes a local news operation will send one of its reporters on an out-of-town story. A local station also may send one of its newswriters along to play a role similar to that of the network field producer. And a local newswriter often will be assigned to work with a reporter on a special report—a series that may run several nights on the news broadcast and usually be about five minutes long each night.

Story Meetings

The top level managers—the news director, assistant news director, executive producers, broadcast producers, assignment editors—all share in deciding what stories will be selected for tape coverage on any particular day. As discussed earlier, there will be a morning meeting, sometime between 9 and 10 A.M., when these news managers get together. The assignment editor will go over a list of stories already being covered and present a list of possible stories for reporters who have not yet been assigned. The people in the morning meeting may decide to change the assignments of those reporters already sent out. And they may go beyond the list of possible stories that the assignment desk has prepared. Any story idea is open for discussion at these meetings.

Usually a second meeting takes place about 4 P.M. for the late night news broadcast. The producer or producers attending this meeting will be assigned to the late news. The early broadcast producers will be too busy working on meeting their deadlines.

At some stations, the news director meets early in the afternoon with the evening news producers to go over the lineup for that broadcast.

Changes will often be made at these meetings. The news director may hold a similar meeting with the late night news producers before going home.

On weekends, the news managers on duty will probably be the assignment editor, the broadcast producer, and perhaps an editor. If problems arise or major stories break, the news director will be called.

The Technical Side

The equivalent to the broadcast producer on the technical or production side of the news operation is the director, the person in charge of technically getting the broadcast on the air. Once the newscast begins, the director is largely responsible for how it will look on the air. Of course, the producer and the editor should provide the director with instructions for special effects and make certain that all the cues, times, and tapes are numbered correctly. But unless the director is able to follow these instructions and gets complete cooperation from other technical people assigned to him, the newscast has no chance of being successful.

To prepare properly for the newscast, the director should have enough time to go over and mark up a copy of the script. Directors have their own assortment of symbols and shorthand that helps them once the broadcast is underway. Without such preparation, the odds of something going wrong increase greatly.

Control room at WBBM–TV in Chicago. (WBBM–TV photo)

CNN Vice President Ed Turner said many producers do not make the best use of their directors. "A director can be very helpful in bringing visual life into a broadcast," Turner said, "but often their talents are ignored." He said the director should be a "full partner" in the news production. Turner said the producer is responsible for the overall look of the newscast, but the director "should be encouraged to add creativity." According to Turner, the director can suggest even little things, such as varying camera shots of the anchors and using unusual bumper shots, that will improve a newscast.

In most markets, the director will be responsible not only for the newscast but also for pushing the buttons and giving the orders to camera operators and the floor manager. At the networks and larger stations, directors will have a number of assistants who will follow their orders. These assistants will set up camera shots in advance and make sure the slide and tape machines are loaded and ready for use on the air. Another assistant—called the technical director—will press the buttons on the control panel that start and stop the videotapes, switch studio camera pictures, and trigger special effects. In the network and very large station control rooms, there also will be assistants who handle only audio and lighting.

The production team also has its version of the desk assistant. This is the production assistant who pulls the slides from the graphics department and sets them up in the slide trays for the broadcast; types a list of the slides for the director, showing in what order they are to appear in the broadcast; rips apart the copy books used to type the script and sorts them for the various people who need them. At most stations, the production assistants—like the desk assistants—are interns and often they share their responsibilities.

The editorial and production people must work together as a team to get the broadcast on the air and to make it a success. When they have worked together as a team for awhile they will be able to anticipate each other's needs. Without the joint effort of all these people, there would be no broadcast.

22

The Lineup

Planning the TV Newscast

The lineup, or rundown, is the plan that guides those involved in getting the news broadcast on the air.

The morning news conference discussed and decided what stories to cover. The assignment or city desk is now sending camera crews and reporters out. The main questions now are: What stories are most important? Which have to be worked on first? How will they be fitted together to make a cohesive broadcast? It is now close to noon and you will be going on the air at 6 P.M. Now is when the news team needs that plan. It is of major importance to the producer and assistants who will help the reporters in putting the stories together and to the director who will technically get the broadcast on the air.

What broadcasters call the lineup is termed the page one dummy on newspapers. In the print media, this is a rough copy of what page one will look like, indicating what stories will go where on page one, how much room they will take up, and how big the headlines will be. Eventually, the newspaper's editions will have a dummy for each page in their edition. In the producer's lineup, each item will represent a page in the final script for the broadcast.

But, remember, there is a difference between reading a newspaper and watching a television news broadcast. A newspaper reader scans the page he is looking at. When his eye spots something that interests him, he can stop and read at his leisure. Not so in TV news. If the story does not interest viewers, they must still watch it, or turn to another channel. The broadcast must have enough variety so that if something does not catch the attention of some viewers there will be other things to interest them.

It is with these points in mind that the producer now drafts his lineup. And he has three important concepts to guide him: peaks and valleys, pacing, and blocks or segments.

Peaks and Valleys

Because everything in the news broadcast will not interest all viewers, it must be thought of as a series of peaks and valleys, or highs and lows. Every news broadcast should start off on a peak or high with the most important, up-to-the-minute, breaking news story of the day. As you progress down the list of news stories, their intensity or news value will diminish. It is at these low points or valleys that you must find ways of giving a lift to the broadcast, bringing it back to a peak.

Pacing means keeping the broadcast flowing in such a manner that it does not reach a point of stagnation or boredom. There is a proper mixture of tape and read stories that gives the broadcast the right kind of movement. It should not be so slow-moving that the viewer becomes bored, and it should not go by so quickly that the viewer becomes confused.

Blocks or segments are the news stories that fit between the commercials. When all segments are put together, they create a whole broadcast.

When you sketch the rough outline of the broadcast, you start with the beginning and the end, the opening and closing of the broadcast. Every broadcast has a formulated opening and closing. They vary from station to station and change within a station. An example follows.

The Opening

When the broadcast begins, the anchor will be on camera reading headlines while tape shows scenes from the most important news stories of the day and from one of the best features in the broadcast. The purpose of this "cold open" is to tease audience interest in four or five stories that will appeal to a wide variety of viewers. This concept of teasers about stories that will appear later on is carried throughout the broadcast. Before the anchor goes to each commercial break, there will be teases for a couple of stories coming up after that commercial. Again, the idea is to keep the viewer interested enough to stay tuned.

The second part of the opening is called the "warm open." This is the identification of the broadcast. It would include a wide shot of the set, a musical introduction, and a flashing station logo over which an announcer is heard to say, "Channel 2 News, the Six O'Clock Report with Jim Jensen and Rolland Smith."

The ending of the broadcast is usually the same. The anchor people say good evening. The last commercial runs and then credits appear over a shot of the set. The one exception might be once a week when the credits of everyone working on the broadcast are run. Because this usually takes one minute or longer, the credits are run over a piece of tape from a feature story that lends itself to music. In its simplest form, it can be weather tape with a track that contains instrumental music. At times, even credits can be used to make a statement that will excite interest among the viewers. During a blizzard one winter, Channel 2 News ran its credits for the week over various shots of the weather story taken over several days and set to the music of the rock song, "We Are the Champions" by Queen.

Draft Lineup

A draft lineup looks like this:

```
1. Cold open  tape
2. Warm open
X. Goodnights
Y. Cx # 7
Z. Credits
```

Note item Y. It is commercial break number 7. Commercials are referred to in TV shorthand as Cx. There are seven commercial breaks in a typical hour-long broadcast. If you pencil in the commercials, you expand the draft to look like this:

```
1. Cold open  tape
2. Warm open
Cx # 1
Cx # 2
Cx # 3
Cx # 4
Cx # 5
Cx # 6
X. Goodnights
Y.  Cx # 7
Z. Credits
```

Seven Segments

The expanded draft outlines seven blocks or segments. The first segment contains everything from the opening to the first commercial. The easiest segment to rough block first is the last one, the one between Cx # 6 and the goodnights. It usually will look like this:

```
Cx # 6
Update   tape
Lead to Wx
Wx live   tape and pix
Feature story   tape
Goodnights
Cx # 7
Credits
```

This segment is based on several theories that have been around broadcast news since it started. First, the update is usually 20 to 30 seconds of headlines, similar to the cold open except it does not mention feature stories. The theory here is that on the six o'clock news the number of viewers increases as the hour progresses. They are people coming home from work and others turning on their sets as they finish their dinners. If they missed the beginning of the broadcast, they missed the major news stories of the day. The update gives them at least the major headlines. If any of those stories change during the hour on the air, you can tell the viewers of those new developments. Just like the cold open, several shots illustrate the news stories. Weather, referred to in TV shorthand as Wx, is put toward the end of the broadcast because almost every viewer wants to know what the weather will be. And the longer you hold the weather report back, in theory, the longer the viewer will stay tuned. The broadcast ends on a feature story or kicker to leave the viewer smiling.

The next easiest segment is the next to last, number six. Sports is usually scheduled in this segment. Most studies show that only one third of the viewers are interested in sports. You want to keep that one third tuned in, but you do not want to turn off the other two thirds. So, you put sports toward the end but leave enough room after sports for items of general interest. The segment will go like this:

```
Cx # 5
News story   possible pix and/or tape
Leads to sports
Sports
News story   possible pix and/or tape
```

```
Pad
Cx # 6
```

The news stories surrounding sports can be "reads." These are 20- or 25-second stories read by the anchors with pictures (pix) shown next to him. There is no tape for the anchors to voice-over. Read stories are dropped in for pacing to give a feel of movement to the broadcast. They are usually placed between or around tape stories by correspondents or regular spots such as sports or weather. Since there are no visuals, the stories are kept tight to avoid a long, dull stretch of air with the anchor on camera.

Pad is an important factor in every TV news broadcast, particularly in the planning stage. You will eventually assign times to each item in the lineup. These times are rough estimates. You might, for example, tell a reporter he has two minutes for his story. But it might be one minute and fifty seconds or two minutes and ten seconds. The anchors often will speed up or slow down as the hour progresses. To take these variables into account, you add the pad factor in your lineups. The pad is an amount of time, usually two to three minutes, out of the hour's broadcast to which nothing is assigned.

So now the draft lineup looks like this:

```
Cold open  tape
Warm open
Cx # 1
Cx #2
Cx # 3
Cx # 4
Cx # 5
News story  possible pix and/or tape
Lead to sports
Sports
News story  possible pix and/or tape
Pad
Cx # 6
Update  tape
Lead to Wx
Wx  tape and pictures
Feature story  tape
Goodnights
Cx # 7
Credits
```

You can now work on the fourth segment, the one between commercials 3 and 4. This segment usually comes just before the 30-minute mark into the hour. You are half-way through the broadcast and usually coming out of a segment that tends to be a valley in the series of ups and downs. You need something to pick up the broadcast. And you usually do that here with a feature segment. So it will look something like this:

```
Cx # 3
News story  pix and/or tape
Feature story  pix and/or tape
Soft news story  tape
People in the News  pix and tapes
Still to come  tape
Cx # 4
```

"People in the News" is television's form of the gossip column, usually containing stories about celebrities. "Still to come" is, in effect, a super tease. You want to keep viewers watching to the end and you try to tease them into doing this by telling them about the features and special reports that are coming up.

The lineup now looks like this:

```
Cold open  tape
Cx # 1
Cx # 2
Cx # 3
News story  pix and/or tape
Feature story  pix and/or tape
Soft news story  tape
People in the News  pix and tapes
Still to come  tape
Cx # 4
Cx # 5
News story  possible pix and/or tape
Lead to sports
Sports
News story  possible pix and/or tape
Pad
Cx # 6
Update  tape
Lead to Wx
```

```
Wx   tape and pix
Feature story   tape
Goodnights
Cx # 7
Credits
```

You can now focus attention on the opening segment, which will set the tone, pace, and personality of the entire broadcast. You should consider three important questions in drafting this segment: What are the major news stories of the day? How long should this opening segment run? On what tone do we want to end the segment?

The opening segment should be the longest of the broadcast. The idea is to hook the viewers and to hold on to them long enough so they lose any thought of flipping the dial. On an hour-long broadcast you should go about eight to ten minutes before the first commercial. How will you end this segment? Usually you have just given viewers the best news stories of the day. The prevalent theory is that this segment should be a miniature broadcast. End it on a somewhat uplifting or dramatic note. Something with a touch of humanity or human interest will do nicely.

You are still left with the second, third, and fifth segments. Mostly breaking news stories go there, combined with informational packages and special reports. This is where specialists such as health and science or consumer reporters enter the picture. This is where television news can break away from the harsh requirements of telling a story in two minutes or less. And two or three nights may be devoted to looking into a topic in depth.

Now you are ready to construct a tentative lineup. It may change as the day progresses.

How the lineup evolves varies from newsroom to newsroom. In metropolitan TV newsrooms, two or three different lineups may be distributed throughout the afternoon to reflect new breaking stories. In some small TV newsrooms, there may not be a formal lineup. The order of stories may be decided by the news director an hour or less before air time by arranging the order of the various packages and read stories that have been turned into him by reporters and the anchor. This method is not to be encouraged.

Usually, the producer of the 6 o'clock news will make up a lineup and distribute copies of it to other members of the staff well in advance of broadcast time. The lineup will reflect the stories that have been assigned to reporters and on-camera crews by the news director or assignment editor. The lineup also will list the read stories to be written by anchors or writers and will indicate where the commercials, weather, and sports are to come. As discussed earlier, many of the ideas for reporter packages or voice-over video stories were developed at staff conferences in the morning, originated by reporters, or assigned by the news director or assignment editor the previous day. In any case, by midday the producer should have a good idea of what packages, voice-over re-ports, and other video stories or footage will be available for use at 6 o'clock. Other stories may break in the next three or four hours that will need coverage, but adjustments will have to be made for them in the lineup later in the afternoon. In order to produce a fast-paced one-hour newscast, you need 10 to 12 packages in addition to sports, weather, "People in the News," read and voice-over stories, and commercials.

Let's look at a list of video stories that might be available on a typical news day and see how to work them into a lineup. The reporter assigned to the story is listed next to a brief description of each.

Tape Outlook

 1. Smith . . . wildcat postal strike.
 2. Rose . . . test tube trial with artist sketches.
 3. Lane . . . beating high food prices . . . with
                live remote from a supermarket.
 4. Cole . . . labor boss goes back to jail.
 5. Johnson . . . doctors working in ghetto clinic.
 6. Stone . . . baby gorilla debuts at zoo.
 7. Rodriguez . . . baseball manager fired.
 8. Goldberg . . . cruise ship walkout.
 9. Jones . . . examines a new diet.
10. Field . . . jogging . . . part 2 . . . all on
                tape since Field is on vacation.
11. Norris . . . killer bees . . . fact or fiction?
12. Crew shoots heavyweight challenger and champ at
    training camps.
13. Checklist: Vet suing government . . . child lives
    after fall from window . . . taxicab driver to get
    hero's medal from mayor.
14. Sportssteps . . . silent voice–over.
15. Also . . . possible story on oyster harvest.

That is the menu the producer will have to work with in deciding what stories will go into the 6 o'clock news. Some of the stories will not make air and some may not even be completed if a late-breaking story necessitates taking a reporter off an assignment to cover it.

In the preceding example, Smith will go to the post office and inter-view workers who are on the picket line after walking off the job. He also will talk to a union leader and a government official. It is an impor-tant story and undoubtedly will make the lineup. The second item on the tape outlook, Rose's story about a test tube baby trial has been going on for more than a week, and some important testimony is expected this day. Good potential. The same is true for the next item, Lane's story on high food prices. The fourth item, Cole's assignment about a labor racketeer going back to jail could be just a voice-over of the man in handcuffs. Item 5, Johnson's story about doctors working in a ghetto clinic, is a good feature but could be held until tomorrow.

This brings us to story 6, baby gorilla debuts. Originally it was thought of as natural sound, voice-over by the anchor. But it also is a good visual human interest or feature story. Everyone likes to look at animals in the zoo, and it is too good an opportunity for reporter Bob Stone to exercise his special light touch to waste it on 20 seconds of voice-over.

Story 7, Rodriguez's report on the local baseball team suddenly firing its popular manager, could provide a lead.

Story 8 about a walkout by the entire crew of a cruise liner has good picture possibilities of the men marching through the city, as well as the unusual story of a ship and its crew stranded in port.

The ninth story about a new diet came up at the morning meeting. A producer saw a mention of it in a newspaper column and got the others to agree to cover it.

The story 10 package was prepared in advance by Bob Field. It is a special report on the fad of running for exercise, the advantages and disadvantages.

For story 11, Tim Norris, the arts editor, is going to take a look at whether the premise of a science-fiction movie on killer bees is scientifically accurate.

A championship heavyweight fight tonight in the city is scheduled as story 12. Camera crews shot both fighters at their training camps.

The story 13 checklist is possible read stories for which silent tape may be shot. The assignment desk will check out the photo opportunities and the feasibility of getting camera crews there in time. They will let the producer know whether or not he will be getting tape on these stories.

Story 14 is silent tape of some sports celebrities leaving their footprints in cement. The anchor will voice-over it.

There are other sources of tape that the producer did not put on his list because the assignment desk will not have to handle them. One is the network's morning news show. This can provide tape of national and international stories for voice-overs or a local angle on a national or international story. There also could be "spec" tape from freelance camerapeople.

It is now about noon and the producer is ready to make the tentative lineup. The producer has the following to work with: the list of tape stories, routine items such as sports and weather, and a list of read stories he wants to get into the broadcast.

Today's list of read stories is as follows:

```
1. A payraise for the mayor is approved by the city
   council.
```

2. A light plane crash in Kalamazoo, Michigan.
3. Contract talks between the city and its firemen.
4. A story about the benefits of a lowfat diet.
5. Wedding in a balloon.
6. Any potential national or international stories that might break and be of interest.

During the day, the following stories broke and were shot on tape:

1. Shooting . . . man found dead in car in apparent gangland–type murder.
2. Fire in a hotel drives two dozen families from their rooms.
3. Parrot burglar . . . some thieves steal a valuable talking bird from a pet store.

And, of course, there are the inevitable changes of plan and surprises. Today the following happened:

Jones was unable to get enough material together to do a story today on dieting and the potential story planned on the oyster harvest fell through. But a story Joan Lane did on swimming safety a few days ago is cut and ready for air. You put it into the broadcast for safety, if it is needed. Rodriguez had planned to concentrate on tonight's heavyweight championship fight, but the manager of the city's major league team was suddenly fired. Rodriguez has two big stories and a busy day and night.

The 6 P.M. Lineup

The lineup for the six o'clock news remained unchanged from the preliminary draft the producer drew up earlier in the day. The producer formalized it about an hour before broadcast. Following is the evening news lineup in final form.

		ON TIME:	6:00:00
1.	Cold open tape	:30	6:00:30
2.	Warm open	:10	:00:40
3.	Story A (open spot for last minute new lead)	--	:00:40
4.	Manager Fired Pix Lead to	:20	1:00
5.	Rodriguez Live in studio and tape	2:30	3:30
6.	Championship Fight Pix Tape	:30	4:00
7.	Cruise Ship Walkout Lead to	:15	4:15

8.	Goldberg tape package	2:15	6:30
9.	Mayor Gets Raise Pix	:25	6:55
10.	Gangland Shooting Pix Tape	:25	7:20
11.	Gorilla Pix Lead to	:15	7:35
12.	Stone package	2:15	9:50
13.	Cx # 1	2:15	12:05
14.	3-Alarmer Pix Tape	:20	12:25
15.	Labor Boss Pix Lead to	:15	12:40
16.	Cole package	2:30	15:10
17.	Kalamazoo Plane Pix or Tape	:20	15:30
18.	Postal Strike Pix Lead to	:15	15:45
19.	Smith Live in studio and tape package	2:15	18:00
20.	Cx # 2	2:15	20:15
21.	Lowfat Diet Pix	:30	20:45
22.	Food Prices Pix Lead to	:15	21:00
23.	Lane package	2:30	23:30
24.	City-Firemen Contract Talks Pix	:20	23:50
25.	Parrot Burglars Pix Tape (SIL/SOT)	:35	24:25
26.	Cx # 3	2:15	26:40
27.	Test Tube Pix Tape	:20	27:00
28.	Jogging Pix Tape package by Field	2:30	29:30
29.	Wedding In A Balloon Pix	:30	30:00
30.	People in the News Pix and Tape	1:00	31:00
31.	Still to Come Tape	:20	31:20
32.	Cx # 4	2:10	33:30
33.	News Read Story Pix	:20	33:50
34.	Ghetto Doctors Pix Lead to	:15	34:05
35.	Johnson live in studio and tape	2:30	36:35
36.	News Read Story Pix	:20	36:55
37.	Swimming Safety Pix Tape package by Lane (2:15 if needed)	--	36:55
38.	Cx # 5	2:15	39:10
39.	Dateline Pix	1:00	40:10
40.	Sports Lead	:10	40:20

41.	Sports Pix and Tapes	4:00	44:20
42.	Sportssteps Tape	:25	44:45
43.	Pad	2:20	47:05
44.	Cx # 6	2:15	49:20
45.	Update Pix Tape	:30	49:50
46.	Wx Lead	:10	50:00
47.	Wx Map with pictures and tape	2:00	52:00
48.	Killer Bees Lead to	:15	52:15
49.	Norris Live in studio and tape	3:00	55:15
50.	Goodnights	:25	55:40
51.	Cx # 7	1:05	56:45
52.	Credits	:15	57:00

Let's analyze this lineup segment by segment. How does the first section fit into the theory discussed earlier in this chapter? First, notice the pacing. There is a package, a voice-over story, another package, a read story, another voice-over story, and the segment ends with a third package. The broadcast does not start off by getting bogged down with one package following another. This would make the broadcast seem heavy. By varying the way the stories are presented, you increase the feeling of movement in the broadcast. It also allows the viewers a chance to feel the presence of the anchor or anchors, the most important on-air people in the broadcast.

Notice that the stories selected for the first segment are those that have tape and are of major interest or have exciting footage. We also listed "story A," without allotting any time to it, for a possible late-breaking lead. Notice also the human interest (baby gorilla) end to the hard section.

In the second segment, the stories begin to lose their mass audience appeal and the picture impact also is less exciting. Two packages were placed in this segment, but a sense of flow was added by starting with a voice-over story, going to a package, doing another voice-over, and ending with a package. Notice that this segment does not end with a human interest or feature. It would make the broadcast appear much too soft. The third segment begins to run out of hard news tape that is of mass interest and exciting to view. Here is where the producer can use consumer reports, science stories and packages of that nature. Notice how the same techniques were used as in the previous segments to keep up the flow and pace. But only one package was used and another way of telling the story (silent-to-sound) was employed. The anchor read the Parrot Burglars story by starting out on camera and then voicing over tape. Then the track was brought up for a quick talking head before the story ended back on camera. This section also makes use of the theory of grouping similar stories together in one section, the lowfat diet and food prices stories.

The fourth section brings the broadcast to the half-way mark. Just before this segment, the broadcast was on a descending slope of peaks and valleys. It started on a peak and has been slowly going downward in intensity ever since. Now, you must try to bring it up for the viewer. One way to do this is with a feature section. This segment grouped stories, using the health and science themes for the first two and light features for the last two. News stories read by the anchor separate them.

In the fifth section, the producer has run out of hard news tape. But he does not want a section that is filled with light stories. One answer is to make use of a couple of hard news stories and reporter packages that provide useful information or tell an interesting story. These packages are neither soft nor hard breaking news. They are more like news features—information or interest in a softer context.

The sixth segment is the sports section. It starts with "Dateline," a headline summary of three or four important national or international stories. This segment also ends on a bright note. It is fine if the bright feature relates to sports, but it can be any kind of a quick, light story with or without a picture or tape.

The final segment is the weather and feature to end the broadcast. Note that just as the broadcast began on the peak of the best news story of the day, it also ends on the peak of what the producer believes is the best feature story of the day.

That's what the 6 P.M. News might look like on a particular day. It is not the same kind of news that you might have discovered on the front page of a daily newspaper. The entire broadcast is a package designed to present stories that visually excite and interest the viewer, along with some useful information and a quick headline look at the major news events.

Some news directors prefer another pattern for blocking a lineup that combines a group of related stories in each segment. The stories about the low-fat diet and food prices, for instance, share food as a common link. Another segment combines a sequence of stories all dealing with money: a raise for the mayor, the stranded ship's crew trying to get their pay, the city's firemen looking for a pay hike in a new contract, and the wildcat postal strike.

Such arrangements place emphasis upon the flow and continuity of news stories but maintain the elements of peaks and valleys and pacing with an intermix of read stories, packages, and voice-overs. Some television producers believe that this philosophy of flow should be the guideline in blocking out the day's newscast.

Critics of flow blocking say it gives a tabloid quality to the broadcast. They cite as an example the lumping together in one segment of all stories dealing with crime, prison, and tragedy. This approach also places some stories too high or too low in the broadcast in terms of news values, according to opponents.

The Late News Lineup

Let's move on to the 11 P.M. broadcast. Traditionally, this has been considered a half-hour summary of all the day's news, the final wrap-up before the viewer goes to bed.

In the early 1970s the 11 P.M. broadcast was a cutdown version of the major packages from the local 6 P.M. news and the half-hour network news. There was not much concern about repetition between the broadcasts. Studies showed that 80 percent of the audience was new. In other words, they did not see a 6 P.M. broadcast.

In the last six years, there has been an increasing trend to update the news at 11 P.M., to present new angles on stories that have been around most of the day, and to hunt out new stories just for the 11 P.M. broadcast. This is similar to the afternoon newspaper doing a second-day angle on a news story, taking a story the reader saw in the morning newspaper and making it appear new. Recent studies show that when one station in town among several goes for the update format at 11 P.M. and promotes it heavily with advertising, the ratings will rise. Another reason for updating at 11 P.M. is the dropoff factor. At 6 P.M., the audience can be considered drop-in, more viewers turning on their sets as they come home or finish the evening meal. But the 11 P.M. is a drop-out broadcast because for most viewers the day is over. This is the last bit of television before going to sleep. The problem at 11 P.M. is to maintain the viewers' interest so as to prevent a large drop-off in the last fifteen minutes of the broadcast.

There are several techniques to updating stories for the 11 P.M. newscast. You can go back to the scene of the daytime story and shoot it at night. Or make some phone calls to find a new angle to the story. Examples would be the condition of a hospitalized victim or the progress of the police investigation of a crime. Sometimes, a story begins in the afternoon and continues into the evening, lending itself naturally to an update. With a new story that is happening that evening, you have a new package by your correspondent with a live studio appearance or remote. If a story is still going on at 11 P.M., then you have a live remote and a tape package by your reporter. Best of all is a new story that breaks within an hour or so of the broadcast. It would be done live from the scene, probably without any earlier tape. And you would go back to the live remote for updates during the course of the broadcast.

However the update is accomplished, its purpose is to convince viewers that the 11 P.M. is a new broadcast with new stories and with repetition limited to a few major stories that must be retold. At the same time, viewers must feel that they still are getting a complete wrap-up of the day and night news or they will feel that they are being cheated.

Time is an even more restricting factor at 11 P.M. The 6 P.M. broadcast had a full hour. The 11 P.M. has a half hour. The 6 P.M. has seven segments, the 11 P.M. only four. This, of course, changes the blocking concept somewhat, although the idea of peaks and valleys continues. Flow blocking also can be applied. Pacing and individual segments still are necessary ingredients. What happens is that everything is condensed or abbreviated.

A typical 11 P.M. draft lineup follows.

1. Open
2. Hard news stories of major interest with exciting tape
3. A human interest story to end the segment
4. Cx #1
5. Secondary news stories, including national and international news
6. Possible news feature stories
7. People in the News or a feature with high interest
8. Still to Come . . . a very important supertease to avoid drop-off
9. Cx #2
10. Sports
11. News feature, entertainment review, or special report
12. Cx #3
13. More news stories, either read or voice-over tape
14. Weather
15. Kicker . . . either a read, voice-over, or package
16. Goodnights
17. Cx #4
18. Credits

The first two segments of the 11 P.M. are similar to the first four segments of the 6 P.M. Sports comes about 17 minutes past the hour, far enough to hold the sports fans, but high enough to leave something of interest for the mass audience. There is no need for a recap in the last section. Most viewers are dropping out, not joining the newscast, and the main aim is to make the viewer feel that the broadcast was a complete wrap-up of the news that occurred that day and night.

Before drafting the lineup for the 11 PM. broadcast, let's take a look at what is being done to update that broadcast. You will recall that many

TV news organizations hold a morning meeting to decide what stories to cover for the 6 P.M. broadcast. Many news directors also like to have an afternoon meeting to decide what new stories to cover or update for the 11 P.M. broadcast.

On the day described earlier it was decided to send Rodriguez to the stadium for the championship fight that probably would still be in progress at 11 P.M. The fight was blacked out but Rodriguez has a ticket and will leave the stadium during the news to do a live standup in the sports section.

It is planned to shoot some natural sound for a voice-over and track up of a free jazz concert in the park. A reporter is sent to cover a rally in the evening by the students and teachers of a high school protesting the firing of their principal. Another reporter will cover the story of an elderly woman who wants to sell her valuable Bible to pay a "few bills." This would be a new feature story. Why do a new feature when you already have at least two from the 6 P.M. broadcast? The answer is to avoid that sense of repetition from the 6 P.M. broadcast. If you replay the features that were aired at 6 P.M., you run the risk of having those who saw that newscast say, "I already know that story," and shut off the TV set.

The producer of the 11 P.M. broadcast also can use stories aired on the evening network news programs and stories provided by network feeds.

Now, let's take a look at what the 11 P.M. producer did that night.

```
 1.  Cold open
 2.  Warm open
 3.  Story A (an open spot for any last-minute new lead)
 4.  Championship fight pix tape tease sports segment
 5.  Manager fired  pix  tape
 6.  Mayor's raise  pix  tape
 7.  Teacher rally  pix  lead to
 8.  Live in studio and tape package
 9.  Cx #1
10.  Postal strike  pix  tape
11.  City-firemen talks pix
12.  Cruise ship walkout  pix  tape
13.  People in the News with voice-over tape on gorilla
     and parrot
14.  Still to come  tape
15.  Cx # 2
16.  Dateline pix  tape
17.  Sports . . . with tape and live remote by Rodriguez
18.  Free jazz concert  tape
```

```
19.  Cx # 3
20.  Pad
21.  Labor boss goes back to jail  pix  tape
22.  Wx lead
23.  Wx . . . live at map with tape and pix
24.  Bible woman pix lead to
25.  Live in studio with tape package
26.  Goodnights
27.  Cx # 4
28.  Credits
```

The first segment switches from the sports stories to the mayor's pay hike to the teacher rally. In the second segment, the money stories are tied together, but there is a switch to the People in the News section. Some hard news is played before sports to avoid an entirely soft feel to the last half of the broadcast. This is done again in the beginning of the fourth section for the same reason. And, of course, the broadcast ends with weather and a feature. Some TV stations will end their 11 P.M. broadcast with the weather, eliminating the feature. They reason that everyone wants to know what the weather will be in the morning, and they hold out to the very last minute to keep the viewers tuned in.

Notice a major difference between the 6 P.M. and 11 P.M. broadcasts. The 6 P.M. is more package heavy. And the packages on the 6 P.M. are longer. The 11 P.M. is a tighter broadcast. To squeeze more stories in and to make room for the one or two new packages shot that evening, many of the 6 P.M. packages are cut or reduced to a voice-over.

The Time Factor

Another important consideration for the producer is the real length of the newscast. When one speaks of an hour newscast or a 30-minute newscast, it does not mean that the audience is really getting that much news. In the one-hour newscast described earlier, there was a total of 13 minutes for commercials. That means the newscast was reduced to 47 minutes. Then there were five ten-second teases, and each one had a five-second fade-in-and-out of black around the commercials. The weather got another two minutes and sports, four minutes. Both the weather and the sports had ten-second lead-ins. More than another minute was eaten up by the opening and the close. And news goes off at 6:57 because it is followed by a three-minute editorial.

Of a 60-minute newscast, less than 37 minutes is left for hard-breaking news and features. There is even less time if you subtract the news update section and the People in the News segment. It's no wonder, then, that the producer must be judicious in the time allocated to the stories that he puts on the air. There is not that much time to give away. Obviously, the challenge is even greater for the producer who must squeeze all the news into a 30-minute newscast that may provide as little as 14 or 15 minutes for hard news and features.

Backtiming

The radio section of this book showed how to backtime the radio news broadcast so that the announcer will get off on time. Getting off on time is even more important in television. The networks and many local stations are run by computers that automatically put the broadcast on and off the air. At the precise second the next scheduled broadcast is to go on, the computer will cut off the program on the air. The computer does not care if the anchors are still saying goodnight. It will cut them off in mid-word.

For this reason, the producer must know at all times when the broadcast is on the air whether it is behind or ahead of time schedule. If short, the producer will have to insert pad items into the broadcast. If long, some items will have to be cut out of the broadcast. Backtiming is the key. Here's how backtiming works. Your lineup lists, item by item, what is in the broadcast. Draw two columns in which you will pencil in figures. The first column will list the actual running time of the item. The second column will be your backtiming, telling you what time you should be going to or finishing an item in the broadcast. A backtiming for the last section of the 6 P.M. news earlier in this chapter would look like this:

Cx # 6	2:00	49:20
Update	:30	49:50
Wx Lead	:10	50:00
Wx	2:00	52:00
Killer Bees Lead to	:15	52:15
Norris--live and tape	3:00	55:15
Goodnights	:25	55:40
Cx # 7	1:05	56:45
Credits	:15	57:00

In this case, the computer will take the broadcast off the air at precisely 57:00 straight up. You can write in the time of each item as it becomes available (weather and commercials will be known in advance), or you can estimate them, making adjustments during the day or even during the broadcast. Write the actual or estimated times in pencil so you can make changes or corrections. Starting with the very last item, *subtract* the time of the item from the time you must be off the air. In this case, take 15 seconds away from 57:00, taking you back to 56:45. Commercial seven will run one minute plus five seconds for the fade in and out of black around the commercial. This will take you back another one minute and five seconds to 55:40. Keep subtracting backwards this way. You see that according to your backtiming you must go into commercial number six at 47:20; you must go into the end feature story at 52:00. The backtiming can be carried up through the first item in the broadcast. For most news broadcasts it will suffice to backtime to the point at which you come out of either the first commercial for the 11 P.M. broadcast or the second commercial for the 6 P.M. broadcast. The less experience you have with backtiming, the closer to the first item in the broadcast you should backtime.

Investigative Reporting

Overuse and misuse of the term *investigative reporting* make it necessary to examine the distinction between reporters' coverage of routine stories and those that involve serious and extensive digging for information. Some journalists point out that every good reporter must investigate in the process of gathering the facts needed to write a story. True enough, but that doesn't mean that all news stories qualify as investigative reporting.

Reporting a routine fire involves no more investigation than asking the fire chief and other authorities standard questions. If authorities suspect arson and if a reporter tracks records to document evidence of insurance fraud, the story may qualify as an investigative report. Without that extra element of dogged pursuit of solid clues and hard evidence, the fire remains a spot news story of the sort that routinely fill radio and television broadcast time.

Neither is the typical work of a station's "action reporter" or "consumer reporter" truly investigative reporting. Consumer complaints or inquiries often require a considerable amount of checking, but usually the reporter is determining basic facts as in any story or finding out where to direct a consumer for further action or resolution of a problem. Sending a reporter and camera crew for a dramatic confrontation with the owner of a rental agency that fails to find housing for clients may appeal to some news directors and viewers, but it is not investigative reporting.

What then is investigative reporting? Bob Greene, a Pulitzer prize-winning reporter for *Newsday*, offers the following definition: "It is the reporting of something that someone or some group is trying to keep secret." But he added quickly, "It has to be your own product."[1] He pointed out that the Pentagon Papers made a good story, but was not investigative reporting because the original work was not done by a reporter but by the Rand Corporation. On the other hand, he said, the Watergate case was "a perfect example, because a group of people was trying to keep information secret and Woodward and Bernstein uncovered it."[2]

Watergate Myths

Carl Bernstein, who with Bob Woodward, broke the Watergate story at the *Washington Post,* said he and Woodward became a "subject of entirely too much mythology." Bernstein tried to "de-mythologize" some of the Watergate story at the first national conference of Investigative Reporters and Editors.[3] "It's important to keep in mind," he said, "that what we did in Watergate was the most basic, empirical police reporting of the kind you first learn when you get into the business, or even that you learn in journalism school."

Bernstein said it probably was an advantage that he and Woodward were not members of the prestigious national staff of the *Post*. "We were outsiders," he said. "We didn't have high-level sources at the White House . . . we were on the metropolitan staff. So we went about the story the same way we would any other story we were assigned to. That is to say, we knocked on a lot of doors."

Bernstein said he and Woodward "started from the bottom. We talked to secretaries, clerks, chauffeurs, administrative assistants, and gradually worked our way up. He said part of the post-Watergate myth is the idea that investigative reporting is a "highly refined, pseudoscience, different and apart from the rest of journalism. I'm not sure I agree," he said.

Bernstein suggested we get away from the term *investigative reporting* and, perhaps, use the term *saturation reporting,* which he described as a "commitment of resources that would enable us to gather every fact, conduct hundreds of interviews if necessary, and really learn our subject before we jump into print or go on the air."[4]

Eugene Roberts, the editor of the *Philadelphia Inquirer,* said, "We don't use the term 'investigative reporter' very often on the *Inquirer*. Not because we don't believe in it or practice it . . . we do . . . but we also find the term misleads and confuses. To many people it means catching a crook . . . ferreting out a wrongdoer . . . and this I think is too narrow a definition. At the *Inquirer*," he said, "investigative reporting means freeing a reporter from normal constraints of time and space, and letting the reporter really inform the public about a situation of vital importance. It means coming to grips with a society far too complex to be covered merely with features or the old inverted pyramid wire service sort of story."[5]

Changing the System

Journalists generally agree that a truly investigative story should attempt to bring about some sort of change, perhaps the rewriting of a law or the firing of a state, local, or federal official. Again, the Woodward and Bernstein series of reports on Watergate is an excellent example because the series led to the downfall of President Nixon and to the jailing of many of his associates. It also should be noted that one of the important considerations in the selection of Pulitzer Prizes for reporting is the "change" that is produced as a result of the stories.

Unfortunately, most investigative reports are conducted by newspapers. As mentioned earlier in this book, one of the major criticisms of broadcast news is that it has failed to come to grips with in-depth reporting. The excuse is always the same: the cost is too great.

An encouraging sign is that a number of innovative TV station managers have hired reporters and assigned them to produce only investigative stories. Some ambitious TV stations have "investigative teams" that are required to produce as few as six stories a year. Unfortunately, such operations are few and restricted mostly to the largest markets.

At the network level, CBS's "60 Minutes" and ABC's "20–20" have come closest to the traditional concept of investigative reporting.

Techniques of Investigative Reporting

Bob Greene, the assistant managing editor at *Newsday*, said that you do not become an investigative reporter until you have established an "absolutely solid, confident, sound ability as a general assignment reporter." [6]

Greene founded *Newsday's* permanent investigative team that has won two Pulitzer Prizes. He said that some people may have "a natural instinct for investigation, but without real strong, heavy grounding in basic reporting they run into problems, usually with sources and judgment." [7]

Greene said that a great many investigative reports begin with a tip but that should be just the start. "The tip must be documented and that is the role of the investigative reporter: to use documents, records, personal interviews, and second and third sources to substantiate the information," Greene said.

Reliable Sources

It also is important that sources be reliable and that the reporter knows the identity of all sources, even if those identities are to be kept secret. Editors and news directors should, at some point in the development of investigative stories, be convinced of the reliability of the sources used by the reporter.

The *Washington Post* was reminded, unfortunately too late, of the importance of checking reporter sources in the unfortunate story, "Jimmy's World." The reporter of that story, Janet Cooke, was forced to resign, and the newspaper had to return a Pulitzer Prize. The embarrassment occurred after it was disclosed that a story about a black child addicted to heroin was not true. Cooke admitted that there really was no Jimmy but claimed that he was a composite character. When her story was published, it shocked the nation's capital. In spite of good writing, it was a lie and an embarrassment to the newspaper and the entire journalism profession. All this occurred because Cooke told her editors that it was necessary to protect the anonymity of her sources. They did not question her account.

Writing about the "Jimmy's World" incident in the Investigative Reporters and Editors *Journal*, the distinguished investigative reporter Clark Mollenhoff said that the story never should have got by the editors.

Mollenhoff, now a professor at Washington and Lee University, said, "Many editors would properly balk at publishing such a story even from an experienced and tested reporter, unless the material from the anonymous source is only one aspect of a story that otherwise could be documented and attributed to specific, credible sources."

Mollenhoff said, "It is well to remember that one good, solid source, a direct witness with no ax to grind (and a record of high credibility) is better than two, three, four or five sources who are relating second or thirdhand hearsay.

"All effective investigative reporters rely, to some degree, upon confidential sources who must remain anonymous for varying times, depending upon the nature of the threat to the source's life or livelihood," said Mollenhoff. "However, every really experienced investigative reporter knows that few informants are totally reliable, even though they may believe they are telling the reporter the full truth."

Mollenhoff said the "only real protection a reporter can give a good informant is to avoid mentioning his existence in a story in which every paragraph is fully supported by documents, independent witnesses, or both. In such cases," Mollenhoff pointed out, "the information taken from the confidential source is used only as a lead to public records, other documents, and direct witnesses that can be quoted to establish the soundness of the informant's allegations."[8]

Soon after the Cooke incident, many news organizations revised their standards, expressly requiring reporters to inform at least one news executive of the true identity of any anonymous source.

Woodward and Bernstein said they required two independent sources before reporting a controversial disclosure as fact.

Although it is essential for an editor or a news director to be aware of the identity of sources before a story is broadcast, that source should not be disclosed widely within your own news organization. If several people know the identity of a sensitive source, the odds increase greatly that someone may inadvertently disclose the source to someone outside the organization. Depending on circumstances, the source may suffer, the reporter's effectiveness may be compromised, and the source may refuse to cooperate further.

Confidentiality of Sources

Bob Greene said he never makes a promise to a source that he cannot keep. If you know that you will be unable to keep a source confidential, then you should never promise to do so, Greene said. If you agree to keep a source confidential, Greene said; "that's a contract as far as I'm concerned, and I won't violate it."

Greene said he would never offer confidentiality to someone involved in a crime. He said if someone offers such information on the basis of confidentiality, he would not write the story. But Greene said he would warn the person that he would "try to catch him in the act."

Greene also takes issue with reporters who insist on withholding from authorities information they may have about an illegal act. "If it's a law enforcement agency, I'll cooperate with it if I have information that will help it to solve a crime," he said.

Many investigative reporters disagree with that, saying it is their job to report about crime and criminals, and cooperating with law enforcement officials could reduce the reporter's effectiveness.

Greene contends that if a reporter goes into court knowing who a criminal is but says he is not going to share that information, then the public will not be supportive. He cited as an example a TV station refusing to surrender film or videotape of rioters who were looting a store. "When the pictures were taken, there was no contract made for confidentiality," Greene stressed, "so there is no reason not to give those pictures to police if they ask for them."

Greene said that when he talks to journalism classes about confidentiality, he conducts a little experiment to get their views on the subject. He first asks the students if they would keep their sources confidential under any circumstances. Almost without exception all say they would. Then, Greene said, "I give them this example. I say suppose that an hour before a man is scheduled to die in the gas chamber a man comes into your office and says to you 'you must call the governor because John Smith did not commit the murder. I know who did.' But, Greene said, "the man then demands that you keep his identity confidential, and you agree. Then, the man tells you that he committed the murder."

Greene then explains to the class, "There is no way that the governor is going to stop the execution unless you give him the name of the person who confessed to you." Greene asks the students how many would now agree to keep the man's identity confidential? Greene said that this time almost all the students say they would reveal the source, rather than let an innocent man die. "And, of course, that's right," Greene added.[9]

Developing Sources

Developing sources and knowing where to find information are probably the most important skills an investigative reporter must learn. How do you get started? Ask other investigative reporters how they operate. Find out how they look up records. Ask them about the people at city hall who are likely to talk to you. Find out which policemen are considered the "most honest." In other words, "pick the brains" of your colleagues. Investigative reporters are eager to encourage beginners. They also enjoy talking about their conquests and are willing to share information about their methods, except with a competing newspaper or TV station.

Greene said investigative reporters must spend a lot of time on the job and off developing sources. He suggested, for example, if you do any social drinking that "it makes more sense to do it where the politicians or cops hang out rather than where other reporters go." And, Greene said that stopping off for a cup of coffee in the morning where city employees have breakfast also is a good idea. "They get to know you in a relaxed atmosphere," Greene said, "and you may discover which ones like to talk."

Greene also said he remembers his sources at Christmas time. Not with gifts, but with Christmas cards. He said he sends out a card to about a thousand sources each year. "Some I have not used or spoken to for years," Greene said, "But it's good to keep in contact because I never know when I will need them again."

James R. Dubro, of CBC–TV in Canada, who produced a successful investigative report on organized crime, called "Connections," said 90 percent of the material for the report came from open sources and information already made public.

Writing in the IRE *Journal*,[10] Dubro said "Connections" was a "result of scholarly research." He said he spent months in libraries reading the literature on organized crime and checking out the sources for information listed in the footnotes and bibliographies. After that, Dubro said, "you have a pretty clear idea who the authorities are and what evidence they have to support what they are saying. Before long," wrote Dubro, "you find yourself dealing with the same basic, raw data used by the authorities you have been reading." Dubro said this process also leads you to some excellent prospects for interviews.

Interviewing followed this research. Dubro advised that in dealing with sources you will be more effective if they have a motive for cooperating: revenge against an enemy, ego gratification, or the glamour of television. He said it is sometimes useful to pretend that you already have the needed information from other sources and only need confirmation. "Sometimes, playing dumb works wonders," according to Dubro. You ask the source to explain everything to you "because you are so naive and ill-informed."

Dubro acknowledged that in TV the problem is finding interview subjects willing to be filmed or taped. And he said it is often a "long and arduous process that requires patience and persistence."

John Spain, news director of WBRZ–TV in Baton Rouge, Louisiana, told a Radio, Television News Directors Association RTNDA convention that about 50 percent of the investigative stories his station works on are "paper stories"—those that are on the public record someplace. "All you have to do," he said, "is turn them over."

Spain cited an example of a crooked sheriff who left a "paper trail." The sheriff had misappropriated money that was supposed to be used for prisoners' food and for youth activities. Instead, Spain said, the sheriff used the money to build a camp for himself and for a tractor and boats. But Spain said the sheriff "stupidly bought all the stuff with public purchase orders. All we had to do was photocopy the papers and he was indicted."

Spain said his investigation of the sheriff was the result of a tip. An out-of-state motorist, picked up by a deputy sheriff, called Spain after the officer refused to accept his credit card's bond service. The deputy said that only one bonding company was acceptable. The motorist thought this was rather strange and alerted Spain who also thought it was unusual and did some investigating. Spain discovered that the bonding company was owned by the sheriff under another name.

After Spain did a TV story on the subject, he received a call from an honest deputy who told him he had more information about the sheriff's illegal activities. Spain said he met the man in another part of the state. "He would have been fired . . . or worse . . . if the sheriff knew he was talking to us," Spain said. "The deputy told us about the misuse of funds . . . and the camp and the tractor . . . and told us there were records to prove it all."

The sheriff refused to turn over the records, so Spain went into court to obtain access to them. Spain broadcast a number of stories about the sheriff, using footage shot from the back of an unmarked van equipped with one-way glass. "We even got some footage of the sheriff riding the tractor. We also got pictures of prisoners working on property owned by the sheriff and one of his deputies."

Spain said the honest deputy sheriff has continued to be a good source and calls him from time to time with other tips. He said that most of the investigative stories done by WBRZ–TV are the result of tips from unhappy and disgruntled civil servants. Spain develops other stories by reading about what is happening elsewhere. "You ask yourself if that could be happening here, and it often is," he said. Spain also gets ideas from talking with investigative reporters in other cities.

Spain's station is in the 94th market. It proves that with the support and encouragement of management, investigative reporting does not have to be limited to the big city news operations. Spain's investigative team includes one reporter, himself, and a "good attorney." He said he tries to do six stories a year.[11]

Adapting Visuals

Lea Thompson, an investigative and consumer reporter for the NBC-owned WRC–TV in Washington, D.C. told a RTNDA convention that many TV stations avoid investigative reporting because they think the reports take too much time and tend to be boring.[12] But she said they need be neither time consuming nor dull. With the new special visual effects equipment, even a series of still pictures can be effective, she pointed out.

Thompson said WRC has used an artist on some investigative stories in situations where cameras could not be used. The artist records observations on a sketch pad as soon as she leaves the story scene. Thompson said a recording from a hidden microphone with such sketches works well. She noted that the FCC has some restrictions on wireless transmissions and that she gets around that by attaching a tiny tape recorder to her body. Thompson also pointed out that state laws on eavesdropping and privacy vary greatly. "It's legal to use a hidden microphone in the District of Columbia and in Virginia," she said, "but you can't use it in Maryland. So sometimes . . . we may go to Virginia because we know that it will be a better story."

If Your Visuals Are Weak

Peter Karl of WLS–TV in Chicago insists that even if you do not have the best kind of visuals for an investigative piece you should still go with the story. He recalled that while working for a TV station in Flint, Michigan, he found out that the police department had records dealing with the personal lives of many people in the city.

Karl did a story on the subject but because he did not have any good visuals the story got buried late in the newscast. "About six weeks later, *Penthouse* magazine did a big article on the story," Karl told the same RTNDA convention.

John Camp, who headed an investigative team at WCVB–TV in Boston and now works with Spain in Baton Rouge, agrees that the substance of the story "should be the overriding consideration, and the visuals should be adapted to the story."

Camp told news directors at the same convention, I ask myself, "am I a television reporter trying to write investigative reports or am I an investigative reporter trying to use TV as a medium?' " Camp said if he is an investigative reporter, "I feel that I have to adapt the visuals to the reports."

Camp said investigative reporters have to use all the resources available, such as effective graphics, documents, talking heads, and location shots to "make a report move." But, he added, that if he has an important investigative story that is not great pictorially, he owes it to the station and himself to tell the story as well as he can, not ignore it.

Ethics of Investigative Reporting

To what lengths should an investigative reporter go to get a story? Some will tell you to go as far as you must, and that the end justifies the means. If it is for the good of the public, they maintain, anything goes if you are trying to uncover corruption. Some reporters argue that it is even permissible for reporters to break the law if that is the only way to get the story.

A large number of investigative reporters are opposed to an "anything goes" attitude. They say such tactics give all reporters a black eye at a time when the profession is under increasing scrutiny and court restraints.

How far should an investigative reporter go to uncover bribes, kickbacks, illegal land transctions, and the like? Peter Karl speaks of a "Chicago style of journalism" that some people say is not ethical. "We lie, we take hidden pictures, we hide in corners and go under cover . . . and we do a lot of other things. But," Karl said, "in Chicago that's the only way you are going to get anything." [13]

Lea Thompson of WRC-TV said she sometimes misrepresents the kind of story she is trying to do—and even her identity—but she added, "we do not break laws." Lea acknowledged that some other tactics raise serious questions. "For example," she asked, "should you use a computer to get somebody's financial records, should you set up phony companies, and should you show how to break into a car or how to make money in computer fraud?"

Thompson said that when she and other investigative reporters at WRC–TV misrepresent themselves while they are doing a story, they always "confess" that they did so when they broadcast the report.

Former *New York Post* Managing Editor John Van Doorn said he would rather have his "reporters miss a story—from a high crime to a misdemeanor—than misrepresent themselves." He said, "It dirties up our business." [14]

New York Times investigative reporter Seymour Hersh agrees. He said, "misrepresentation is wrong and dishonest—particularly now when it's clear to everyone that we're less than perfect." [15]

The syndicated columnist and investigative reporter Jack Anderson said he disagrees with those who would steal, cheat, break the law, and do whatever else is necessary to get a story. He also expressed concern that such tactics would make life more difficult for reporters because people are not too fond of reporters to begin with.

Anderson also expressed concern over what he described as "too many of our young reporters who are eager to become Woodward and Bernsteins overnight." [16] Anderson said these young reporters look upon investigative reporting as a "romantic expressway to fame and fortune" and said this often results in bad stories. Anderson said they "puff it up with air and they play it up when they ought to play it down."

Anderson said that when new reporters join his staff he tells them "to look at the facts as they are. Not as you hope they are. Not as you think they are. Not as you wish they are. Not even as someone tells you they are."

Anderson also had this warning. "Most of the stories I've worked on have fallen flat. After you've invested several weeks in a story, it's a hard thing to lay it down. But," Anderson said, "if the story isn't true, if you have been going up a dead end, drop it." He said, "When we publish a story, at least we believe it. And, if we don't believe it, we don't write it."

The People's Right to Know

Anderson's insistence on fairness is shared by most investigative reporters. But many say that in such a complex society, unless you "bend the rules" somewhat, you may never get the facts that the people have a right to know. Almost without exception investigative reporters seem to have no problem with going "undercover."

One of the most controversial and successful examples of undercover investigative reporting was the "Mirage" series by reporters at the *Chicago Sun-Times*. To expose municipal corruption *Sun-Times* reporters, in conjunction with the Better Government Association, opened a bar, which they called, appropriately, the "Mirage." The investigative team pretended to be operating the bar while photographers with hidden cameras snapped pictures of various inspectors soliciting bribes from the reporters. The series produced the desired results. City investigations followed, and many journalists believed that a Pulitzer Prize would go to the *Sun-Times*. But not so. According to the *Columbia Journalism Review,* part of the reason the Pulitzer went elsewhere was the feeling on the part of some members of the Pulitzer committee that the investigative team's "deception" went too far. [17]

Faking an Accident

Earlier, we mentioned that Peter Karl, an investigative reporter for WLS–TV in Chicago, admitted that deception poses no problems for his station if it is necessary to bring out the truth. Karl described how, in one investigative report, "faking" an accident helped his investigative team nail an ambulance chaser and uncover an insurance racket. The subject of the investigation was Paul Skidmore, who made a lucrative living convincing accident victims that he could get them extra insurance claim awards.

With the help of the Chicago police and Allstate Insurance Company, Karl's investigative reporter team, in cooperation with the *Sun-Times,* arranged an "accident" on a vacant lot. Skidmore was alerted to the "accident" and made contact with the supposed victims, who really were reporters from WLS–TV and the *Sun-Times*.

Skidmore did not know the investigative team had acquired an apartment that had been bugged with hidden microphones and cameras. A rendezvous was arranged in the apartment, and the ambulance chaser fell into the trap.

The cameras and microphones recorded Skidmore explaining how the "victims" should fake pain when they were examined by "his" doctors. The doctors, he said, would report to their insurance companies that the injuries were serious. Skidmore assured them that the settlements would be much larger than they could normally expect.

WLS–TV and the *Sun-Times* purchased the cars that were used in the faked accident. They also bought insurance policies and paid thousands of dollars in medical bills to illustrate how the insurance scam worked. The reporters were treated at eight hospitals for their imaginary injuries.

"Not including manpower," Karl said, "the investigative series cost WLS–TV and the *Sun-Times* around $38,000." More than 400 videotapes were shot during the story, which took eight months to complete. On the day the story broke the State Attorney's office and other groups launched an investigation.

Karl warns that if you are going to "pull a stunt" like this, you must be aware of the law. "Don't be afraid of the law," Karl said, "but journalists must make sure that they do not give the courts precedent cases that affect what we do as journalists."[18]

Karl says WLS–TV has counsel who constantly check to make sure that the investigative team does not violate the law.

Soul-Searching by "60 Minutes"

After 13 years of "dishing it out," as the CBS announcer phrased it, "60 Minutes" decided in the fall of 1981 to begin its fourteenth year on the air by examining its investigative techniques. Industry and newspaper representatives and TV critic Jeff Greenfield joined "60 Minutes" correspondent Mike Wallace and Executive Producer Don Hewitt on a special soul-searching edition of "60 Minutes."

It was not because Hewitt and the program's other producers and correspondents believed any of their techniques were improper that they decided to invite criticism. "It was because we realized that we have an excessive amount of influence in this country," said Hewitt. "Because of our popularity, we have become a topic of conversation at the dinner table."

Despite the disclaimer, the "60 Minutes" debate about its investigative techniques followed the embarrassing Janet Cooke incident and a well-publicized debate on investigative methods between the CBS-owned-and-operated Chicago station WBBM–TV and "20–20," the ABC counterpart of "60 Minutes." The CBS station had accused "20–20" of using some

CBS News correspondent Mike Wallace. (CBS News photo)

questionable techniques in producing its award-winning report, "Arson and Profit." The producers of "20–20," in turn, claimed that WBBM–TV was guilty of many of the same charges it had made against ABC.

Correspondent Mike Wallace began the program with a review of some of the controversial techniques employed not only by "60 Minutes" reporters but also by most investigative reporters. He acknowledged that these techniques have "raised some serious questions" about investigative reporting: Should reporters go undercover? Should they use anonymous sources? Should they confront the object of an inquiry with surprise witnesses and surprise documents?

And, Wallace asked, should reporters withhold vital information from a prospective interviewee; pose as someone other than a reporter to get a story; set up an enterprise—a sting operation, in effect—to lure unsuspecting subjects before the cameras; and infiltrate a factory or labor union to find out what is really going on inside? Is all of this fair, proper, right? asked Wallace.

Misrepresentation

Newsday's Bob Greene said he had no problems with a "60 Minutes" researcher who assumed the identity of a child who had been dead almost 20 years in order to demonstrate how easy it was to obtain a passport and other official documents.

But Ellen Goodman, a syndicated columnist for the *Boston Globe*, wondered if there was no other way to pursue the story. Was it done this way, she suggested, because it was the "best way to present it dramatically" on television?

The editor of the *St. Petersburg Times*, Eugene Patterson, argued that the story could have been covered without misrepresentation. He said the passport office probably had lots of cases that "60 Minutes" could have followed up, but, agreeing with Goodman, he said that would not have been as dramatic. Patterson said he was concerned about the theatrical element in TV reporting and feared that "misrepresenting one's self, misleading, camouflaging one's identity will become a way of life."

Infiltration

What about planting a producer and camera crew inside an allegedly phony cancer clinic to find out what really was going on inside? "60 Minutes" did just that. Was it right? Critic Jeff Greenfield pointed out that this was deception on an "ambitious scale" but he wondered if there really was any other way to "conclusively demonstrate" that the clinic was endangering the health of people who went there without putting someone through that clinic. Obviously, Greenfield said, if a CBS reporter identified himself, he would not find out how they treated patients.

Patterson's response: "Good story, great television, awful journalism." He suggested the way the story should have been done was to find and interview people who had been victimized by the clinic.

Hewitt said "60 Minutes" did do that. But, he said, that would not have satisfied television viewers. He said interviews are sufficient to convince newspaper readers, but television viewers "to be convinced want as much documentation as you can give them. This was the only way we could document that what we were told (by our sources) was in fact true and the only way we could convince viewers that it was in fact true."

Patterson charged that this approach had an element of entrapment, but Hewitt denied this. He said what happened inside that clinic would have happened regardless of whether CBS people did or did not show up.

Patterson said the Janet Cooke fiasco proved there is a "point of diminishing returns in theatrical journalism." He said the print media learned this the hard way when the Janet Cooke story "blew up in the face of the *Washington Post*. It was a phony story that read good," Patterson said, "but it wasn't true."

Hewitt objected that there was no comparison between the Janet Cooke story and the reports broadcast by "60 Minutes." He noted that Janet Cooke had "concocted" a story. "Nobody has concocted a fictitious story on '60 Minutes,' " Hewitt stressed. "You may object to the way we told the story, but nobody did anything dishonest," Hewitt added.

Impersonation

The impersonation technique concerns many journalists. Mike Wallace recalled how "60 Minutes" carried out a sting operation in Chicago to expose allegedly fraudulent and expensive Medicaid practices that involved kickbacks from laboratories. Renting an empty storefront, "60 Minutes" set up its own bogus clinic, staffed not by doctors but by members of Chicago's Better Government Association. It set up a one-way mirror in the store to film the illegal kickbacks. And it worked. But was it proper? Was it good journalism?

Jeff Greenfield viewed it as "very close to pure entrapment. There is nothing that that medical clinic was doing but trying to entice people in to prove kickbacks," he said.

Hewitt responded that it all comes down to a simple proposition: "Does the end justify the means? We are in the business of providing our viewers with documentary evidence of wrongdoing, misdeeds, and we can do it better this way than if Mike Wallace gets on camera and says 'Let me tell you what happened to me last week in Chicago'."

Bob Greene said he is "constantly troubled by the loose use of the word *entrapment*." He said the TV cameras set up by "60 Minutes" in the Chicago clinic "did not show anybody doing anything that they wouldn't be disposed to do." As for the one-way mirror, Greene said he did not see why it was any different or less fair than a reporter listening through a door to a conversation and taking notes.

Wallace was asked how he would like it if he was on the receiving end with a camera suddenly pointed at him as he was asked embarrassing questions. The CBS News correspondent replied, "I would not like it." But he added quickly with a chuckle, "That's why I lead a life beyond reproach." The only reason "60 Minutes" began the Chicago investigation was because it had good reason to believe that the kickbacks in Medicaid were going on and were costing taxpayers millions of dollars. The one-way mirror and other techniques did sting some people who, it could be argued, deserved to be stung. Should investigative reporters be concerned about embarrassing those who break the law?

When Ellen Goodman asked Hewitt if he would do the Chicago clinic story the same way if he had it to do over again, he said, "I think that we have tempered and changed some of our techniques because I think what we felt we did with care is now . . . widespread, rampant, epidemic." Hewitt added, "I think we are taking a second look at a lot of this stuff."

The Ambush Interview

Some of this "stuff" includes the "ambush interview." Criticism was unanimous on the "60 Minutes" debate about the practice of confronting interview subjects by surprise at their homes or places of business. Familiar to all are TV reports that show a reporter chasing a subject down the street, shoving a microphone through a car window. In one such incident, the subject rolled up the window of his car, trapping the mike inside as the delighted reporter ran beside the moving vehicle. The reporter obviously was enjoying this "dramatic" confrontation. So was his producer as he watched the report on the 6 o'clock news that evening. Some producers and news directors encourage such behavior because they believe viewers like it. The theory is that it shows the audience that reporters are really doing their job aggressively. Others find such interviews repulsive.

CBS's Don Hewitt said that the "ambush interview probably has been abused and that reporters probably should not try to get people to talk who obviously don't want to talk." But Hewitt stressed that "60 Minutes" reporters never "walked up to anyone" while the camera was shooting without trying for weeks or months to reach the person by letter or telephone.

Bob Greene said the "ambush interview" uses a medium to "distort something out of proportion."

The Trap Interview

Is it proper to trick an unsuspecting subject into an interview in order to create a confrontation? Dan Rather employed the technique to get an interview with a man who allegedly used a counterfeit grading stamp to cheat customers at a California meat packing plant. "60 Minutes" already had evidence the man was engaged in the practice when it arranged to interview him inside a meat storage locker. The unsuspecting man granted the interview because he thought Rather wanted to learn more about the meat grading procedure. As the camera moved in for a close-up, Rather showed the man the counterfeit stamp and said there was reason to believe it belonged to him and that he had used it to misgrade meat.

Critic Jeff Greenfield said what bothered him about the scene was the way the man was shown squirming once the trap was sprung. He was "like a butterfly impaled on a pin," said Greenfield. "It seems to me," he said, "that that's good television at the expense of some sense of what you want to see on television, of how one ought to treat a subject."

Eugene Patterson agreed. He said it was a "cruel thing to do. You already have the guy cold, so what do you want?" asked Patterson. Greenfield charged that "60 Minutes" cornered the man in the meat locker because it needed pictures to make the program exciting and dramatic. Hewitt disputed that. He said it was just part of the documentation. Bob Greene defended "60 Minutes." He said the man could have stood his ground, denied he misgraded meat, and told Rather "if you go on television and say I did, I'll sue you." But, Greene noted, the man did not do that; he just walked away from Rather.

Withholding Information

The "60 Minutes" self-examination also took a look at the practice of withholding information from an investigation witness, even when a crime or wrongdoing is not involved. An example was a story "60 Minutes" broadcast on nuclear plant safety. The producers had been criticized in some quarters for not revealing before an interview with the head of the Nuclear Regulatory Commission that one of his employees was resigning over the issue of nuclear power plant safety.

Should you share any derogatory information you may have before confronting a witness? Eugene Patterson said it helps a reporter occasionally to take an interviewee by surprise.

Ellen Goodman agreed that a reporter should not put all the cards on the table. But Mobil Oil Vice-President Herbert Schmertz disagreed. He said surprising the NRC official put him at a severe disadvantage and "shortchanged the public" because it did not get as much information as it might have if "60 Minutes" had leveled with the official before the interview. Schmertz pointed out that there was in this case no charge of illegality or corruption, only a complex policy issue. And he said under such circumstances, "You will not get useful information to the public on those kinds of complex issues" by surprising the person with information that is not known to him.[19]

Revealing Your Purpose

Soon after the "60 Minutes" debate, we asked Hewitt about the ethics of a reporter misrepresenting the purpose of a story. Hewitt insisted that "60 Minutes" has never misrepresented its purpose. But officials at a Rochester, New York hospital complained that "60 Minutes" producers led them to believe they wanted to do a story that would be favorable to the hospital. Hewitt said it was the hospital's mistake for thinking that, adding, "We only do stories that tell the truth."

The truth in this case, according to "60 Minutes," was that surgeons at the hospital were allowing other doctors to replace them in the operating room without the knowledge of the patients. That's the story that "60 Minutes" was after from the start. "But all we told the hospital," admitted Hewitt, "was that we wanted to do a story about surgery." Was that fair? Hewitt said yes. "I don't think you have to divulge to anybody the broad outline of your story."

Hewitt defended his position with another example: "If you know a bank president is embezzling funds and you say to him 'I want to talk to you about your bank and your relationship to it,' you are under no obligation to say 'and I also want to talk to you about your embezzlement of money'."

The "60 Minutes" executive producer also noted that business and government often complain about investigative reporters' techniques because they want to present only one picture: what their public relations

Don Hewitt, Executive Producer of CBS News' "60 Minutes". (CBS News photo)

or advertising people say about them. "They don't want anyone to go beyond that," he added.

To support that point, Hewitt recalled a report that "60 Minutes" did about the making of the motion picture, "Tora, Tora, Tora." The film, produced by Twentieth-Century-Fox, was about the attack on Pearl Harbor, and "60 Minutes" had learned that the extras in the movie were sailors, provided free (at taxpayers' expense) to the filmmaker.

Producers of "60 Minutes" decided to do an investigative report but told Twentieth-Century-Fox only that it wanted to do a story about the making of the film. The company was delighted by the prospect for free publicity for the movie. But it was shocked and angered when the "60 Minutes" report was aired. Should Hewitt have revealed what he was up to? "Absolutely not," he said. "We told them we were going to do a story about the making of the movie. We were not obliged to tell them we were going to concentrate on the use of navy personnel at taxpayers' expense."

In the final analysis, Hewitt told us, investigative reporting comes down to the basic question: are you doing any violence to the truth by any of the techniques that you use? He said "60 Minutes" has never knowingly done this.

"The only criterion for any reporter," Hewitt concluded, "is to decide whether his story is a fair representation of what he's investigating. Everything else," he insisted, "is just nuance."

When asked if it is getting harder to do investigative reports because subjects are becoming "gun-shy" at the sight of a "60 Minutes" reporter or camera crew, Hewitt said, "No, but a lot of subjects have been exhausted after 13 years." He also said there is increased competition for subjects because other networks and local stations are doing more investigative reporting.

Finding the Records—The Paper Trail

Investigative reporters David Anderson and Peter Benjaminson wrote in their book *Investigative Reporting* that there are three kinds of records: "those the law entitles the public to see, those the law prohibits the public from seeing, and those not mentioned by the law. Good investigators," said the authors, "do not admit the existence of a category of records that they will never see." The only important distinctions among the three kinds of records, they wrote, "involve the method best suited to getting them and the relative difficulty in doing so." They noted, as an example, that income tax records are hard to get whereas property tax records are easily obtained.

Anderson and Benjaminson also said that gaining access to public records "is only part of the battle. Knowing what kinds of information are kept on record is even more important. Too often, they wrote, "reporters presume that because they have not previously heard of a record, it does not exist. Fortunately, ours is a society of paper shufflers; there is hardly a deal made, an action taken, or an official statement uttered that is not committed to paper and filed somewhere," they noted.[20]

Much of that paper work is conducted in government, at the federal, state, and local levels. It is shuffled about in the various departments, agencies, and courts in Washington, in the state capitols, and in the cities, towns, and county seats. And the great majority of these records are open to the public.

Let us look at the various repositories of public records and how to locate them.

The Courts

Information concerning pending trials can be obtained at the court's docket room. Those who staff the offices will help you find the following:

1. The names and addresses of the plaintiffs and defendants.
2. The names and addresses of the lawyers or legal firms representing both sides.

3. The nature of the charge (if the case is criminal) or the complaint if suit is brought by a private individual in a civil dispute.
4. The "prayer for relief," or what the complainant seeks in civil actions, particularly damage suits.
5. Exhibit lists in criminal cases. In both criminal and civil cases, the transcripts of trials are also available for inspection. The documents, of course, cannot be removed, but as long as you are willing to pay, you can get as many copies as you wish. This is true of most public records.

Special Courts

Investigative reporters also will find useful information in many of the special courts throughout the nation: probate courts that deal with wills, estates, and trusts; U.S. Tax Courts that handle Internal Revenue Service tax cases; the U.S. Court of Claims in which an individual or company can sue the government; divorce and bankruptcy courts; and some less familiar courts such as the U.S. Court of Military Appeals and the U.S. Court of Temporary Emergency appeals, which hears energy cases.

Government Publications

John Ullmann, executive director of Investigative Reporters and Editors (IRE), said a variety of government manuals, directories, and libraries can help an investigative reporter find the information he needs. He cited the following:

1. The *U.S. Government Manual.* Outlines the responsibilities and organization of the federal government.
2. The *Federal Regional Directory.* Helpful when you want to make Freedom of Information Act (FOI) requests. It shows additional federal government offices that are most likely to have the records held on local activities.
3. The *Code of Federal Regulations.* An annual compilation of the *Federal Register.* It contains an agency description of how laws and regulations are to be enforced and the mechanism for doing so.
4. The *Congressional Source Book* series (three volumes), produced by the Government Accounting Office (GAO.) It contains information about what the federal agencies do and what sort of information they collect. The series also includes performance audits of federal departments and regulatory agencies.
5. *Washington Information Directory.* Produced by the *Congressional Quarterly.* It provides additional nongovernment sources not listed in the Government Manual.
6. Government Depository Libraries. There are 1,300 of these throughout the nation, and 68 percent of them are located on college campuses. Most federal government publications and studies, may be found in these libraries, according to Ullmann. But he sug-

gested seeking the help of the government document librarian for specific information.

Among the useful documents in the depository libraries, Ulmann said, are the reports issued by the GAO. The congressional watchdog isues 1,110 reports a year. Its recommendations to Congress provide valuable story tips. Ullmann said, "I can't imagine starting on a problem without checking this library to see what government GAO investigators have found."

Ullmann noted that the congressional hearings also are in the government document sections of libraries. He said these hearings are especially useful because the experts who are called to testify "make excellent sources."

Ullmann also reminded reporters that library computers can be particularly helpful in locating information quickly. The computer also can give you access to bibliographies. Ullmann recalled that on one occasion he was able to locate in six minutes ten articles in newspapers and magazines on a particular subject he was researching. The articles, he said, also gave him the names of five experts on the subject.[21]

Checking on Business

Business organizations, both private and corporations, also leave paper trails. The corporations are easier to follow because more laws and regulations control and guide their business dealings. But an energetic reporter also can follow the trail left by partnerships and individual entrepreneurs.

Every state requires articles of incorporation if a company makes its headquarters in the state. The corporation must list the officers and directors of the firm. Corporations also are required to file papers in any state in which they are doing business. General Motors, for example, must register in California although its headquarters is in Detroit.

A license to do business also is required by city and county governments if the company operates within their boundaries. Individuals in business and partnerships file such papers.

Most county offices also maintain *Universal Commercial Code Indexes* which list the debts and obligations against companies.

Securities and Exchange Commission

Anytime a corporation makes a major change in its operations, it must file papers with the Securities and Exchange Commission (SEC), all available to the public. If control of a corporation changes hands or the company is forced into receivership or bankruptcy, such actions are recorded with the SEC. The same is true if a major law suit is filed against a corporation or if there is a change in the corporation's accounting firm.

A corporation also must inform the SEC if more than 5 percent of its stock is traded or if more than a million dollars of its stock is traded or sold. Every time a proxy statement is sent to stockholders seeking new funds or to acquire a new company, the SEC must be told. This is useful information to a reporter who is working on a story involving a major corporation.

Trade Publications

Hundreds of magazines and newspapers are devoted to business and industry news. They are often helpful sources of information about companies, especially smaller organizations that are not listed with the SEC. Many of these trade publications are the voices of industry associations and lobbies. The information they publish is often biased, but they still can be useful in finding out more about a firm and in leading a reporter to additional sources of information. Many other trade publications are completely independent of trade associations. Often their editors are willing to share information, both favorable and unfavorable, about a particular company.

Such respected business newspapers and magazines as the *Wall Street Journal, Forbes, Fortune,* and *Business Week* are an asset to any investigative reporter concentrating on the business world. The trade record books, such as *Standard and Poor's* and *Moody's,* also keeps track of officers and directors of corporations and other vital corporate information.

Land Deals

Much of the crime, corruption, and questionable business dealings that occur in this country involve land transactions. When they are exposed, it is frequently because an investigative reporter knew how to use the public records concerning real estate transactions. This can be challenging. Those determined to conceal their identity can complicate the paper trail by buying property in other people's names or by setting up what is known as a "blind trust."

Investigative reporter Jack Tobin, who has done numerous reports for *Sports Illustrated* and *Time Magazine,* related how he tried for a year to find out details concerning the purchase of property in San Clemente, California, by President Nixon.[22] It was known that Nixon had acquired the ranch, but Tobin could not find any records of the sale because he was looking for the Nixon name on the papers. Nixon had not acquired the property in his name. One day, Tobin was discussing his dilemma with a retired land recording official who advised Tobin to work backwards, using the location of the property to find out who owned it.

Using a land plat map, Tobin found the tiny street on which Nixon's ranch was located. He took that information to the assessor's office. But that office could not help without the exact identification of the parcel of land. Tobin obtained that information from the engineering office and returned to the assessor's office. There he found a tax bill, which, in turn, gave him a code number leading to the grantee-grantor file. Finally, that file told Tobin that the Title Insurance & Trust Company, acting as a blind trust, had acquired the property for persons unknown. When Tobin confronted a title company official about the purchase, he refused to discuss the matter. However, Tobin knew he had located the Nixon property in the records and had discovered how it was purchased.

Tobin said that almost every business has something hidden in a blind trust. It may be a hunting lodge or a playground in Palm Springs. But Tobin noted that such properties rarely are listed under the corporate name. The "reversing-to-a-blind trust" technique used by Tobin usually will produce results.

Of course, it is a lot easier when you know the identity of the person in whose name the property is recorded. The grantee-grantor files are listed alphabetically. Those records will tell you who is getting the tax bills. You also will be able to find out the date of the sale; the names of the buyer and seller; a description of the property; and an IRS tax stamp that will give you the approximate value of the property.

Freedom of Information Act

In 1967 Congress enacted the Freedom of Information (FOI) Act which opened to the public all but the most sensitive federal documents. Since then, all 50 states also have enacted "sunshine" laws that allow the public to examine and copy most records maintained by the state governments. But the laws vary from state to state. In some, the laws include local governments within the state and also require school boards and other municipal executive boards to hold all their meetings in public.

At the federal level, the FOI Act was amended in 1974 by Congress to require federal agencies to prove that a document should not be released to the public, either for national security or other valid reasons.

In recent years the FOI Act has been under increasing attack from government agencies and some members of Congress. Pressure to soften the act grew stronger when the Reagan Administration took office in 1981. The government has argued that the news media have not used the act to great advantage in the last decade. It also says the FOI Act is being used in ways not intended by Congress. The government claims, for example, that companies are reluctant to provide information about product development because other companies can file FOI requests to spy on their activities. The CIA and FBI complain that informants and undercover agents are more reluctant to share information because of fears of being uncovered through FOI requests.

Journalists dispute these claims, maintaining that without the FOI Act much crime and corruption would have gone unreported.

Let's examine the FOI Act in greater detail. As the law now stands, documents are to be open to the public except when the information concerns the following:

1. National security and foreign policy.
2. Advice and recommendations made within a federal agency or between federal agencies.
3. Unwarranted invasion of privacy.
4. Files dealing with criminal cases that are current or pending.

Obtaining the Information

You must first determine which branch of your state or local government has the information you are seeking. Most state FOI laws closely resemble the federal Act. If you are seeking information from a state authority, you must obtain a copy of that state's FOI law to determine the proper method for requesting information. Often, it will be necessary to file FOI requests with more than one agency.

Sometimes you will have to file a number of FOI requests for additional information. This is particularly true when the information you have received as a result of your first FOI request provides leads to additional information. FOI requests often produce a snowball effect.

An example is provided by one of the country's leading investigative reporters, Jack Taylor of the *Denver Post*. Before joining the *Post*, Taylor conducted numerous investigative reports for the *Daily Oklahoman*, and over a ten-year period he used the FOI Act 2,500 times. Taylor won a Pulitzer Prize nomination for his report on My Lai in which he filed 750 FOI requests. During an investigation of Indian affairs he made 850 FOI requests.

A copy of Taylor's original FOI request to the Bureau of Indian affairs is reprinted on the next page along with his suggestions for filing an FOI.

The Assault on the FOI Act

In 1981, the U.S. Department of Justice took steps that made it more difficult to obtain information from federal agencies. Until then, the Justice Department had instructed federal agencies to release information (even when they could justify noncompliance under FOI Act restrictions) unless they could show that release of the information would cause serious harm. But Attorney General William French Smith informed federal agencies to defend most challenges to an agency's decision to refuse access to its records under the FOI Act unless doing so would jeopardize another agency's ability to protect its files.

John Ullmann, the executive director of IRE, says the Justice Department's action was "only the first salvo designed to weaken the act." He predicted that pressure on Congress to water down the Act will increase.[23]

Eugene Roberts, executive editor of the *Philadelphia Inquirer*, which

THE OKLAHOMA PUBLISHING COMPANY
THE DAILY OKLAHOMAN·OKLAHOMA CITY TIMES
OKLAHOMA CITY, OKLAHOMA 73125

28 September 1979

Mr. Walter R. Mills
Superintendent
Colorado River Agency
Bureau of Indian Affairs
U.S. Department of the Interior
Parker, Arizona 85344

re: FREEDOM of INFORMATION ACT REQUEST

Dear Sir:

Your attention is invited to the Freedom of Information Act [5
U.S.C. 552], as amended, and to implementing Department of the
Interior and Bureau of Indian Affairs instructions and regula-
tions.

Under provisions of the above cited authority, request that we
be provided with copies of the following documents. We are willing to provide reimbursement for reproduction costs, but request
waiver of all fees, under provisions of 43 CFR 2.19(c)(3)(f),
since release of the information would be in the public interest.

1.   SUMMARY of TRUST FUNDS monthly report most recently filed
with your office for each of the tribes under your jurisdiction.

2.   DETAIL of TRUST FUNDS monthly report most recently filed
with your office for each of the tribes under your jurisdiction.

3.   TRUST FUNDS INVESTMENTS report most recently filed with
your office for each of the tribes under your jurisdiction.

Sincerely,

JACK H. TAYLOR JR.
Special Assignments/
  Investigations

Although it is not necessary, it is nevertheless a good idea to label both your letter and the envelope as a Freedom of Information Act Request. In many cases this facilitates and expedites handling of your request.

Although it is not necessary to cite both the Freedom of Information Act and the agency's implementing regulations, it is useful to call attention to the agency recipient that you may be familiar with them. It is also a good idea to review the agency's own regulations before filing a request. Copies of the regulations are usually available from the agency or are readily accessible in the Federal Register in most libraries.

Some agencies have been known to use excessive fees in an effort to thwart Freedom of Information Act requests. A requester should be aware that the law does not permit charging fees for the time it takes to process a Freedom of Information Act request, or deliberate over whether or not to make the requested documents available. Fees can be legitimately assessed for the time it takes to locate the requested documents and for reproduction costs. Most agencies, however, have provisions written into their implementing regulations authorizing waiver of fees in cases where the release of the information is in the public interest or is made to the news media.

It is a good idea to indicate in your initial request a willingness to pay repro-duction costs. That can serve to avoid unnecessary correspondence—and the resulting delay in obtaining the information—at the outset, since many agen-cies will automatically write for an indication or such a willingness to pay fees. You can include a ceiling amount, such as $25, to insure that you don't get trapped into an obligation for fees that may be more than you would ordinarily be willing (or able) to pay. Although reproduction costs are seldom that much, short of obtaining several thousand pages of documents, search fees can mount quickly. Note that a willingness to pay search fees has not been expressed. That was a deliberate omission designed to avoid being backed into a corner. While reasonable search fees should not be resisted when they have been in-cluded with reproduction costs, the wording in this expression of willingness gives the requester a fall-back position to resist exorbitant search fees by arguing that the requester never agreed to pay search fees to begin with.

It is always a good idea to be as specific as you can in describing the documents you want. That serves several purposes. It can direct an agency official more quickly to the proper file, thus easing the pain of any resulting search fees. It can head off at the outset any temptation on the part of a reluctant bureaucrat to avoid responding by claiming you weren't specific enough. It can get you the information more quickly. In the sample letter, these are the exact names of the documents. The entities to which these documents pertain are easily identified by the addressee, though it may be expeditious to list them separately when more than one entity is involved. In this case the entities are the Chemehuevi, Colorado River, Fort Mojave, Cocopah and Quechan Indian Tribes.

has won six Pulitzer Prizes for reporting under his leadership, said he is "disquieted and alarmed" by such attacks on the FOI Act. He said the act was not strong enough originally and that government agencies have been violating its provisions for years. He noted that it often takes reporters three to four months to get routine information from federal agencies although the act says it should be provided within ten working days.

Roberts also recalled that the Library of Congress compiled 276 news stories that might not have been disclosed without FOI requests. Without a strong FOI Act, he said, "some of the most important reporting efforts would not have been possible."[24]

Roberts posed this question: "Do we really want government so airtight or leakproof that the only information that gets to us passes through a narrow funnel and is stamped with an administration seal of approval as right and fit for public consumption?"

Privacy Act of 1974

One of the exemptions to the Freedom of Information Act, mentioned earlier, is unwarranted invasion of privacy. In 1974, Congress passed a Privacy Act in an effort to prevent the government from improperly using or disclosing information from its files about individuals. An obvious conflict exists between the FOI Act and the Privacy Act. Some journalists complain that the government has used the Privacy Act unnecessarily in an effort to withhold information from the public. Most journalists, however, agree that there are times when an individual's privacy should be protected.

In considering a person's privacy, ask yourself these questions:

1. Am I intruding on a person's seclusion, solitude, or private affairs without good cause?
2. Am I disclosing embarrassing private facts about a person needlessly without advancing or improving my report?
3. Am I broadcasting information that places a person in a false light in the public eye?

Good reporters would not deliberately do any of these. Doing so could be both embarrassing and costly to a news organization.

The Risks of Investigative Reporting

Most investigative reporters say they think about the possibilities of physical injury but do not dwell on the subject. The tragic assassination in 1976 of Don Bolles, an investigative reporter for the *Arizona Republic,* made it plain that risks do exist.

Professor Clark Mollenhoff of Washington and Lee University writes that until Bolles' death "for years we had proceeded about our business ignoring threats to our lives and our job, more or less assuming that the bosses of organized crime and politics would 'be too smart' to kill a reporter or editor and stir up the whole communnity."[25]

Lea Thompson of WRC–TV said there have been threats on her life, and John Spain of WBRZ–TV said he was threatened by the sheriff and deputies he was investigating in Louisiana. But Thompson said if reporters worry about the threats to their lives, "their objectivity ceases."[26]

Fortunately, most threats made against investigative reporters are just that, threats. Investigative reporting for the most part carries little risk. The danger is far greater in covering a war, rebellion, or a riot.

IRE

The Investigative Reporters and Editors, Inc., (IRE) is a dedicated organization and the *IRE Journal* should be read regularly by all journalists.

In addition to annual meetings, IRE organizes frequent seminars throughout the year, many in cooperation with the Radio and Television News Directors Association, Sigma Delta Chi, and other professional societies. The nation's top investigative reporters share their expertise at such meetings. Students serious about becoming investigative reporters should attend as many seminars as possible.

IRE also maintains at the University of Missouri an elaborate resources center, which houses more than 6,000 newspaper stories and television transcripts that are available for a small duplicating cost. The organization also maintains a directory of all IRE members along with the types of investigative reports they have conducted during their careers. If you are working on a story about illegal drug traffic, for example, the IRE directory would tell you which IRE members have worked on such stories in the past.

24

Looking Ahead and Summing Up

This is the most exciting period in the history of broadcast news. Never before have the opportunities been greater for young people entering the profession. Broadcast news grew at a slow pace during the 1960s and 1970s, as mentioned previously, and then found new vitality in 1980 when the Cable News Network made its debut. The influence of CNN on television news has been significant for many reasons. It proved for the first time that there was a market for more than 30 minutes of national news. CNN turned skeptics into believers. In 1980, few believed that CNN would "make it." But within two years, other organizations—ABC and Westinghouse—announced plans to launch round-the-clock news services, and CBS, NBC, and ABC greatly expanded their news. A CBS news executive admitted that none of this would have happened if CNN had not entered the picture. In 1981, CNN launched a second news service.

These exciting developments mean more opportunities than ever before for broadcast journalists. Hundreds of new jobs already have been created at the network level since 1980. The creation of those jobs (and quite possibly hundreds more) means that people will be "moving up." It usually takes many years to reach the major markets and the networks.

Master control at Cable News Network (CNN) headquarters in Atlanta. (Photo courtesy of CNN)

But when there is a great demand for additional personnel in those larger markets, news managers look to the smaller stations for help.

This period in broadcast news also is exciting because of the changing technology. When today's established veterans began their careers, film was the backbone of every news operation. The potential of videotape and microwave was not realized until the mid-1970s and, as remarkable as it now seems, film was still the predominant force in broadcast news at most local TV stations until 1980 when the price of silver skyrocketed. That was a good year for ENG salesmen, and the variety of new hardware that has appeared in newsrooms around the nation since then has been bountiful. Keeping up with the new technology has become a challenge in itself. The explosion in technology experienced in the past few years will continue.

Television news gathering equipment of the future promises to be smaller, lighter, and probably cheaper as demand and production increase. In the not distant future, an electronic component called a charge coupled device (CCD) seems destined to replace conventional tubes used to electronically sense an image and convert it into a signal. A one-inch size CCD will do the work of a flashlight-size plumbicon tube. Quality should be even better than at present. It should be possible to shoot usable pictures with available light more often than is now the case.

The one-piece camera-recorder will, of course, make one-man crews more common than at present, at least at the local station level. This development is welcome because there are too few crews to cover all the

Sony Betacam camera has a built-in videotape recorder. (Sony photo)

stories at hand. There are now more reporters than crews at both local stations and networks. When the ratio of television reporters to crews becomes more nearly equal, it should become more common for television news operations to find original stories more frequently.

Television news may become less dependent upon the spadework of newspapers and also less imitative. Newspapers will likely continue to lose readership and television will be an even more important news source for the public.

Television news greatly benefited from the introduction of relatively small, mobile microwave units in the late 1970s. Mobile satellite ground stations were available by the 1970s but were much larger and more difficult to move than the microwave truck.

Many foresee a portable satellite ground station in a couple of suitcases, something shippable on a scheduled airline, that a network could use to originate audio and video from anywhere in the world. The gear could provide coordination circuits to network headquarters, as well as broadcast channels and even a facsimile or data link for transmitting scripts, rundowns, and so forth.

Those on the technical side of broadcast news have even more ambitious dreams about the future and, no doubt, many of those dreams will become reality.

Some of the information in this book may change within a short time. Change is the very nature of the profession. But most of the book's content will remain valid because it is based on fundamental journalism that has not changed a great deal over the years and is not likely to undergo major change. These basics are good writing, solid reporting, and an awareness of what it takes to produce honest, objective, and exciting broadcast news programs with integrity. Developing good news judgment is as important today as in the past.

It is hoped that you will not be content to rip and read newscasts. Another hope is that you will want and need the contentment that comes from seeing your work improve and being recognized as superior by your audience and your peers. If you are physically attractive, that will be a plus for you. But it is hoped that you will achieve not on your looks but because you have developed your mind and journalistic skills, because you have a desire to know more today than you did the day before, because you understand that the world is not always quite right and that changing it for the better, no matter how slightly, is reward in itself, and because you have learned to be fair, compassionate, and understanding about what you see while seeking the truth.

ENG Checklist

If you're using ENG equipment in your broadcast news classes for the actual packaging of news stories, then you already know that ENG is an extremely complex, often frustrating assortment of hardware. If it is any consolation, all the things that seem to go wrong when you are using ENG equipment also are going wrong in the professional world, where cameras and recorders are probably five to ten times more expensive than the devices you are handling. But cables break and even professional cameras and recorders sometimes do strange things. To keep your frustrations to a minimum, the following checklist should help you to avoid most of the mistakes students make when they are shooting a story with ENG equipment:

1. **Check all your equipment before you leave on a story.** Do not assume that everything is working. The chances are more likely that something is broken. Make sure that you are getting a picture and that your deck is working properly. Shoot something and play it back in the camera viewfinder. Be certain that your microphone is operating properly. Check your lights.

2. **You need videotape.** Sound silly? You may be surprised at the number of times we have had students call us from the scene of a story to say they forgot to take tape. Or, that they forgot to take a red button for the back of the cassette that is necessary to make the tape work. (You can stick some masking tape over the hole in an emergency.)

3. **Bring a tripod.** Few students, or professionals, can hold a camera

steady for long periods of time without wobbling. There is nothing worse than a talking head that bounces all over the screen.

4. Batteries have a way of giving out just when you need them. Take some extra ones. And please put them on charge when you return from a story. Do not remove them until the light shows they are completely charged. Otherwise, the batteries will lose their memories. That means you will have less time to shoot with them next time. Whenever you can, use your AC adaptor when shooting a story. You can usually find AC power inside an office or building. This will save your batteries. Also, remember to carry an AC extension cord and a three-prong adaptor. Some old buildings will not accept the new three-prong plugs.

5. Take an audio tape recorder. If you are at a news conference or conducting an interview, place the tape recorder in a spot close to the person who is speaking so that the condenser microphone will pick up the conversation. You are not interested in broadcast quality. The recording will help you in the editing process. You can listen to the tape recording on your way back to the newsroom and select the sound bites that you will want to use in your story. And it will help you if no editing stations are available when you return to base. When one does open up, you will be ready to select your sound bites quickly.

6. Make sure you have earphones. Do not rely only on the indicator on the VCR's audio level gauge. Often it will appear that you are getting sound when you are not. Unless you hear the voices in the earphones, be suspicious. Replay the tape to make sure you have audio.

7. Lavaliere microphones are preferable to the hand-held kind, but, of course, in a breaking news story you will be forced to use the latter. Don't stick the microphone in the middle of a person's face. If you hold it about chest level, it should work just fine and your cameraperson will be most appreciative. Carry a windscreen. Many an interview and stand-up has been ruined because wind made it unusable.

8. Get natural sound. Nothing is more disturbing than watching a parade and hearing no music or watching a barking dog without hearing the dog.

9. Don't forget to set your white balance. The best way to do this is to hold a white piece of paper in front of the subject or scene that you are going to shoot. Then have the cameraperson push the white balance switch until the signal light comes on in the viewfinder.

10. Use the right filter. Many students ruin good interviews and cover footage because they have the indoor filter on when they are shooting outside, and vice versa.

11. Many stories must be reshot or killed because they are out of focus. Remember to zoom in on the farthest object you intend to shoot and then adjust your focus. For example, if you are shooting an interview, focus on the newsmaker's tie or dress. Then, when you pull back for a two-shot of the reporter and the interviewee, both will remain in focus.

12. Let the VCR lockup. Remember to run off about ten seconds of videotape before you cue your reporter to speak. That lock up time also is necessary when shooting cover footage.

13. Stay on the head. If you are the photographer, get your establishing shots before the interview. When your reporter asks if you are ready, be prepared to zoom in slowly from a two-shot to the head of the interviewee. You should have a good tight shot of the interviewee by the time the reporter has finished the first question. Do not leave the head once the interview begins. When the reporter asks questions, you can and should change the head shot for variety. Don't be afraid to experiment. Move in closely on the head if it is particularly interesting or emotional. Don't be afraid to chop off part of the head and neck. You are not taking snapshots. Your camera can explore the weathered face of a bearded seaman and can find the years of joy and suffering in the face of a fading movie star. But be kind. Don't overdo those shots.

14. To make your editing easier, get your reverse questions. You may not need them, but if you have the time and your interviewee will cooperate, ask some of your questions again with the camera shooting you over the shoulder of the interviewee. Remember, reversals should not show only you. Also, have your cameraperson get some over-the-shoulder shots of you just listening.

15. For cutaways, get some shots of other people in the room. Another cameraperson attending the news conference is an old standby, along with the reporter taking notes. A wide shot of the audience also will do. At best, such shots are weak and are to be avoided if possible, but if you must edit a speaker's comments, you may have no choice unless you are prepared to live with a jump cut.

16. Most of the time you will return without enough cover footage. In the professional world, you will be expected to limit the amount of cover footage that you shoot in order to reduce editing problems. But most of you will start out needing as much good cover footage as you can find. Avoid the quick zoom-ins and outs. Make sure that you remain on important objects for at least ten seconds before cutting to another shot.

17. Interviews: Make sure that when you leave on assignment you have prepared some questions. But don't get locked in with those questions. Follow up on responses. And *listen* to what the person says. There also should be some logic about the order of your questions. You should be headed in some direction and know what kind of information you are looking for. Young reporters have a bad habit of drifting too much from their original line of questioning. It is a waste of time at the scene and in the screening room. Also, learn when to stop. Remember that it makes little sense to ask 20 minutes of questions if you know that you will be able to use no more than 40 seconds in your story.

18. A final note that will save you much grief: put a label on your videotape as soon as you use it. It is not a bad idea to stick the label on before you leave for the story, but certainly do it as soon as you remove the cassette. Without labels, tapes are misplaced or recorded over, even in a professional news operation. Develop good habits now. Mark your tapes so you do not lose or wipe them by accident.

Glossary

ADDA A system that electronically stores graphic and video images on discs in a computer for andom recall. Also ESS.

AFTRA American Federation of Television and Radio Artists. Union that represents on-air people in larger markets.

AP Associated Press, one of the two major wire services in the United States.

Affiliates Radio and TV stations that are serviced by networks.

Actuality The voices of people involved in a news story. Also called a sound cut or sound bite.

Ambush interview Cornering someone and asking questions on camera without any advance notice.

Anchorperson Someone who reads news on the TV set.

Assignment Editor Newsperson who is responsible for assigning stories to reporters and camera crews.

Attribution The source for a news story.

Audio The sound used in a radio or TV broadcast.

B-roll A film term still used to describe use of videotape to cover an interview or narration.

B-wire Secondary AP and UPI news wires.

Back-timing The timing of the final part of a radio or TV program to help the newscaster get off the air on time.

Beat An assignment given to a reporter on a continuing basis, such as city hall, the legislature, or police headquarters.

Beeper An interview recorded over the phone. Most stations have eliminated the beep sound that was to let the person who is being interviewed know that the conversation is being recorded. But the term continues to be used to describe telephone interviews.

Black Control track on a videotape. Also, "going to black," which refers to the cutting or fading from picture to a blank screen.

Blind Lead-in A general lead-in to a report from the field when you do not know what the reporter will lead with.

Bridge Words that connect one piece of narration or sound bite to another.

Broadcast wire The news wire written in broadcast style by AP and UPI. Also known as the radio wire.

Budget A list of stories that the wire services are planning to send to their customers. Also, sometimes referred to by assignment editors to indicate story possibilities.

Bulletin Late-breaking news of importance.

Bumper shot Shot of the TV newsroom or studio before going to a commercial.

Character generator Electronic equipment used to produce supers (see *Fonts*).

Chroma or key Abbreviation for chromakey. The electronic placement of pictures behind the newscaster.

Close The ending of a reporter's news story, usually one or two sentences that include the reporter's name and station call letters. Also, the end of a newscast.

Close-up Also called a tight shot that shows the subject's head or head and shoulders.

Color Imaginative use of words in a news story.

Copy Material written for broadcast. Also, wire copy that is sent on teletype by AP, UPI, and other wire services.

Cosmetics The "show-biz" aspects of TV news.

Cover footage Video shot at scene of news story. It is called *cover* footage because it is used to cover or replace the picture of the newsmaker and the reporter while their voices are heard.

Crash Colloquialism for serious problems in a newscast, meaning it fell apart.

Cue Signal from floor manager to anchors. Usually to let them know when they should start reading prompter and which camera they should be looking into.

Cue words The words at the beginning or at the end of audiotape or videotape to identify how a sound cut begins and ends.

Cutaway A video shot used to avoid a jump cut.

Cutoff time The point at which a reporter knows he must leave the scene of a story in order to make broadcast.

Delayed lead Holding the most important information in a story until the middle or end to achieve suspense.

Degauss To wipe or clean audiotape or videotape electronically before reusing.

Depth of field The range in which objects will appear in focus.

Dissolve Special video effect that slowly replaces one image on the screen with another.

Dub To copy or record audio or video material.

Electronic newsroom A newsroom equipped with video display terminals and computers.

Enterprise story A news story that involves more than routine spot news research. A more in-depth examination of a subject.

Establishing shot A wide shot of a scene, usually used at the beginning of a news story. Also, a shot of a reporter and interviewee used to set up a sound cut. Also called an establishing two-shot.

ESS See ADDA.

Evergreen A story that can be used anytime. Usually a dateless feature.

Fade A dissolve from picture to darkness or black. Fade to black is used between news stories and commercials.

Feeds Broadcast material distributed by networks to affiliates and owned stations for use on local newscasts. Also called syndication feeds.

Freedom of Information Act Passed by Congress in 1967 and amended in 1974. All states also have passed similar "sunshine laws" that open all but the most sensitive government documents to the public.

Fill copy News copy that is relatively unimportant for use near end of newscast if needed to fill time. Also called pad copy.

Flash Brief headline used by wire services to describe news of extreme urgency such as the death of a president or the outbreak of war.

Font See *Super.*

Freeze frame A still video image seen next to or behind the anchor while the broadcaster is reading the lead into a story. On cue from the director, the freeze usually is released and the tape plays.

Future file Folder used by the assignment editor to keep track of stories that may be covered during the month.

Gain Volume of an audio or video signal.

Graphics Photos, graphs, maps, or any other visuals used in a TV news story.

Happy Talk   Transition lines exchanged by anchors during a newscast.

Hard lead   A lead that includes the most important information in the first sentence.

Head shot   Video shot of a person's head.

Headlines   Usually a series of one-line sentences describing news events or comments from newsmakers. Used at the top of a newscast or during breaks in TV entertainment programming.

High-angle shot   Video shot with camera looking down on a subject or scene.

Hold for release   Wire service story or press release that is embargoed until the time specified.

IBEW   International Brotherhood of Electrical Workers. The union that represents many broadcast technicians in larger markets.

Information overload   Putting too much information or needless words into a story.

Intro   Copy read by an anchor that leads into a reporter's story. Also, copy written by a reporter for the start of a story.

Investigative reporting   Developing news reports about something that someone is trying to hide.

Jump cut   An erratic movement of a head that results when video is edited internally to eliminate some of the speaker's words.

Key light   The main light used in shooting video.

Kicker   A light story used at the end of a newscast.

Laserphoto   Photos transmitted by wire from AP.

Lead   The first line or two of a news story. Also, the first story in a newscast.

Leading question   Phrasing a question during an interview so as to elicit the answer *you* want to hear rather than what the interviewee has to say.

Lineup   The arrangement of the stories in a newscast. Also called the rundown.

Live   Broadcasting on air from the studio or scene of a story.

Local angle   Finding the details of a news story that are of special interest to the audience in your town or city.

Local news   Stories dealing with your immediate listening area.

Locking up   The time it takes for a videocassette recorder to stabilize.

Long shot   Camera shot that shows most of the scene.

Low-angle shot   Camera shot taken from below a subject.

Medium shot   Camera shot that shows about half of a person's body. Also called a waist shot. A scene that shows two or more people but not the complete background.

Microwave   Beaming of a TV signal between two points with the use of microwave antennaes.

Minicam   A lightweight video camera used in the field.

Montage   A series of audio or video segments edited together. Used frequently in reaction or "man-in-the-street" interviews.

NABET   National Association of Broadcast Employees and Technicians, the union that represents many broadcast technicians in larger markets.

Negative lead   A lead that contains the word *not*. To be avoided in broadcast copy.

News director   The person in charge of the news operation at a radio or TV station.

News judgment   Ability to recognize and make decisions concerning the relative importance of news.

O & O   Abbreviation for stations that are owned and operated by networks, as contrasted to stations that are network affiliates.

O/C   Abbreviation for *on camera*. Used on the video side of the TV split page to indicate that the anchor is seen on camera.

Out cue   Last words in an audio or video sound bite.

Package   A story put together by a reporter that usually includes an interview, narration, and cover footage.

Pad copy   News stories of limited interest that are written for the end of a newscast if it runs short. Also called fill copy.

Pan   Camera moving in a horizontal position.

Peaks and valleys   A TV production technique that arranges stories in a newscast so that the most exciting stories are not grouped together.

Pic or **pix**   Abbreviation for pictures.

Pool   Sharing of equipment, lines, satellite, and sometimes people by networks during coverage of news events.

Prime time   The time of day or night when radio and TV have their largest audiences.

Privacy Act   Passed by Congress in 1974 to prevent unwarranted invasion of a person's privacy.

Producer   The newsperson responsible for deciding which material will go into a newscast and the order in which each story will appear.

Promo   Publicity material produced by a radio or TV station to promote one of its programs.

Prompter   Electronic device that projects news script on monitors attached to studio cameras so the scripts can be read by anchors.

PSA   Abbreviation for Public Service Announcement. Time donated by radio and TV stations to nonprofit organizations.

Radio mike   Transmits a short distance on a radio frequency to a recorder. Also known as a wireless mike.

Radio wire   News wire written in broadcast style by AP and UPI.

Rear Projection   Graphic material seen on a screen behind or next to anchors.

Reporter involvement   The use of the reporter on camera during a news story. Some involvement is considered acceptable; some types are not.

Reuters   British news agency.

Reversal   A shot of the reporter looking at the person being interviewed. Shot over the shoulder of the interviewee. An editing device.

Reverse question   Shot of the reporter repeating questions asked during an interview. Usually shot over the shoulder of the interviewee. Like the reversal, it is an editing technique.

Rip and read   The broadcasting of the AP or UPI radio wire copy without any rewrite.

Roll   A signal to start a tape machine either in the studio or in the field.

RTNDA   Radio and Television News Directors Association.

Running story   A news story in which there are new developments for more than one consecutive day.

Screen   To look at videotape.

Script   Radio or TV broadcast copy.

SDX   Society of Professional Journalists. (Sigma Delta Chi)

Shot   Scene taken by a video camera.

Shotgun lead   A news story lead that deals with two or more related news items.

SIL   Abbreviation for silent. It is used on the video side of the TV split page to indicate the use of videotape that has no sound.

SL   Abbreviation for slide. It is used on the video side of the TV split page to indicate that a slide is to be used.

Slug   Word or two identifying a news story. It is written in the upper left-hand corner of a script.

Soft lead   A lead in which the most important information in a story is not given immediately.

SOT   Abbreviation for sound on tape. It is used on the video side of the TV split page to indicate the use of videotape that has sound.

Sound bite or **cut**   Portion of statement or interview that is broadcast in a radio or TV news story.

Sound under   Keeping the natural sound low, under the voice of the reporter or newscaster.

Source   The provider of information used in a news story. Most sources are identified, but sometimes they are kept secret.

Spec people   Usually refers to free-lance reporters and camera people who file stories on speculation. Most of the time they will be paid only if the story gets on the air.

Splice   Connecting two pieces of audiotape together, usually with an ''Edit-all'' block.

Split page   The standard TV news script. The left side of the page is used for video directions and the right side is for the script and audio cues.

Split screen   Two pictures on the screen at the same time.

Spot   Colloquialism for a commercial.

Squeeze frame   Reducing a picture on camera until it takes up only a part of the screen. Also known as a squeeze zoom.

Staging   Unethical practice of asking people to behave in a certain way while you record or videotape them.

Stand-up   A report given by a reporter on camera from the scene.

Still   Any graphic material used on camera during a newscast.

Super   Short for superimposing lettering over graphics or videotape. Most commonly used to give the names and titles of the newsmakers while they are shown on the screen. Also called a *font*.

Suspense lead   When the most important information in a news story is kept until the end or nearly the end.

Syndication   The sale and distribution of news material to radio and TV stations by independent companies. The networks also provide syndicated material to their affiliates and some independent stations.

Tag   Sentence or two used by reporter or anchor to end a news story.

Talking Head   Jargon for person being interviewed for television news report.

Tease   A short headline-type sentence that describes the story to follow a commercial. In TV, usually accompanied by a few seconds of the upcoming video story or a shot of the newsroom (a bumper shot).

Time coding   The recording of the time of day on the edge of videotape as it is being shot to assist the editing process.

Tight shot   Close-up camera shot of individual or object.

Trap interview   Asking surprise and sometimes embarrassing questions of someone on camera.

Trend story   A news report that examines a new trend or fad.

Two-shot   Camera shot of two people.

Umbrella lead   Same as a shotgun lead.

Upcut   The loss of words at the beginning of a videotape.

Update   New details in a news story that require a rewrite or new treatment.

Unifax   The wire picture service of UPI.

UPI   United Press International, one of the two major wire services in the United States.

VCR   Videocassette recorder. Machine that records the pictures produced by a video camera.

VDT   Video display terminal.

V/O   Abbreviation for voice-over. It is used on the video half of the split page TV script to indicate that the anchor's voice is being heard over video. Also, reporter narration over cover footage.

Voicer   A report from the scene by a radio newsperson.

VTR   Videotape recorder. Usually refers to a one- or two-inch machine used in studio.

WGA   Writers Guild of America Union that represents broadcast newswriters and some assignment editors in major markets.

Wild track   Sound recorded at the scene that may be used later for background noise in a story.

Wire   News services provided by AP, UPI, Reuters, and other organizations.

Word processing   The use of computers and video display terminals to write and store information.

Wrap   To complete work on a story. Or abbreviation for wraparound in which reporter's voice is heard at the beginning and end of a sound bite.

Zoom   Changing the camera lenses' focal length in order to move closer to or farther from the subject.

Source Notes

Chapter 1

1. Vernon Stone, report for the Radio and Television News Directors Association (RTNDA), January 1981.
2. Quoted in Journalism section, *Broadcasting,* 7 April 1980, p. 100.
3. Ibid.
4. Ibid.
5. Vernon Stone, RTNDA report, February 1980.
6. Vernon Stone, personal interview with the author.
7. Quoted in "Washington Watch," *Broadcasting,* 10 November 1980, p. 82.

Chapter 13

1. Walter Cronkite, third annual Frank E. Gannett lecture, sponsored by the Washington Journalism Center, 9 December 1980.
2. Quoted in Larry Weymouth, "Walter Cronkite Remembers," *Washington Journalism Review,* Jan./Feb. 1981, p. 24.
3. Weymouth, op. cit.
4. Jeff Greenfield, on "Sunday Morning" broadcast, CBS News, 9 February 1981.
5. Quoted in John Huey, "Screen Test," *The Wall Street Journal,* 23 May 1980.

6. Quoted in Harry F. Walters, "Ted Turner Tackles TV News," *Newsweek*, 16 June 1980, p. 59.

7. Quoted in "Rebel with a Cause," *Broadcasting*, 19 May 1980, p. 44.

Chapter 20

1. Desmond Smith, "Is This the Future of TV News?" *New York Magazine*, 22 February 1982.

2. Ibid.

3. Quoted in *TV Guide*, article by Sally Bedell, 6 February 1982, p. 8.

4. Charles Kuralt, address to the RTNDA convention, New Orelans, December 1981.

5. Quoted in Tony Schwartz, "The Turmult in TV News," *The New York Times*, 1 March 1982, p. c15.

6. Quoted in *TV Guide*, article by Sally Bedell, 6 February 1982, p. 8.

7. Quoted in Roger Piantadosi, "Profile—Roone Arledge," *Washington Journalism Review*, May 1982, p. 46.

Chapter 23

1. Robert Greene, personal interview with author.

2. Ibid.

3. Carl Bernstein, address to national convention of Investigative Reporters and Editors (IRE), Columbus, Ohio, June 1977.

4. Ibid.

5. Eugene Roberts, address to IRE convention, San Diego, June 1981.

6. Greene, op. cit.

7. Greene, op. cit.

8. Clark Mollenhoff, "R.I.P., Press Credibility," *The IRE Journal*, Spring 1981, p. 5.

9. Greene, op. cit.

10. James R. Dubro, "Organized Crime, Part III," *The IRE Journal*, Spring 1981, pp. 20–21.

11. John Spain, at RTNDA convention, Hollywood, Florida, December 1980.

12. Lea Thompson, at RTNDA convention, Hollywood, Florida, December 1980.

13. Peter Karl, at RTNDA convention, Hollywood, Florida, December 1980.

14. Quoted in Ann Zimmerman, "By Any Other Name," *Washington Journalism Review*, December 1979, p. 34.

15. Zimmerman, op. cit.

16. Jack Anderson, address to IRE convention, Columbus, Ohio, June 1977.

17. "Publisher's Notes," *Columbia Journalism Review*, Sept./Oct. 1979, p. 20.

18. Peter Karl, at RTNDA convention, Hollywood, Florida, December 1980.
19. CBS News, "60 Minutes," 27 September 1981.
20. David Anderson and Peter Benjamin, *Investigative Reporting* (Bloomington: Indiana University Press, 1976), pp. 39–41.
21. John Ullmann, at IRE convention, San Diego, June 1981.
22. Jack Tobin, at IRE convention, San Diego, June 1981.
23. John Ullmann, "Making the F.O.I.A. Less Useful, by Fiat," *The IRE Journal*, Spring 1981.
24. Eugene Roberts, address to IRE convention, San Diego, June 1981.
25. Clark Mollenhoff, *Investigative Reporting* (New York: Macmillan, 1981), pp. 340–341.
26. Thompson, op. cit.

Index